ns*Against the Arians*

356–360 AD

By

St. Athanasius,

Bishop of Alexandria

From *Nicene and Post-Nicene Fathers, Series II, Volume IV*

By John Henry Newman, Archibald Robertson, Alexander Roberts, James Donaldson, Arthur Cleveland Coxe, Philip Schaff and Henry Wace. (Buffalo, NY, United States: *Christian Literature Publishing Co.*, 1885.)

"If the whole world is against the Truth of God's Word,;
in the strength of the Lord, Athanasius is Against the World!"
-St. Athanasius, Bishop of Alexandria

CONTENTS

Discourse I — p. 7

Chapter I. Introduction. — p. 7

Chapter II. Extracts from the Thalia of Arius. — p. 14

Chapter III. The Importance of the Subject. — p. 20

Chapter IV. That the Son is Eternal and Increate. — p. 27

Chapter V. Subject Continued. — p. 35

Chapter VI. Subject Continued. — p. 41

Chapter VII. Objections to the Foregoing Proof. — p. 53

Chapter VIII. Objections Continued. — p. 60

Chapter IX. Objections Continued. — p. 68

Chapter X. Objections Continued. — p. 77

Chapter XI. Texts Explained; And First, Phil. II. 9, 10 — p. 82

Chapter XII. Texts Explained; Secondly, Psalm XLV. 7, 8. — p. 100

Chapter XIII. Texts Explained; Thirdly, Hebrews I. 4. — p. 116

Discourse II — p. 141

Chapter XIV. Texts Explained; Fourthly, Hebrews III. 2. — p. 141

Chapter XV. Texts Explained; Fifthly, Acts II. 36. — p. 163

Chapter XVI. Introductory to Proverbs VIII. 22, that the Son is Not a Creature. p. 177

Chapter XVII. Introduction to Proverbs VIII. 22 Continued. p. 190

Chapter XVIII. Introduction to Proverbs VIII. 22 Continued. p. 203

Chapter XIX. Texts Explained; Sixthly, Proverbs VIII. 22. p. 229

Chapter XX. Texts Explained; Sixthly, Proverbs VIII. 22 Continued. p. 243

Chapter XXI. Texts Explained; Sixthly, Proverbs VIII. 22, Continued. p. 255

Chapter XXII. Texts Explained; Sixthly, the Context of Proverbs VIII. 22 Vz. 22-30. p. 287

Discourse III p. 309

Chapter XXIII. Texts Explained; Seventhly, John XIV. 10. p. 309

Chapter XXIV. Texts Explained; Eighthly, John XVII. 3. And the Like. p. 321

Chapter XXV. Texts Explained; Ninthly, John X. 30; XVII. 11, Etc. p. 327

Chapter XXVI. Introductory to Texts from the Gospels on the Incarnation. p. 359

Chapter XXVII. Texts Explained; Tenthly, Matthew XI. 27: John III. 35, Etc. p. 378

Chapter XXVIII. Texts Explained; Eleventhly, Mark XIII. 32 And Luke II. 52. p. 390

Chapter XXIX. Texts Explained; Twelfthly, Matthew XXVI. 39; John XII. 27, Etc. p. 412

Chapter XXX. Objections Continued, as in Chapters VII.-X. p. 421

Discourse IV p. 442

Discourse I

Chapter I. Introduction.

Reason for writing; certain persons indifferent about Arianism; Arians not Christians, because sectaries always take the name of their founder.

1. Of all other heresies which have departed from the truth it is acknowledged that they have but devised a madness, and their irreligiousness has long since become notorious to all men. For that their authors went out from us, it plainly follows, as the blessed John has written, that they never thought nor now think with us. Wherefore, as says the Saviour, in that they gather not with us, they scatter with the devil, and keep an eye on those who slumber, that, by this second sowing of their own mortal poison, they may have companions in death. But, whereas one heresy, and that the last, which has now risen as harbinger of Antichrist, the Arian, as it is called, considering that other heresies, her elder sisters, have been openly proscribed, in her craft and cunning, affects to array herself in Scripture language , like her father the devil, and

is forcing her way back into the Church's paradise — that with the pretence of Christianity, her smooth sophistry (for reason she has none) may deceive men into wrong thoughts of Christ — nay, since she has already seduced certain of the foolish, not only to corrupt their ears, but even to take and eat with Eve, till in their ignorance which ensues they think bitter sweet, and admire this loathsome heresy, on this account I have thought it necessary, at your request, to unrip 'the folds of its breast-plate ,' and to show the ill savour of its folly. So while those who are far from it may continue to shun it, those whom it has deceived may repent; and, opening the eyes of their heart, may understand that darkness is not light, nor falsehood truth, nor Arianism good; nay, that those who call these men Christians are in great and grievous error, as neither having studied Scripture, nor understanding Christianity at all, and the faith which it contains.

2. For what have they discovered in this heresy like to the religious Faith, that they vainly talk as if its supporters said no evil? This in truth is to call even Caiaphas a Christian, and to reckon the traitor Judas still among the Apostles,

and to say that they who asked Barabbas instead of the Saviour did no evil, and to recommend Hymenæus and Alexander as right-minded men, and as if the Apostle slandered them. But neither can a Christian bear to hear this, nor can he consider the man who dared to say it sane in his understanding. For with them for Christ is Arius, as with the Manichees Manichæus; and for Moses and the other saints they have made the discovery of one Sotades, a man whom even Gentiles laugh at, and of the daughter of Herodias. For of the one has Arius imitated the dissolute and effeminate tone, in writing Thaliæ on his model; and the other he has rivalled in her dance, reeling and frolicking in his blasphemies against the Saviour; till the victims of his heresy lose their wits and go foolish, and change the Name of the Lord of glory into the likeness of the 'image of corruptible man,' and for Christians come to be called Arians, bearing this badge of their irreligion. For let them not excuse themselves; nor retort their disgrace on those who are not as they, calling Christians after the names of their teachers, that they themselves may appear to have that Name in the same way. Nor let them make a jest of it, when they feel shame at their disgraceful appellation; rather, if they be ashamed, let them hide their faces, or let them recoil from their own irreligion. For never at any time did Christian people take their title from the Bishops among them, but from the Lord, on whom we rest our faith. Thus, though the blessed Apostles have become our teachers, and have ministered the Saviour's Gospel, yet not from them have we our title, but from Christ we are and are named Christians. But for those who derive the faith which they profess from others, good reason is it they should bear their name, whose property they have become.

3. Yes surely; while all of us are and are called Christians after Christ, Marcion broached a heresy a long time since and was cast out; and those who continued with him who ejected him remained Christians; but those who followed Marcion were called Christians no more, but henceforth Marcionites. Thus Valentinus also, and Basilides, and Manichæus, and Simon Magus, have imparted their own name to their followers; and some are accosted as Valentinians, or as Basilidians, or as Manichees, or as Simonians; and other, Cataphrygians from Phrygia, and from Novatus Novatians. So too Meletius, when ejected

by Peter the Bishop and Martyr, called his party no longer Christians, but Meletians , and so in consequence when Alexander of blessed memory had cast out Arius, those who remained with Alexander, remained Christians; but those who went out with Arius, left the Saviour's Name to us who were with Alexander, and as to them they were hence-forward denominated Arians. Behold then, after Alexander's death too, those who communicate with his successor Athanasius, and those with whom the said Athanasius communicates, are instances of the same rule; none of them bear his name, nor is he named from them, but all in like manner, and as is usual, are called Christians. For though we have a succession of teachers and become their disciples, yet, because we are taught by them the things of Christ, we both are, and are called, Christians all the same. But those who follow the heretics, though they have innumerable successors in their heresy, yet anyhow bear the name of him who devised it. Thus, though Arius be dead, and many of his party have succeeded him, yet those who think with him, as being known from Arius, are called Arians. And, what is a remarkable evidence of this, those of the Greeks who even at this time come into the Church, on giving up the superstition of idols, take the name, not of their catechists, but of the Saviour, and begin to be called Christians instead of Greeks: while those of them who go off to the heretics, and again all who from the Church change to this heresy, abandon Christ's name, and henceforth are called Arians, as no longer holding Christ's faith, but having inherited Arius's madness.

4. How then can they be Christians, who for Christians are Ario-maniacs ? Or how are they of the Catholic Church, who have shaken off the Apostolical faith, and become authors of fresh evils? Who, after abandoning the oracles of divine Scripture, call Arius's Thaliæ a new wisdom? And with reason too, for they are announcing a new heresy. And hence a man may marvel, that, whereas many have written many treatises and abundant homilies upon the Old Testament and the New, yet in none of them is a Thalia found; nay nor among the more respectable of the Gentiles, but among those only who sing such strains over their cups, amid cheers and jokes, when men are merry, that the rest may laugh; till this marvellous Arius, taking no grave pattern, and ignorant even of what is respectable, while he stole largely from other heresies,

would be original in the ludicrous, with none but Sotades for his rival. For what beseemed him more, when he would dance forth against the Saviour, than to throw his wretched words of irreligion into dissolute and loose metres? That, while 'a man,' as Wisdom says, 'is known from the utterance of his word ,' so from those numbers should be seen the writer's effeminate soul and corruption of thought. In truth, that crafty one did not escape detection; but, for all his many writhings to and fro, like the serpent, he did but fall into the error of the Pharisees. They, that they might transgress the Law, pretended to be anxious for the words of the Law, and that they might deny the expected and then present Lord, were hypocritical with God's name, and were convicted of blaspheming when they said, 'Why do You, being a man, make Yourself God,' and say, 'I and the Father are one John 10:30?' And so too, this counterfeit and Sotadean Arius, feigns to speak of God, introducing Scripture language , but is on all sides recognised as godless Arius, denying the Son, and reckoning Him among the creatures.

Chapter II. Extracts from the Thalia of Arius.

Ariusmaintains that God became a Father, and the Son was not always; the Son out of nothing; once He was not; He was not before his generation; He was created; named Wisdom and Word after God's attributes; made that He might make us; one out of many powers of God; alterable; exalted on God's foreknowledge of what He was to be; not very God; but called so as others by participation; foreign in essence from the Father; does not know or see the Father; does not know Himself.

5. Now the commencement of Arius's Thalia and flippancy, effeminate in tune and nature, runs thus:—

'According to faith of God's elect, God's prudent ones,

Holy children, rightly dividing, God's Holy Spirit receiving,

Have I learned this from the partakers of wisdom,

Accomplished, divinely taught, and wise in all things.

Along their track, have I been walking, with like opinions.

I the very famous, the much suffering for God's glory;

And taught of God, I have acquired wisdom and knowledge.'

And the mockeries which he utters in it, repulsive and most irreligious, are such as these :— 'God was not always a Father.' but 'once God was alone, and not yet a Father, but afterwards He became a Father.' 'The Son was not always;' for, whereas all things were made out of nothing, and all existing creatures and works were made, so the Word of God Himself was 'made out of nothing,' and 'once He was not,' and 'He was not before His origination,' but He as others 'had an origin of creation.' 'For God,' he says, 'was alone, and the Word as yet was not, nor the Wisdom. Then, wishing to form us, thereupon He made a certain one, and named Him Word and Wisdom and Son, that He might form us by means of Him.' Accordingly, he says that there are two wisdoms, first, the attribute co-existent with God, and next, that in this wisdom the Son was originated, and was only named Wisdom and Word as partaking of it. 'For Wisdom,' says he, 'by the will of the wise God, had its existence in Wisdom.' In like manner, he says, that there is another

Word in God besides the Son, and that the Son again, as partaking of it, is named Word and Son according to grace. And this too is an idea proper to their heresy, as shown in other works of theirs, that there are many powers; one of which is God's own by nature and eternal; but that Christ, on the other hand, is not the true power of God; but, as others, one of the so-called powers, one of which, namely, the locust and the caterpillar , is called in Scripture, not merely the power, but the 'great power.' The others are many and are like the Son, and of them David speaks in the Psalms, when he says, 'The Lord of hosts' or 'powers.' And by nature, as all others, so the Word Himself is alterable, and remains good by His own free will, while He chooses; when, however, He wills, He can alter as we can, as being of an alterable nature. For 'therefore,' says he, 'as foreknowing that He would be good, did God by anticipation bestow on Him this glory, which afterwards, as man, He attained from virtue. Thus in consequence of His works fore-known , did God bring it to pass that He being such, should come to be.'

6. Moreover he has dared to say, that 'the Word is not the very God;' 'though He is called God, yet He is not very God,' but 'by participation of grace, He, as others, is God only in name.' And, whereas all beings are foreign and different from God in essence, so too is 'the Word alien and unlike in all things to the Father's essence and propriety,' but belongs to things originated and created, and is one of these. Afterwards, as though he had succeeded to the devil's recklessness, he has stated in his Thalia, that 'even to the Son the Father is invisible,' and 'the Word cannot perfectly and exactly either see or know His own Father.' but even what He knows and what He sees, He knows and sees 'in proportion to His own measure,' as we also know according to our own power. For the Son, too, he says, not only knows not the Father exactly, for He fails in comprehension , but 'He knows not even His own essence;'— and that 'the essences of the Father and the Son and the Holy Ghost, are separate in nature, and estranged, and disconnected, and alien , and without participation of each other ;' and, in his own words, 'utterly unlike from each other in essence and glory, unto infinity.' Thus as to 'likeness of glory and essence,' he says that the Word is entirely diverse from both the Father

and the Holy Ghost. With such words has the irreligious spoken; maintaining that the Son is distinct by Himself, and in no respect partaker of the Father. These are portions of Arius's fables as they occur in that jocose composition.

7. Who is there that hears all this, nay, the tune of the Thalia, but must hate, and justly hate, this Arius jesting on such matters as on a stage ? Who but must regard him, when he pretends to name God and speak of God, but as the serpent counselling the woman? Who, on reading what follows in his work, but must discern in his irreligious doctrine that error, into which by his sophistries the serpent in the sequel seduced the woman? Who at such blasphemies is not transported? 'The heaven,' as the Prophet says, 'was astonished, and the earth shuddered Jeremiah 2:12 ' at the transgression of the Law. But the sun, with greater horror, impatient of the bodily contumelies, which the common Lord of all voluntarily endured for us, turned away, and recalling his rays made that day sunless. And shall not all human kind at Arius's blasphemies be struck speechless, and stop their ears, and

shut their eyes, to escape hearing them or seeing their author? Rather, will not the Lord Himself have reason to denounce men so irreligious, nay, so unthankful, in the words which He has already uttered by the prophet Hosea, 'Woe unto them, for they have fled from Me; destruction upon them, for they have transgressed against Me; though I have redeemed them, yet they have spoken lies against Me Hosea 7:13.' And soon after, 'They imagine mischief against Me; they turn away to nothing.' For to turn away from the Word of God, which is, and to fashion to themselves one that is not, is to fall to what is nothing. For this was why the Ecumenical Council, when Arius thus spoke, cast him from the Church, and anathematized him, as impatient of such irreligion. And ever since has Arius's error been reckoned for a heresy more than ordinary, being known as Christ's foe, and harbinger of Antichrist. Though then so great a condemnation be itself of special weight to make men flee from that irreligious heresy, as I said above, yet since certain persons called Christian, either in ignorance or pretence, think it, as I then said, little different from the Truth, and call its professors Christians; proceed we to put some questions to them, according to our powers, thereby to expose the unscrupulousness of the heresy. Perhaps, when thus caught, they will be silenced, and flee from it, as from the sight of a serpent.

Chapter III. The Importance of the Subject.

The Ariansaffect Scripture language, but their doctrine new, as well as unscriptural. Statement of the Catholic doctrine, that the Son is proper to the Father's substance, and eternal. Restatement of Arianismin contrast, that He is a creature with a beginning: the controversy comes to this issue, whether one whom we are to believein as God, can be so in name only, and is merely a creature. What pretence then for being indifferent in the controversy? The Ariansrely on state patronage, and dare not avow their tenets

8. If then the use of certain phrases of divine Scripture changes, in their opinion, the blasphemy of the Thalia into reverent language, of course they ought also to deny Christ with the present Jews, when they see how they study the Law and the Prophets; perhaps too they will deny the Law

and the Prophets like Manichees , because the latter read some portions of the Gospels. If such bewilderment and empty speaking be from ignorance, Scripture will teach them, that the devil, the author of heresies, because of the ill savour which attaches to evil, borrows Scripture language, as a cloak wherewith to sow the ground with his own poison also, and to seduce the simple. Thus he deceived Eve; thus he framed former heresies; thus he persuaded Arius at this time to make a show of speaking against those former ones, that he might introduce his own without observation. And yet, after all, the man of craft did not escape. For being irreligious towards the Word of God, he lost his all at once , and betrayed to all men his ignorance of other heresies too ; and having not a particle of truth in his belief, does but pretend to it. For how can he speak truth concerning the Father, who denies the Son, that reveals concerning Him? Or how can he be orthodox concerning the Spirit, while he speaks profanely of the Word that supplies the Spirit? And who will trust him concerning the Resurrection, denying, as he does, Christ for us the first-begotten from the dead? And how shall he not err in respect to His incarnate presence, who is simply ignorant of the Son's genuine and true generation from the Father? For thus, the former Jews also, denying the Word, and saying, 'We have no king but Cæsar John 19:15,' were immediately stripped of all they had, and forfeited the light of the Lamp, the odour of ointment, knowledge of prophecy, and the Truth itself; till now they understand nothing, but are walking as in darkness. For who was ever yet a hearer of such a doctrine ? Or whence or from whom did the abettors and hirelings of the heresy gain it? Who thus expounded to them when they were at school ? Who told them, 'Abandon the worship of the creation, and then draw near and worship a creature and a work ?' But if they themselves own that they have heard it now for the first time, how can they deny that this heresy is foreign, and not from our fathers ? But what is not from our fathers, but has come to light in this day, how can it be but that of which the blessed Paul has foretold, that 'in the latter times some shall depart from the sound faith, giving heed to seducing spirits and doctrines of devils, in the hypocrisy of liars; cauterized in their own conscience, and turning from the truth ?'

9. For, behold, we take divine Scripture, and thence discourse with freedom of the religious Faith, and set it up as a light upon its candlestick, saying:— Very Son of the Father, natural and genuine, proper to His essence, Wisdom Only-begotten, and Very and Only Word of God is He; not a creature or work, but an offspring proper to the Father's essence. Wherefore He is very God, existing one in essence with the very Father; while other beings, to whom He said, 'I said you are Gods ,' had this grace from the Father, only by participation of the Word, through the Spirit. For He is the expression of the Father's Person, and Light from Light, and Power, and very Image of the Father's essence. For this too the Lord has said, 'He that has seen Me, has seen the Father John 14:9.' And He ever was and is and never was not. For the Father being everlasting, His Word and His Wisdom must be everlasting. On the other hand, what have these persons to show us from the infamous Thalia? Or, first of all, let them read it themselves, and copy the tone of the writer; at least the mockery which they will encounter from others may instruct them how low they have fallen; and then let them proceed to explain themselves. For what can they say from it, but that 'God was not always a Father,

but became so afterwards; the Son was not always, for He was not before His generation; He is not from the Father, but He, as others, has come into subsistence out of nothing; He is not proper to the Father's essence, for He is a creature and work?' And 'Christ is not very God, but He, as others, was made God by participation; the Son has not exact knowledge of the Father, nor does the Word see the Father perfectly; and neither exactly understands nor knows the Father. He is not the very and only Word of the Father, but is in name only called Word and Wisdom, and is called by grace Son and Power. He is not unalterable, as the Father is, but alterable in nature, as the creatures, and He comes short of apprehending the perfect knowledge of the Father.' Wonderful this heresy, not plausible even, but making speculations against Him that is, that He be not, and everywhere putting forward blasphemy for reverent language! Were any one, after inquiring into both sides, to be asked, whether of the two he would follow in faith, or whether of the two spoke fitly of God — or rather let them say themselves, these abettors of irreligion, what, if a man be asked concerning God (for 'the Word was God?'), it were fit to answer. For from this one question the whole case on both sides may be determined, what is fitting to say — He was, or He was not; always, or before His birth; eternal, or from this and from then; true, or by adoption, and from participation and in idea ; to call Him one of things originated, or to unite Him to the Father; to consider Him unlike the Father in essence, or like and proper to Him; a creature, or Him through whom the creatures were originated; that He is the Father's Word, or that there is another word beside Him, and that by this other He was originated, and by another wisdom; and that He is only named Wisdom and Word, and has become a partaker of this wisdom, and second to it?

10. Which of the two theologies sets forth our Lord Jesus Christ as God and Son of the Father, this which you vomited forth, or that which we have spoken and maintain from the Scriptures? If the Saviour be not God, nor Word, nor Son, you shall have leave to say what you will, and so shall the Gentiles, and the present Jews. But if He be Word of the Father and true Son, and God from God, and 'over all blessed for ever Romans 9:5,' is it not becoming to obliterate and blot out those other phrases and that Arian Thalia, as but a pattern of evil, a store of all

irreligion, into which, whoever falls, 'knows not that giants perish with her, and reaches the depths of Hades?' This they know themselves, and in their craft they conceal it, not having the courage to speak out, but uttering something else. For if they speak, a condemnation will follow; and if they be suspected, proofs from Scripture will be cast at them from every side. Wherefore, in their craft, as children of this world, after feeding their so-called lamp from the wild olive, and fearing lest it should soon be quenched (for it is said, 'the light of the wicked shall be put out Job 18:5,') they hide it under the bushel of their hypocrisy, and make a different profession, and boast of patronage of friends and authority of Constantius, that what with their hypocrisy and their professions, those who come to them may be kept from seeing how foul their heresy is. Is it not detestable even in this, that it dares not speak out, but is kept hidden by its own friends, and fostered as serpents are? For from what sources have they got together these words? Or from whom have they received what they venture to say? Not any one man can they specify who has supplied it. For who is there in all mankind, Greek or Barbarian, who ventures to rank among creatures One whom he confesses the while to be

God and says, that He was not till He was made? Or who is there, who to the God in whom he has put faith, refuses to give credit, when He says, 'This is My beloved Son Matthew 3:17,' on the pretence that He is not a Son, but a creature? Rather, such madness would rouse an universal indignation. Nor does Scripture afford them any pretext; for it has been often shown, and it shall be shown now, that their doctrine is alien to the divine oracles. Therefore, since all that remains is to say that from the devil came their mania (for of such opinions he alone is sower), proceed we to resist him — for with him is our real conflict, and they are but instruments — that, the Lord aiding us, and the enemy, as he is wont, being overcome with arguments, they may be put to shame, when they see him without resource who sowed this heresy in them, and may learn, though late, that, as being Arians, they are not Christians.

Chapter IV. That the Son is Eternal and Increate.

These attributes, being the points in dispute, are first proved by direct texts of Scripture. Concerning the 'eternal power' of God in Romans 1:20, which is shown to mean the Son. Remarks on the Arian formula, 'Once the Son was not,' its supporters not daring to speak of 'a time when the Son was not.'

11. At his suggestion then you have maintained and you think, that 'there was once when the Son was not;' this is the first cloke of your views of doctrine which has to be stripped off. Say then what was once when the Son was not, O slanderous and irreligious men ? If you say the Father, your blasphemy is but greater; for it is impious to say that He was 'once,' or to signify Him by the word 'once.' For He is ever, and is now, and as the Son is, so is He, and is Himself He that is, and Father of the Son. But if you say that the Son was once, when He Himself was not, the answer is foolish and unmeaning. For how could He both be and not be? In this difficulty, you can but answer, that there was a time when the Word was not; for your very adverb 'once' naturally signifies this. And your other, 'The Son was not before His generation,' is equivalent to saying, 'There was once when He was not,' for both the one and the other signify that there is a time

before the Word. Whence then this your discovery? Why do you, as 'the heathen, rage, and imagine vain phrases against the Lord and against His Christ.' for no holy Scripture has used such language of the Saviour, but rather 'always' and 'eternal' and 'coexistent always with the Father.' For, 'In the beginning was the Word, and the Word was with God, and the Word was God John 1:1.' And in the Apocalypse he thus speaks ; 'Who is and who was and who is to come.' Now who can rob 'who is' and 'who was' of eternity? This too in confutation of the Jews has Paul written in his Epistle to the Romans, 'Of whom as concerning the flesh is Christ, who is over all, God blessed for ever Romans 9:5;' while silencing the Greeks, he has said, 'The visible things of Him from the creation of the world are clearly seen, being understood by the things that are made, even His eternal Power and Godhead ;' and what the Power of God is, he teaches us elsewhere himself, 'Christ the Power of God and the Wisdom of God.' Surely in these words he does not designate the Father, as you often whisper one to another, affirming that the Father is 'His eternal power.' This is not so; for he says not, 'God Himself is the power,' but 'His is the power.' Very plain is it to all that 'His' is not 'He;' yet not something alien but rather proper to Him. Study too the context and 'turn to the Lord.' now 'the Lord is that Spirit ;'and you will see that it is the Son who is signified.

12. For after making mention of the creation, he naturally speaks of the Framer's Power as seen in it, which Power, I say, is the Word of God, by whom all things have been made. If indeed the creation is sufficient of itself alone, without the Son, to make God known, see that you fall not, from thinking that without the Son it has come to be. But if through the Son it has come to be, and 'in Him all things consist Colossians 1:17,' it must follow that he who contemplates the creation rightly, is contemplating also the Word who framed it, and through Him begins to apprehend the Father. And if, as the Saviour also says, 'No one knows the Father, save the Son, and he to whom the Son shall reveal Him Matthew 11:27,' and if on Philip's asking, 'Show us the Father,' He said not, 'Behold the creation,' but, 'He that has seen Me, has seen the Father John 14:8-9,' reasonably does Paul — while accusing the Greeks of contemplating the harmony and order of the creation without reflecting on the Framing Word within it

(for the creatures witness to their own Framer) so as through the creation to apprehend the true God, and abandon their worship of it — reasonably has he said, 'His Eternal Power and Godhead Romans 1:20,' thereby signifying the Son. And where the sacred writers say, 'Who exists before the ages,' and 'By whom He made the ages Hebrews 1:2,' they thereby as clearly preach the eternal and everlasting being of the Son, even while they are designating God Himself. Thus, if Isaiah says, 'The Everlasting God, the Creator of the ends of the earth Isaiah 40:28;' and Susanna said, 'O Everlasting God ;' and Baruch wrote, 'I will cry unto the Everlasting in my days,' and shortly after, 'My hope is in the Everlasting, that He will save you, and joy has come unto me from the Holy One ;' yet forasmuch as the Apostle, writing to the Hebrews, says, 'Who being the radiance of His glory and the Expression of His Person Hebrews 1:3;' and David too in the eighty-ninth Psalm, 'And the brightness of the Lord be upon us,' and, 'In Your Light shall we see Light ,' who has so little sense as to doubt of the eternity of the Son ? For when did man see light without the brightness of its radiance, that he may say of the Son, 'There was once, when He was not,' or 'Before His generation He was not.' And the words addressed to the Son in the hundred and forty-fourth Psalm, 'Your kingdom is a kingdom of all ages ,' forbid any one to imagine any interval at all in which the Word did not exist. For if every interval in the ages is measured, and of all the ages the Word is King and Maker, therefore, whereas no interval at all exists prior to Him , it were madness to say, 'There was once when the Everlasting was not,' and 'From nothing is the Son.' And whereas the Lord Himself says, 'I am the Truth ,' not 'I became the Truth.' but always, 'I am — I am the Shepherd, — I am the Light,'— and again, 'Call Me not, Lord and Master? And you call Me well, for so I am,' who, hearing such language from God, and the Wisdom, and Word of the Father, speaking of Himself, will any longer hesitate about the truth, and not immediately believe that in the phrase 'I am,' is signified that the Son is eternal and without beginning?

13. It is plain then from the above that the Scriptures declare the Son's eternity; it is equally plain from what follows that the Arian phrases 'He was not,' and 'before' and 'when,' are in the same Scriptures predicated of

creatures. Moses, for instance, in his account of the generation of our system, says, 'And every plant of the field, before it was in the earth, and every herb of the field before it grew; for the Lord God had not caused it to rain upon the earth, and there was not a man to till the ground Genesis 2:5.' And in Deuteronomy, 'When the Most High divided to the nations Deuteronomy 32:8.' And the Lord said in His own Person, 'If you loved Me, you would rejoice because I said, I go unto the Father, for My Father is greater than I. And now I have told you before it come to pass, that when it has come to pass, you might believe John 14:28-29.' And concerning the creation He says by Solomon, 'Or ever the earth was, when there were no depths, I was brought forth; when there were no fountains abounding with water. Before the mountains were settled, before the hills, was I brought forth Proverbs 8:23.' And, 'Before Abraham was, I am John 8:58.' And concerning Jeremiah He says, 'Before I formed you in the womb, I knew you Jeremiah 1:5.' And David in the Psalm says, 'Before the mountains were brought forth, or ever the earth and the world were made, You are, God from everlasting and world without end.' And in Daniel, 'Susanna cried out with a loud voice and said, O everlasting God, that know the secrets, and know all things before they be.' Thus it appears that the phrases 'once was not,' and 'before it came to be,' and 'when,' and the like, belong to things originate and creatures, which come out of nothing, but are alien to the Word. But if such terms are used in Scripture of things originate, but 'ever' of the Word, it follows, O you enemies of God, that the Son did not come out of nothing, nor is in the number of originated things at all, but is the Father's Image and Word eternal, never having not been, but being ever, as the eternal Radiance of a Light which is eternal. Why imagine then times before the Son? Or why blaspheme the Word as after times, by whom even the ages were made? For how did time or age at all subsist when the Word, as you say, had not appeared, 'through' whom 'all things have been made and without' whom 'not one thing was made John 1:3?' Or why, when you mean time, do you not plainly say, 'a time was when the Word was not?' But while you drop the word 'time' to deceive the simple, you do not at all conceal your own feeling, nor, even if you did, could you escape discovery. For you still simply mean times, when you say, 'There was when He was not,' and 'He was not before His generation.'

Chapter V. Subject Continued.

Objection, that the Son's eternity makes Him coordinate with the Father, introduces the subject of His Divine Sonship, as a second proof of His eternity. The word Son is introduced in a secondary, but is to be understood in real sense. Since all things partake of the Father in partaking of the Son, He is the whole participation of the Father, that is, He is the Son by nature; for to be wholly participated is to beget.

14. When these points are thus proved, their profaneness goes further. 'If there never was, when the Son was not,' say they, 'but He is eternal, and coexists with the Father, you call Him no more the Father's Son, but brother.' O insensate and contentious! For if we said only that He was eternally with the Father, and not His Son, their pretended scruple would have some plausibility; but if, while we say that He is eternal, we also confess Him to be Son from the Father, how can He that is begotten be considered brother of Him who begets? And if our faith is in Father and Son, what brotherhood is there between them? And how can

the Word be called brother of Him whose Word He is? This is not an objection of men really ignorant, for they comprehend how the truth lies; but it is a Jewish pretence, and that from those who, in Solomon's words, 'through desire separate themselves Proverbs 18:1 ' from the truth. For the Father and the Son were not generated from some pre-existing origin , that we may account Them brothers, but the Father is the Origin of the Son and begot Him; and the Father is Father, and not born the Son of any; and the Son is Son, and not brother. Further, if He is called the eternal offspring of the Father, He is rightly so called. For never was the essence of the Father imperfect, that what is proper to it should be added afterwards ; nor, as man from man, has the Son been begotten, so as to be later than His Father's existence, but He is God's offspring, and as being proper Son of God, who is ever, He exists eternally. For, whereas it is proper to men to beget in time, from the imperfection of their nature , God's offspring is eternal, for His nature is ever perfect. If then He is not a Son, but a work made out of nothing, they have but to prove it; and then they are at liberty, as if imagining about a creature, to cry out, 'There was once when He was not;' for things which are originated were not, and have come to be. But if

He is Son, as the Father says, and the Scriptures proclaim, and 'Son' is nothing else than what is generated from the Father; and what is generated from the Father is His Word, and Wisdom, and Radiance; what is to be said but that, in maintaining 'Once the Son was not,' they rob God of His Word, like plunderers, and openly predicate of Him that He was once without His proper Word and Wisdom, and that the Light was once without radiance, and the Fountain was once barren and dry ? For though they pretend alarm at the name of time, because of those who reproach them with it, and say, that He was before times, yet whereas they assign certain intervals, in which they imagine He was not, they are most irreligious still, as equally suggesting times, and imputing to God an absence of Reason.

15. But if on the other hand, while they acknowledge with us the name of 'Son,' from an unwillingness to be publicly and generally condemned, they deny that the Son is the proper offspring of the Father's essence, on the ground that this must imply parts and divisions ; what is this but to deny that He is very Son, and only in name to call Him

Son at all? And is it not a grievous error, to have material thoughts about what is immaterial, and because of the weakness of their proper nature to deny what is natural and proper to the Father? It does but remain, that they should deny Him also, because they understand not how God is , and what the Father is, now that, foolish men, they measure by themselves the Offspring of the Father. And persons in such a state of mind as to consider that there cannot be a Son of God, demand our pity; but they must be interrogated and exposed for the chance of bringing them to their senses. If then, as you say, 'the Son is from nothing,' and 'was not before His generation,' He, of course, as well as others, must be called Son and God and Wisdom only by participation; for thus all other creatures consist, and by sanctification are glorified. You have to tell us then, of what He is partaker. All other things partake of the Spirit, but He, according to you, of what is He partaker? Of the Spirit? Nay, rather the Spirit Himself takes from the Son, as He Himself says; and it is not reasonable to say that the latter is sanctified by the former. Therefore it is the Father that He partakes; for this only remains to say. But this, which is participated, what is it or whence ? If it be something external provided by the

Father, He will not now be partaker of the Father, but of what is external to Him; and no longer will He be even second after the Father, since He has before Him this other; nor can He be called Son of the Father, but of that, as partaking which He has been called Son and God. And if this be unseemly and irreligious, when the Father says, 'This is My Beloved Son Matthew 3:17,' and when the Son says that God is His own Father, it follows that what is partaken is not external, but from the essence of the Father. And as to this again, if it be other than the essence of the Son, an equal extravagance will meet us; there being in that case something between this that is from the Father and the essence of the Son, whatever that be.

16. Such thoughts then being evidently unseemly and untrue, we are driven to say that what is from the essence of the Father, and proper to Him, is entirely the Son; for it is all one to say that God is wholly participated, and that He begets; and what does begetting signify but a Son? And thus of the Son Himself, all things partake according to the grace of the Spirit coming from Him ; and this shows that the Son Himself partakes of nothing, but what

is partaken from the Father, is the Son; for, as partaking of the Son Himself, we are said to partake of God; and this is what Peter said 'that you may be partakers in a divine nature 2 Peter 1:4;' as says too the Apostle, 'Do you not know, that you are a temple of God.' and, 'We are the temple of a living God.' And beholding the Son, we see the Father; for the thought and comprehension of the Son, is knowledge concerning the Father, because He is His proper offspring from His essence. And since to be partaken no one of us would ever call affection or division of God's essence (for it has been shown and acknowledged that God is participated, and to be participated is the same thing as to beget); therefore that which is begotten is neither affection nor division of that blessed essence. Hence it is not incredible that God should have a Son, the Offspring of His own essence; nor do we imply affection or division of God's essence, when we speak of 'Son' and 'Offspring;' but rather, as acknowledging the genuine, and true, and Only-begotten of God, so we believe. If then, as we have stated and are showing, what is the Offspring of the Father's essence be the Son, we cannot hesitate, rather we must be certain, that the same is the Wisdom and Word of the Father, in and through whom He creates and makes all things; and His Brightness too, in whom He enlightens all things, and is revealed to whom He will; and His Expression and Image also, in whom He is contemplated and known, wherefore 'He and His Father are one John 10:30,' and whoever looks on Him looks on the Father; and the Christ, in whom all things are redeemed, and the new creation wrought afresh. And on the other hand, the Son being such Offspring, it is not fitting, rather it is full of peril, to say, that He is a work out of nothing, or that He was not before His generation. For he who thus speaks of that which is proper to the Father's essence, already blasphemes the Father Himself; since he really thinks of Him what he falsely imagines of His offspring.

Chapter VI. Subject Continued.

Third proof of the Son's eternity, viz. from other titles indicative of His coessentiality; as the Creator; One of the Blessed Trinity; as Wisdom; as Word; as Image. If the Son is a perfect Image of the Father, why is He not a Father also? Because God, being perfect, is not the origin of a race. Only the Father a Father because the Only Father, only the Son a Son because the Only Son. Men are not really fathers and really sons, but shadows of the True. The Son does not become a Father, because He has received from the Father to be immutable and ever the same

17. This is of itself a sufficient refutation of the Arian heresy; however, its heterodoxy will appear also from the following:— If God be Maker and Creator, and create His works through the Son, and we cannot regard things which come to be, except as being through the Word, is it not blasphemous, God being Maker, to say, that His Framing Word and His Wisdom once was not? It is the same as saying, that God is not Maker, if He had not His proper Framing Word which is from Him, but that that by which He frames, accrues to Him from without , and is alien from Him, and unlike in essence. Next, let them tell us this — or rather learn from it how irreligious they are in saying, 'Once He was not,' and, 'He was not before His generation;'— for if the Word is not with the Father from everlasting, the Triad is not everlasting; but a Monad was first, and afterwards by addition it became a Triad; and so

as time went on, it seems what we know concerning God grew and took shape. And further, if the Son is not proper offspring of the Father's essence, but of nothing has come to be, then of nothing the Triad consists, and once there was not a Triad, but a Monad; and a Triad once with deficiency, and then complete; deficient, before the Son was originated, complete when He had come to be; and henceforth a thing originated is reckoned with the Creator, and what once was not has divine worship and glory with Him who was ever. Nay, what is more serious still, the Triad is discovered to be unlike Itself, consisting of strange and alien natures and essences. And this, in other words, is saying, that the Triad has an originated consistence. What sort of a religion then is this, which is not even like itself, but is in process of completion as time goes on, and is now not thus, and then again thus? For probably it will receive some fresh accession, and so on without limit, since at first and at starting it took its consistence by way of accessions. And so undoubtedly it may decrease on the contrary, for what is added plainly admits of being subtracted.

18. But this is not so: perish the thought; the Triad is not originated; but there is an eternal and one Godhead in a Triad, and there is one Glory of the Holy Triad. And you presume to divide it into different natures; the Father being eternal, yet you say of the Word which is seated by Him, 'Once He was not;' and, whereas the Son is seated by the Father, yet you think to place Him far from Him. The Triad is Creator and Framer, and you fear not to degrade It to things which are from nothing; you scruple not to equal servile beings to the nobility of the Triad, and to rank the King, the Lord of Sabaoth with subjects. Cease this confusion of things unassociable, or rather of things which are not with Him who is. Such statements do not glorify and honour the Lord, but the reverse; for he who dishonours the Son, dishonours also the Father. For if the doctrine of God is now perfect in a Triad, and this is the true and only Religion, and this is the good and the truth, it must have been always so, unless the good and the truth be something that came after, and the doctrine of God is completed by additions. I say, it must have been eternally so; but if not eternally, not so at present either, but at present so, as you suppose it was from the beginning — I mean, not a Triad now. But such heretics no Christian

would bear; it belongs to Greeks, to introduce an originated Triad, and to level It with things originate; for these do admit of deficiencies and additions; but the faith of Christians acknowledges the blessed Triad as unalterable and perfect and ever what It was, neither adding to It what is more, nor imputing to It any loss (for both ideas are irreligious), and therefore it dissociates It from all things generated, and it guards as indivisible and worships the unity of the Godhead Itself; and shuns the Arian blasphemies, and confesses and acknowledges that the Son was ever; for He is eternal, as is the Father, of whom He is the Eternal Word, — to which subject let us now return again.

19. If God be, and be called, the Fountain of wisdom and life — as He says by Jeremiah, 'They have forsaken Me the Fountain of living waters Jeremiah 2:13;' and again, 'A glorious high throne from the beginning, is the place of our sanctuary; O Lord, the Hope of Israel, all that forsake You shall be ashamed, and they that depart from Me shall be written in the earth, because they have forsaken the Lord, the Fountain of living waters ;' and in the book of

Baruch it is written, 'You have forsaken the Fountain of wisdom Baruch 3:12,'— this implies that life and wisdom are not foreign to the Essence of the Fountain, but are proper to It, nor were at any time without existence, but were always. Now the Son is all this, who says, 'I am the Life John 14:6,' and, 'I Wisdom dwell with prudence Proverbs 8:12.' Is it not then irreligious to say, 'Once the Son was not?' for it is all one with saying, 'Once the Fountain was dry, destitute of Life and Wisdom.' But a fountain it would then cease to be; for what begets not from itself, is not a fountain. What a load of extravagance! For God promises that those who do His will shall be as a fountain which the water fails not, saying by Isaiah the prophet, 'And the Lord shall satisfy your soul in drought, and make your bones fat; and you shall be like a watered garden, and like a spring of water, whose waters fail not Isaiah 58:11.' And yet these, whereas God is called and is a Fountain of wisdom, dare to insult Him as barren and void of His proper Wisdom. But their doctrine is false; truth witnessing that God is the eternal Fountain of His proper Wisdom; and, if the Fountain be eternal, the Wisdom also must needs be eternal. For in It were all things made, as David says in the Psalm, 'In Wisdom have

You made them all ;' and Solomon says, 'The Lord by Wisdom has formed the earth, by understanding has He established the heavens Proverbs 3:19.' And this Wisdom is the Word, and by Him, as John says, 'all things were made,' and 'without Him was made not one thing.' And this Word is Christ; for 'there is One God, the Father, from whom are all things, and we for Him; and One Lord Jesus Christ, through whom are all things, and we through Him 1 Corinthians 8:6.' And if all things are through Him, He Himself is not to be reckoned with that 'all.' For he who dares to call Him, through whom are things, one of that 'all,' surely will have like speculations concerning God, from whom are all. But if he shrinks from this as unseemly, and excludes God from that all, it is but consistent that he should also exclude from that all the Only-Begotten Son, as being proper to the Father's essence. And, if He be not one of the all , it is sin to say concerning Him, 'He was not,' and 'He was not before His generation.' Such words may be used of the creatures; but as to the Son, He is such as the Father is, of whose essence He is proper Offspring, Word, and Wisdom. For this is proper to the Son, as regards the Father, and this shows that the Father is proper to the Son; that we may neither say that God was ever without Word, nor that the Son was non-existent. For wherefore a Son, if not from Him? Or wherefore Word and Wisdom, if not ever proper to Him?

20. When then was God without that which is proper to Him? Or how can a man consider that which is proper, as foreign and alien in essence? For other things, according to the nature of things originate, are without likeness in essence with the Maker; but are external to Him, made by the Word at His grace and will, and thus admit of ceasing to be, if it so pleases Him who made them; for such is the nature of things originate. But as to what is proper to the Father's essence (for this we have already found to be the Son), what daring is it in irreligion to say that 'This comes from nothing,' and that 'It was not before generation,' but was adventitious, and can at some time cease to be again? Let a person only dwell upon this thought, and he will discern how the perfection and the plenitude of the Father's essence is impaired by this heresy; however, he will see its unseemliness still more clearly, if he considers that the Son is the Image and Radiance of the Father, and

Expression, and Truth. For if, when Light exists, there be withal its Image, viz. Radiance, and, a Subsistence existing, there be of it the entire Expression, and, a Father existing, there be His Truth (viz. the Son); let them consider what depths of irreligion they fall into, who make time the measure of the Image and Form of the Godhead. For if the Son was not before His generation, Truth was not always in God, which it were a sin to say; for, since the Father was, there was ever in Him the Truth, which is the Son, who says, 'I am the Truth John 14:6.' And the Subsistence existing, of course there was immediately its Expression and Image; for God's Image is not delineated from without, but God Himself has begotten it; in which seeing Himself, He has delight, as the Son Himself says, 'I was His delight Proverbs 8:30.' When then did the Father not see Himself in His own Image? Or when had He not delight, that a man should dare to say, 'the Image is out of nothing,' and 'The Father had not delight before the Image was originated?' and how should the Maker and Creator see Himself in a created and originated essence? For such as is the Father, such must be the Image.

21. Proceed we then to consider the attributes of the Father, and we shall come to know whether this Image is really His. The Father is eternal, immortal, powerful, light, King, Sovereign, God, Lord, Creator, and Maker. These attributes must be in the Image, to make it true that he 'that has seen' the Son 'has seen the Father John 14:9.' If the Son be not all this, but, as the Arians consider, originate, and not eternal, this is not a true Image of the Father, unless indeed they give up shame, and go on to say, that the title of Image, given to the Son, is not a token of a similar essence , but His name only. But this, on the other hand, O you enemies of Christ, is not an Image, nor is it an Expression. For what is the likeness of what is out of nothing to Him who brought what was nothing into being? Or how can that which is not, be like Him that is, being short of Him in once not being, and in its having its place among things originate? However, such the Arians wishing Him to be, devised for themselves arguments such as this —'If the Son is the Father's offspring and Image, and is like in all things to the Father, then it necessarily holds that as He is begotten, so He begets, and He too becomes father of a son. And again, he who is begotten from Him, begets in his turn, and so on without limit; for

this is to make the Begotten like Him that begot Him.' Authors of blasphemy, verily, are these foes of God! Who, sooner than confess that the Son is the Father's Image , conceive material and earthly ideas concerning the Father Himself, ascribing to Him severings and effluences and influences. If then God be as man, let Him become also a parent as man, so that His Son should be father of another, and so in succession one from another, till the series they imagine grows into a multitude of gods. But if God be not as man, as He is not, we must not impute to Him the attributes of man. For brutes and men, after a Creator has begun them, are begotten by succession; and the son, having been begotten of a father who was a son, becomes accordingly in his turn a father to a son, in inheriting from his father that by which he himself has come to be. Hence in such instances there is not, properly speaking, either father or son, nor do the father and the son stay in their respective characters, for the son himself becomes a father, being son of his father, but father of his son. But it is not so in the Godhead; for not as man is God; for the Father is not from a father; therefore does He not beget one who shall become a father; nor is the Son from effluence of the Father, nor is He begotten from a father that was begotten; therefore neither is He begotten so as to beget. Thus it belongs to the Godhead alone, that the Father is properly father, and the Son properly son, and in Them, and Them only, does it hold that the Father is ever Father and the Son ever Son.

22. Therefore he who asks why the Son is not to beget a son, must inquire why the Father had not a father. But both suppositions are unseemly and full of impiety. For as the Father is ever Father and never could become Son, so the Son is ever Son and never could become Father. For in this rather is He shown to be the Father's Expression and Image, remaining what He is and not changing, but thus receiving from the Father to be one and the same. If then the Father change, let the Image change; for so is the Image and Radiance in its relation towards Him who begot It. But if the Father is unalterable, and what He is that He continues, necessarily does the Image also continue what He is, and will not alter. Now He is Son from the Father; therefore He will not become other than is proper to the Father's essence. Idly then have the foolish ones devised this objection also, wishing to separate the

Image from the Father, that they might level the Son with things originated.

Chapter VII. Objections to the Foregoing Proof.

Whether, in the generation of the Son, God made One that was already, or One that was not.

22 (continued). Ranking Him among these, according to the teaching of Eusebius, and accounting Him such as the things which come into being through Him, Arius and his fellows revolted from the truth, and used, when they commenced this heresy, to go about with dishonest phrases which they had got together; nay, up to this time some of them , when they fall in with boys in the market-place, question them, not out of divine Scripture, but thus, as if bursting with 'the abundance of their heart Matthew 12:34;'— 'He who is, did He make him who was not, from that which was [not], or him who was? Therefore did He make the Son, whereas He was, or whereas He was not ?' And again, 'Is the Unoriginate one or two?' and 'Has He free will, and yet does not alter at His own

choice, as being of an alterable nature? For He is not as a stone to remain by Himself unmoveable.' Next they turn to silly women, and address them in turn in this womanish language; 'Had you a son before bearing? Now, as you had not, so neither was the Son of God before His generation.' In such language do the disgraceful men sport and revel, and liken God to men, pretending to be Christians, but changing God's glory 'into an image made like to corruptible man.'

23. Words so senseless and dull deserved no answer at all; however, lest their heresy appear to have any foundation, it may be right, though we go out of the way for it, to refute them even here, especially on account of the silly women who are so readily deceived by them. When they thus speak, they should have inquired of an architect, whether he can build without materials; and if he cannot, whether it follows that God could not make the universe without materials. Or they should have asked every man, whether he can be without place; and if he cannot, whether it follows that God is in place, that so they may be brought to shame even by their audience. Or why is it that, on

hearing that God has a Son, they deny Him by the parallel of themselves; whereas, if they hear that He creates and makes, no longer do they object their human ideas? They ought in creation also to entertain the same, and to supply God with materials, and so deny Him to be Creator, till they end in grovelling with Manichees. But if the bare idea of God transcends such thoughts, and, on very first hearing, a man believes and knows that He is in being, not as we are, and yet in being as God, and creates not as man creates, but yet creates as God, it is plain that He begets also not as men beget, but begets as God. For God does not make man His pattern; but rather we men, for that God is properly, and alone truly , Father of His Son, are also called fathers of our own children; for of Him 'is every fatherhood in heaven and earth named Ephesians 3:15.' And their positions, while unscrutinized, have a show of sense; but if any one scrutinize them by reason, they will be found to incur much derision and mockery.

24. For first of all, as to their first question, which is such as this, how dull and vague it is! They do not explain who it is they ask about, so as to allow of an answer, but they

say abstractedly, 'He who is,' 'him who is not.' Who then 'is,' and what 'are not,' O Arians? Or who 'is,' and who 'is not?' what are said 'to be,' what 'not to be?' for He that is, can make things which are not, and which are, and which were before. For instance, carpenter, and goldsmith, and potter, each, according to his own art, works upon materials previously existing, making what vessels he pleases; and the God of all Himself, having taken the dust of the earth existing and already brought to be, fashions man; that very earth, however, whereas it was not once, He has at one time made by His own Word. If then this is the meaning of their question, the creature on the one hand plainly was not before its origination, and men, on the other, work the existing material; and thus their reasoning is inconsequent, since both 'what is' becomes, and 'what is not' becomes, as these instances show. But if they speak concerning God and His Word, let them complete their question and then ask, Was the God, 'who is,' ever without Reason? And, whereas He is Light, was He ray-less? Or was He always Father of the Word? Or again in this manner. Has the Father 'who is' made the Word 'who is not,' or has He ever with Him His Word, as the proper offspring of His substance? This will show them that they do but presume and venture on sophisms about God and Him who is from Him. Who indeed can bear to hear them say that God was ever without Reason? This is what they fall into a second time, though endeavouring in vain to escape it and to hide it with their sophisms. Nay, one would fain not hear them disputing at all, that God was not always Father, but became so afterwards (which is necessary for their fantasy, that His Word once was not), considering the number of the proofs already adduced against them; while John besides says, 'The Word was John 1:1,' and Paul again writes, 'Who being the brightness of His glory Hebrews 1:3,' and, 'Who is over all, God blessed forever. Amen Romans 9:5.'

25. They had best have been silent; but since it is otherwise, it remains to meet their shameless question with a bold retort. Perhaps on seeing the counter absurdities which beset themselves, they may cease to fight against the truth. After many prayers then that God would be gracious to us, thus we might ask them in turn; God who is, has He so become, whereas He was not? Or is He also before His coming into being? Whereas He is, did He

make Himself, or is He of nothing, and being nothing before, did He suddenly appear Himself? Unseemly is such an enquiry, both unseemly and very blasphemous, yet parallel with theirs; for the answer they make abounds in irreligion. But if it be blasphemous and utterly irreligious thus to inquire about God, it will be blasphemous too to make the like inquiries about His Word. However, by way of exposing a question so senseless and so dull, it is necessary to answer thus:— whereas God is, He was eternally; since then the Father is ever, His Radiance ever is, which is His Word. And again, God who is, has from Himself His Word who also is; and neither has the Word been added, whereas He was not before, nor was the Father once without Reason. For this assault upon the Son makes the blasphemy recoil upon the Father; as if He devised for Himself a Wisdom, and Word, and Son from without ; for whichever of these titles you use, you denote the offspring from the Father, as has been said. So that this their objection does not hold; and naturally; for denying the Logos they in consequence ask questions which are illogical. As then if a person saw the sun, and then inquired concerning its radiance, and said, 'Did that which is make that which was, or that which was not,' he would be held not to reason sensibly, but to be utterly mazed, because he fancied what is from the Light to be external to it, and was raising questions, when and where and whether it were made; in like manner, thus to speculate concerning the Son and the Father and thus to inquire, is far greater madness, for it is to conceive of the Word of the Father as external to Him, and to idly call the natural offspring a work, with the avowal, 'He was not before His generation.' Nay, let them over and above take this answer to their question — The Father who was, made the Son who was, for 'the Word was made flesh John 1:14;' and, whereas He was Son of God, He made Him in consummation of the ages also Son of Man, unless forsooth, after the Samosatene, they affirm that He did not even exist at all, till He became man.

26. This is sufficient from us in answer to their first question. And now on your part, O Arians, remembering your own words, tell us whether He who was needed one who was not for the framing of the universe, or one who was? You said that He made for Himself His Son out of nothing, as an instrument whereby to make the universe.

Which then is superior, that which needs or that which supplies the need? Or does not each supply the deficiency of the other? You rather prove the weakness of the Maker, if He had not power of Himself to make the universe, but provided for Himself an instrument from without , as carpenter might do or shipwright, unable to work anything without adze and saw! Can anything be more irreligious? Yet why should one dwell on its heinousness, when enough has gone before to show that their doctrine is a mere fantasy?

Chapter VIII. Objections Continued.

Whether we may decide the question by the parallel of human sons, which are born later than their parents. No, for the force of the analogy lies in the idea of connaturality. Time is not involved in the idea of Son, but is adventitious to it, and does not attach to God, because He is without parts and passions. The titles Word and Wisdom guard our thoughts of Him and His Son from this misconception. God not a Father, as a Creator, in posse from eternity, because creation does not relate to the essence of God, as generation does.

26. (continued). Nor is answer needful to their other very simple and foolish inquiry, which they put to silly women; or none besides that which has been already given, namely, that it is not suitable to measure divine generation by the nature of men. However, that as before they may pass judgment on themselves, it is well to meet them on the same ground, thus:— Plainly, if they inquire of parents concerning their son, let them consider whence is the child which is begotten. For, granting the parent had not a son before his begetting, still, after having him, he had him, not as external or as foreign, but as from himself, and proper to his essence and his exact image, so that the former is beheld in the latter, and the latter is contemplated in the former. If then they assume from human examples that generation implies time, why not from the same infer that it implies the Natural and the Proper , instead of extracting serpent-like from the earth only what turns to poison? Those who ask of parents, and say, 'Had you a son before you begot him?' should add, 'And if you had a son, did you purchase him from without

as a house or any other possession.' And then you would be answered, 'He is not from without, but from myself. For things which are from without are possessions, and pass from one to another; but my son is from me, proper and similar to my essence, not become mine from another, but begotten of me; wherefore I too am wholly in him, while I remain myself what I am.' For so it is; though the parent be distinct in time, as being man, who himself has come to be in time, yet he too would have had his child ever coexistent with him, but that his nature was a restraint and made it impossible. For Levi too was already in the loins of his great-grandfather, before his own actual generation, or that of his grandfather. When then the man comes to that age at which nature supplies the power, immediately, with nature, unrestrained, he becomes father of the son from himself.

27. Therefore, if on asking parents about children, they get for answer, that children which are by nature are not from without, but from their parents, let them confess in like manner concerning the Word of God, that He is simply from the Father. And if they make a question of the time,

let them say what is to restrain God — for it is necessary to prove their irreligion on the very ground on which their scoff is made — let them tell us, what is there to restrain God from being always Father of the Son; for that what is begotten must be from its father is undeniable. Moreover, they will pass judgment on themselves in attributing such things to God, if, as they questioned women on the subject of time, so they inquire of the sun concerning its radiance, and of the fountain concerning its issue. They will find that these, though an offspring, always exist with those things from which they are. And if parents, such as these, have in common with their children nature and duration, why, if they suppose God inferior to things that come to be , do they not openly say out their own irreligion? But if they do not dare to say this openly, and the Son is confessed to be, not from without, but a natural offspring from the Father, and that there is nothing which is a restraint to God (for not as man is He, but more than the sun, or rather the God of the sun), it follows that the Word is from Him and is ever co-existent with Him, through whom also the Father caused that all things which were not should be. That then the Son comes not of nothing but is eternal and from the Father, is certain even from the nature of the case; and the question of the heretics to parents exposes their perverseness; for they confess the point of nature, and now have been put to shame on the point of time.

28. As we said above, so now we repeat, that the divine generation must not be compared to the nature of men, nor the Son considered to be part of God, nor the generation to imply any passion whatever; God is not as man; for men beget passibly, having a transitive nature, which waits for periods by reason of its weakness. But with God this cannot be; for He is not composed of parts, but being impassible and simple, He is impassibly and indivisibly Father of the Son. This again is strongly evidenced and proved by divine Scripture. For the Word of God is His Son, and the Son is the Father's Word and Wisdom; and Word and Wisdom is neither creature nor part of Him whose Word He is, nor an offspring passibly begotten. Uniting then the two titles, Scripture speaks of 'Son,' in order to herald the natural and true offspring of His essence; and, on the other hand, that none may think of the Offspring humanly, while signifying His essence, it

also calls Him Word, Wisdom, and Radiance; to teach us that the generation was impassible, and eternal, and worthy of God. What affection then, or what part of the Father is the Word and the Wisdom and the Radiance? So much may be impressed even on these men of folly; for as they asked women concerning God's Son, so let them inquire of men concerning the Word, and they will find that the word which they put forth is neither an affection of them nor a part of their mind. But if such be the word of men, who are passible and partitive, why speculate they about passions and parts in the instance of the immaterial and indivisible God, that under pretence of reverence they may deny the true and natural generation of the Son? Enough was said above to show that the offspring from God is not an affection; and now it has been shown in particular that the Word is not begotten according to affection. The same may be said of Wisdom; God is not as man; nor must they here think humanly of Him. For, whereas men are capable of wisdom, God partakes in nothing, but is Himself the Father of His own Wisdom, of which whoever partake are given the name of wise. And this Wisdom too is not a passion, nor a part, but an Offspring proper to the Father. Wherefore He is ever

Father, nor is the character of Father adventitious to God, lest He seem alterable; for if it is good that He be Father, but has not ever been Father, then good has not ever been in Him.

29. But, observe, say they, God was always a Maker, nor is the power of framing adventitious to Him; does it follow then, that, because He is the Framer of all, therefore His works also are eternal, and is it wicked to say of them too, that they were not before origination? Senseless are these Arians; for what likeness is there between Son and work, that they should parallel a father's with a maker's function? How is it that, with that difference between offspring and work, which has been shown, they remain so ill-instructed? Let it be repeated then, that a work is external to the nature, but a son is the proper offspring of the essence; it follows that a work need not have been always, for the workman frames it when he will; but an offspring is not subject to will, but is proper to the essence. And a man may be and may be called Maker, though the works are not as yet; but father he cannot be called, nor can he be, unless a son exist. And if they curiously inquire

why God, though always with the power to make, does not always make (though this also be the presumption of madmen, for 'who has known the mind of the Lord, or who has been His Counsellor?' or how 'shall the thing formed say to' the potter, 'why did you make me thus?' however, not to leave even a weak argument unnoticed), they must be told, that although God always had the power to make, yet the things originated had not the power of being eternal. For they are out of nothing, and therefore were not before their origination; but things which were not before their origination, how could these coexist with the ever-existing God? Wherefore God, looking to what was good for them, then made them all when He saw that, when originated, they were able to abide. And as, though He was able, even from the beginning in the time of Adam, or Noah, or Moses, to send His own Word, yet He sent Him not until the consummation of the ages (for this He saw to be good for the whole creation), so also things originated did He make when He would, and as was good for them. But the Son, not being a work, but proper to the Father's offspring, always is; for, whereas the Father always is, so what is proper to His essence must always be; and this is His

Word and His Wisdom. And that creatures should not be in existence, does not disparage the Maker; for He has the power of framing them, when He wills; but for the offspring not to be ever with the Father, is a disparagement of the perfection of His essence. Wherefore His works were framed, when He would, through His Word; but the Son is ever the proper offspring of the Father's essence.

Chapter IX. Objections Continued.

Whether is the Unoriginate one or two? Inconsistent in Ariansto use an unscriptural word; necessary to define its meaning. Different senses of the word. If it means 'without Father,' there is but One Unoriginate; if 'without beginning or creation,' there are two. Inconsistency of Asterius. 'Unoriginate' a title of God, not in contrast with the Son, but with creatures, as is 'Almighty,' or 'Lord of powers.' 'Father' is the truer title, as not only Scriptural, but implying a Son, and our adoption as sons

30. These considerations encourage the faithful, and distress the heretical, perceiving, as they do, their heresy overthrown thereby. Moreover, their further question, 'whether the Unoriginate be one or two ,' shows how false are their views, how treacherous and full of guile. Not for the Father's honour ask they this, but for the dishonour of the Word. Accordingly, should any one, not aware of their craft, answer, 'the Unoriginated is one,' immediately they spirit out their own venom, saying, 'Therefore the Son is among things originated,' and well have we said, 'He was not before His generation.' Thus they make any kind of disturbance and confusion, provided they can but separate the Son from the Father, and reckon the Framer of all among His works. Now first they may be convicted on this score, that, while blaming the Nicene Bishops for their use of phrases not in Scripture, though these not injurious, but subversive of their irreligion, they themselves went off upon the same fault, that is, using words not in Scripture , and those in contumely of the Lord, knowing 'neither what they say nor whereof they affirm 1 Timothy 1:7.' For instance, let them ask the Greeks, who have been their instructors (for it is a word of their invention, not Scripture), and when they have been instructed in its

various significations, then they will discover that they cannot even question properly, on the subject which they have undertaken. For they have led me to ascertain that by 'unoriginate' is meant what has not yet come to be, but is possible to be, as wood which is not yet become, but is capable of becoming, a vessel; and again what neither has nor ever can come to be, as a triangle quadrangular, and an even number odd. For a triangle neither has nor ever can become quadrangular; nor has even ever, nor can ever, become odd. Moreover, by 'unoriginate' is meant, what exists, but has not come into being from any, nor having a father at all. Further, Asterius, the unprincipled sophist, the patron too of this heresy, has added in his own treatise, that what is not made, but is ever, is 'unoriginate.' They ought then, when they ask the question, to add in what sense they take the word 'unoriginate,' and then the parties questioned would be able to answer to the point.

31. But if they still are satisfied with merely asking, 'Is the Unoriginate one or two?' they must be told first of all, as ill-educated men, that many are such and nothing is such, many, which are capable of origination, and nothing,

which is not capable, as has been said. But if they ask according as Asterius ruled it, as if 'what is not a work but was always' were unoriginate, then they must constantly be told that the Son as well as the Father must in this sense be called unoriginate. For He is neither in the number of things originated, nor a work, but has ever been with the Father, as has already been shown, in spite of their many variations for the sole sake of speaking against the Lord, 'He is of nothing' and 'He was not before His generation.' When then, after failing at every turn, they betake themselves to the other sense of the question, 'existing but not generated of any nor having a father,' we shall tell them that the unoriginate in this sense is only one, namely the Father; and they will gain nothing by their question. For to say that God is in this sense Unoriginate, does not show that the Son is a thing originated, it being evident from the above proofs that the Word is such as He is who begot Him. Therefore if God be unoriginate, His Image is not originated, but an Offspring , which is His Word and His Wisdom. For what likeness has the originated to the unoriginate? (one must not weary of using repetition;) for if they will have it that the one is like the other, so that he who sees the one beholds the other, they are like to say that the Unoriginate is the image of creatures; the end of which is a confusion of the whole subject, an equalling of things originated with the Unoriginate, and a denial of the Unoriginate by measuring Him with the works; and all to reduce the Son into their number.

32. However, I suppose even they will be unwilling to proceed to such lengths, if they follow Asterius the sophist. For he, earnest as he is in his advocacy of the Arian heresy, and maintaining that the Unoriginate is one, runs counter to them in saying, that the Wisdom of God is unoriginate and without beginning also. The following is a passage out of his work : 'The Blessed Paul said not that he preached Christ the power of God or the wisdom of God, but, without the article, 'God's power and God's wisdom 1 Corinthians 1:24;' thus preaching that the proper power of God Himself, which is natural to Him and co-existent with Him unoriginatedly, is something besides.' And again, soon after: 'However, His eternal power and wisdom, which truth argues to be without beginning and unoriginate; this must surely be one.' For though, misunderstanding the Apostle's words, he

considered that there were two wisdoms; yet, by speaking still of a wisdom coexistent with Him, he declares that the Unoriginate is not simply one, but that there is another Unoriginate with Him. For what is coexistent, coexists not with itself, but with another. If then they agree with Asterius, let them never ask again, 'Is the Unoriginate one or two,' or they will have to contest the point with him; if, on the other hand, they differ even from him, let them not rely upon his treatise, lest, 'biting one another, they be consumed one of another Galatians 5:15.' So much on the point of their ignorance; but who can say enough on their crafty character? Who but would justly hate them while possessed by such a madness? For when they were no longer allowed to say 'out of nothing' and 'He was not before His generation,' they hit upon this word 'unoriginate,' that, by saying among the simple that the Son was 'originate,' they might imply the very same phrases 'out of nothing,' and 'He once was not;' for in such phrases things originated and creatures are implied.

33. If they have confidence in their own positions, they should stand to them, and not change about so variously ;

but this they will not, from an idea that success is easy, if they do but shelter their heresy under color of the word 'unoriginate.' Yet after all, this term is not used in contrast with the Son, clamour as they may, but with things originated; and the like may be found in the words 'Almighty,' and 'Lord of the Powers.' For if we say that the Father has power and mastery over all things by the Word, and the Son rules the Father's kingdom, and has the power of all, as His Word, and as the Image of the Father, it is quite plain that neither here is the Son reckoned among that all, nor is God called Almighty and Lord with reference to Him, but to those things which through the Son come to be, and over which He exercises power and mastery through the Word. And therefore the Unoriginate is specified not by contrast to the Son, but to the things which through the Son come to be. And excellently: since God is not as things originated, but is their Creator and Framer through the Son. And as the word 'Unoriginate' is specified relatively to things originated, so the word 'Father' is indicative of the Son. And he who names God Maker and Framer and Unoriginate, regards and apprehends things created and made; and he who calls God Father, thereby conceives and contemplates the Son. And hence one might marvel at the obstinacy which is added to their irreligion, that, whereas the term 'unoriginate' has the aforesaid good sense, and admits of being used religiously , they, in their own heresy, bring it forth for the dishonour of the Son, not having read that he who honours the Son honours the Father, and he who dishonours the Son, dishonours the Father. John 5:23 If they had any concern at all for reverent speaking and the honour due to the Father, it became them rather, and this were better and higher, to acknowledge and call God Father, than to give Him this name. For, in calling God unoriginate, they are, as I said before, calling Him from His works, and as Maker only and Framer, supposing that hence they may signify that the Word is a work after their own pleasure. But that he who calls God Father, signifies Him from the Son being well aware that if there be a Son, of necessity through that Son all things originate were created. And they, when they call Him Unoriginate, name Him only from His works, and know not the Son any more than the Greeks; but he who calls God Father, names Him from the Word; and knowing the Word, he acknowledges Him to be Framer of all, and understands that through Him all things have been made.

34. Therefore it is more pious and more accurate to signify God from the Son and call Him Father, than to name Him from His works only and call Him Unoriginate. For the latter title, as I have said, does nothing more than signify all the works, individually and collectively, which have come to be at the will of God through the Word; but the title Father has its significance and its bearing only from the Son. And, whereas the Word surpasses things originated, by so much and more does calling God Father surpass the calling Him Unoriginate. For the latter is unscriptural and suspicious, because it has various senses; so that, when a man is asked concerning it, his mind is carried about to many ideas; but the word Father is simple and scriptural, and more accurate, and only implies the Son. And 'Unoriginate' is a word of the Greeks, who know not the Son; but 'Father' has been acknowledged and vouchsafed by our Lord. For He, knowing Himself whose Son He was, said, 'I am in the Father, and the Father is in Me;' and, 'He that has seen Me, has seen the Father,' and 'I and the Father are One ;' but nowhere is He found to call the Father Unoriginate. Moreover, when He teaches us to pray, He says not, 'When you pray, say, O God Unoriginate,' but rather, 'When you pray, say, Our Father,

which art in heaven Luke 11:2.' And it was His will that the Summary of our faith should have the same bearing, in bidding us be baptized, not into the name of Unoriginate and originate, nor into the name of Creator and creature, but into the Name of Father, Son, and Holy Ghost. For with such an initiation we too, being numbered among works, are made sons, and using the name of the Father, acknowledge from that name the Word also in the Father Himself. A vain thing then is their argument about the term 'Unoriginate,' as is now proved, and nothing more than a fantasy.

Chapter X. Objections Continued.

How the Word has free will, yet without being alterable. He is unalterable because the Image of the Father, proved from texts.

35. As to their question whether the Word is alterable, it is superfluous to examine it; it is enough simply to write down what they say, and so to show its daring irreligion. How they trifle, appears from the following questions:—

'Has He free will, or has He not? Is He good from choice according to free will, and can He, if He will, alter, being of an alterable nature? Or, as wood or stone, has He not His choice free to be moved and incline hither and there?' It is but agreeable to their heresy thus to speak and think; for, when once they have framed to themselves a God out of nothing and a created Son, of course they also adopt such terms, as being suitable to a creature. However, when in their controversies with Churchmen they hear from them of the real and only Word of the Father, and yet venture thus to speak of Him, does not their doctrine then become the most loathsome that can be found? Is it not enough to distract a man on mere hearing, though unable to reply, and to make him stop his ears, from astonishment at the novelty of what he hears them say, which even to mention is to blaspheme? For if the Word be alterable and changing, where will He stay, and what will be the end of His development? How shall the alterable possibly be like the Unalterable? How should he who has seen the alterable, be considered to have seen the Unalterable? At what state must He arrive, for us to be able to behold in Him the Father? For it is plain that not at all times shall we see the Father in the Son, because the Son is ever altering, and is of changing nature. For the Father is unalterable and unchangeable, and is always in the same state and the same; but if, as they hold, the Son is alterable, and not always the same, but of an ever-changing nature, how can such a one be the Father's Image, not having the likeness of His unalterableness ? How can He be really in the Father, if His purpose is indeterminate? Nay, perhaps, as being alterable, and advancing daily, He is not perfect yet. But away with such madness of the Arians, and let the truth shine out, and show that they are foolish. For must not He be perfect who is equal to God? And must not He be unalterable, who is one with the Father, and His Son proper to His essence? And the Father's essence being unalterable, unalterable must be also the proper Offspring from it. And if they slanderously impute alteration to the Word, let them learn how much their own reason is in peril; for from the fruit is the tree known. For this is why he who has seen the Son has seen the Father; and why the knowledge of the Son is knowledge of the Father.

36. Therefore the Image of the unalterable God must be unchangeable; for 'Jesus Christ is the same yesterday,

today, and for ever Hebrews 13:8.' And David in the Psalm says of Him, 'Thou, Lord, in the beginning hast laid the foundation of the earth, and the heavens are the work of Your hands. They shall perish, but You remain; and they all shall wax old as does a garment. And as a vesture shall Thou fold them up, and they shall be changed, but You are the same, and Your years shall not fail.' And the Lord Himself says of Himself through the Prophet, 'See now that I, even I am He,' and 'I change not.' It may be said indeed that what is here signified relates to the Father; yet it suits the Son also to say this, specially because, when made man, He manifests His own identity and unalterableness to such as suppose that by reason of the flesh He is changed and become other than He was. More trustworthy are the saints, or rather the Lord, than the perversity of the irreligious. For Scripture, as in the above-cited passage of the Psalter, signifying under the name of heaven and earth, that the nature of all things originate and created is alterable and changeable, yet excepting the Son from these, shows us thereby that He is no wise a thing originate; nay teaches that He changes everything else, and is Himself not changed, in saying, 'You are the same, and Your years shall not fail Hebrews 1:12.' And with reason; for things originate, being from nothing , and not being before their origination, because, in truth, they come to be after not being, have a nature which is changeable; but the Son, being from the Father, and proper to His essence, is unchangeable and unalterable as the Father Himself. For it were sin to say that from that essence which is unalterable was begotten an alterable word and a changeable wisdom. For how is He longer the Word, if He be alterable? Or can that be Wisdom which is changeable? Unless perhaps, as accident in essence , so they would have it, viz. as in any particular essence, a certain grace and habit of virtue exists accidentally, which is called Word and Son and Wisdom, and admits of being taken from it and added to it. For they have often expressed this sentiment, but it is not the faith of Christians; as not declaring that He is truly Word and Son of God, or that the wisdom intended is true Wisdom. For what alters and changes, and has no stay in one and the same condition, how can that be true? Whereas the Lord says, 'I am the Truth John 14:6.' If then the Lord Himself speaks thus concerning Himself, and declares His unalterableness, and the Saints have learned and testify this, nay and our notions of God acknowledge it as religious, whence did these men of irreligion draw this novelty? From their heart as from a seat of corruption did they vomit it forth.

Chapter XI. Texts Explained; And First, Phil. II. 9, 10

Whether the words 'Wherefore God has highly exalted' prove moral probation and advancement. Argued against, first, from the force of the word 'Son;' which is inconsistent with such an interpretation. Next, the passage examined. Ecclesiastical sense of 'highly exalted,' and 'gave,' and 'wherefore;' viz. as being spoken with reference to our Lord's manhood. Secondary sense; viz. as implying the Word's 'exaltation' through the resurrection in the same sense in which Scripture speaks of His descent in the Incarnation; how the phrase does not derogate from the nature of the Word.

37. But since they allege the divine oracles and force on them a misinterpretation, according to their private sense , it becomes necessary to meet them just so far as to

vindicate these passages, and to show that they bear an orthodox sense, and that our opponents are in error. They say then, that the Apostle writes, 'Wherefore God also has highly exalted Him, and given Him a Name which is above every name; that in the Name of Jesus every knee should bow, of things in heaven and things in earth and things under the earth Philippians 2:9-10;' and David, 'Wherefore God even Your God, has anointed You with the oil of gladness above Your fellows.' Then they urge, as something acute: 'If He was exalted and received grace, on a 'wherefore,' and on a 'wherefore' He was anointed, He received a reward of His purpose; but having acted from purpose, He is altogether of an alterable nature.' This is what Eusebius and Arius have dared to say, nay to write; while their partizans do not shrink from conversing about it in full market-place, not seeing how mad an argument they use. For if He received what He had as a reward of His purpose, and would not have had it, unless He had needed it, and had His work to show for it, then having gained it from virtue and promotion, with reason had He 'therefore' been called Son and God, without being very Son. For what is from another by nature, is a real offspring, as Isaac was to Abraham, and Joseph to Jacob, and the radiance to the sun; but the so called sons from virtue and grace, have but in place of nature a grace by acquisition, and are something else besides the gift itself; as the men who have received the Spirit by participation, concerning whom Scripture says, 'I begot and exalted children, and they rebelled against Me.' And of course, since they were not sons by nature, therefore, when they altered, the Spirit was taken away and they were disinherited; and again on their repentance that God who thus at the beginning gave them grace, will receive them, and give light, and call them sons again.

38. But if they say this of the Saviour also, it follows that He is neither very God nor very Son, nor like the Father, nor in any wise has God for a Father of His being according to essence, but of the mere grace given to Him, and for a Creator of His being according to essence, after the similitude of all others. And being such, as they maintain, it will be manifest further that He had not the name 'Son' from the first, if so be it was the prize of works done and of that very same advance which He made when He became man, and took the form of the servant; but

then, when, after becoming 'obedient unto death,' He was, as the text says, 'highly exalted,' and received that 'Name' as a grace, 'that in the Name of Jesus every knee should bow Philippians 2:8.' What then was before this, if then He was exalted, and then began to be worshipped, and then was called Son, when He became man? For He seems Himself not to have promoted the flesh at all, but rather to have been Himself promoted through it, if, according to their perverseness, He was then exalted and called Son, when He became man. What then was before this? One must urge the question on them again, to make it understood what their irreligious doctrine results in. For if the Lord be God, Son, Word, yet was not all these before He became man, either He was something else beside these, and afterwards became partaker of them for His virtue's sake, as we have said; or they must adopt the alternative (may it return upon their heads!) that He was not before that time, but is wholly man by nature and nothing more. But this is no sentiment of the Church. but of the Samosatene and of the present Jews. Why then, if they think as Jews, are they not circumcised with them too, instead of pretending Christianity, while they are its foes? For if He was not, or was indeed, but afterwards was promoted, how were all things made by Him, or how in Him, were He not perfect, did the Father delight Proverbs 8:30? And He, on the other hand, if now promoted, how did He before rejoice in the presence of the Father? And, if He received His worship after dying, how is Abraham seen to worship Him in the tent , and Moses in the bush? And, as Daniel saw, myriads of myriads, and thousands of thousands were ministering unto Him? And if, as they say, He had His promotion now, how did the Son Himself make mention of that His glory before and above the world, when He said, 'Glorify Thou Me, O Father, with the glory which I had with You before the world was John 17:5.' If, as they say, He was then exalted, how did He before that 'bow the heavens and come down;' and again, 'The Highest gave His thunder ?' Therefore, if, even before the world was made, the Son had that glory, and was Lord of glory and the Highest, and descended from heaven, and is ever to be worshipped, it follows that He had not promotion from His descent, but rather Himself promoted the things which needed promotion; and if He descended to effect their promotion, therefore He did not receive in reward the name of the Son and God, but rather He Himself has made us sons of the Father, and deified men by becoming Himself man.

39. Therefore He was not man, and then became God, but He was God, and then became man, and that to deify us. Since, if when He became man, only then He was called Son and God, but before He became man, God called the ancient people sons, and made Moses a god of Pharaoh (and Scripture says of many, 'God stands in the congregation of Gods '), it is plain that He is called Son and God later than they. How then are all things through Him, and He before all? Or how is He 'first-born of the whole creation ,' if He has others before Him who are called sons and gods? And how is it that those first partakers do not partake of the Word? This opinion is not true; it is a device of our present Judaizers. For how in that case can any at all know God as their Father? For adoption there could not be apart from the real Son, who says, 'No one knows the Father, save the Son, and he to whomsoever the Son will reveal Him Matthew 11:27.' And how can there be deifying apart from the Word and before Him? Yet, says He to their brethren the Jews, 'If He called them gods, unto whom the Word of God came

John 10:35.' And if all that are called sons and gods, whether in earth or in heaven, were adopted and deified through the Word, and the Son Himself is the Word, it is plain that through Him are they all, and He Himself before all, or rather He Himself only is very Son, and He alone is very God from the very God, not receiving these prerogatives as a reward for His virtue, nor being another beside them, but being all these by nature and according to essence. For He is Offspring of the Father's essence, so that one cannot doubt that after the resemblance of the unalterable Father, the Word also is unalterable.

40. Hitherto we have met their irrational conceits with the true conceptions implied in the Word 'Son,' as the Lord Himself has given us. But it will be well next to cite the divine oracles, that the unalterableness of the Son and His unchangeable nature, which is the Father's, as well as their perverseness, may be still more fully proved. The Apostle then, writing to the Philippians, says, 'Have this mind in you, which was also in Christ Jesus; who, being in the form of God, thought it not a prize to be equal with God; but emptied Himself, taking the form of a servant, being

made in the likeness of men. And, being found in fashion as a man, He humbled Himself, becoming obedient to death, even the death of the cross. Wherefore God also highly exalted Him, and gave Him a Name which is above every name; that in the Name of Jesus every knee should bow, of things in heaven, and things in earth, and things under the earth, and that every tongue should confess that Jesus Christ is Lord, to the glory of God the Father Philippians 2:5-11.' Can anything be plainer and more express than this? He was not from a lower state promoted: but rather, existing as God, He took the form of a servant, and in taking it, was not promoted but humbled Himself. Where then is there here any reward of virtue, or what advancement and promotion in humiliation? For if, being God, He became man, and descending from on high He is still said to be exalted, where is He exalted, being God? This withal being plain, that, since God is highest of all, His Word must necessarily be highest also. Where then could He be exalted higher, who is in the Father and like the Father in all things ? Therefore He is beyond the need of any addition; nor is such as the Arians think Him. For though the Word has descended in order to be exalted, and so it is written, yet what need was there that He should humble Himself, as if to seek that which He had already? And what grace did He receive who is the Giver of grace ? Or how did He receive that Name for worship, who is always worshipped by His Name? Nay, certainly before He became man, the sacred writers invoke Him, 'Save me, O God, for Your Name's sake ;'and again, 'Some put their trust in chariots, and some in horses, but we will remember the Name of the Lord our God.' And while He was worshipped by the Patriarchs, concerning the Angels it is written, 'Let all the Angels of God worship Him Hebrews 1:6.'

41. And if, as David says in the 71st Psalm, 'His Name remains before the sun, and before the moon, from one generation to another ,' how did He receive what He had always, even before He now received it? Or how is He exalted, being before His exaltation the Most High? Or how did He receive the right of being worshipped, who before He now received it, was ever worshipped? It is not a dark saying but a divine mystery. 'In the beginning was the Word, and the Word was with God, and the Word was

God;' but for our sakes afterwards the 'Word was made flesh.' And the term in question, 'highly exalted,' does not signify that the essence of the Word was exalted, for He was ever and is 'equal to God Philippians 2:6,' but the exaltation is of the manhood. Accordingly this is not said before the Word became flesh; that it might be plain that 'humbled' and 'exalted' are spoken of His human nature; for where there is humble estate, there too may be exaltation; and if because of His taking flesh 'humbled' is written, it is clear that 'highly exalted' is also said because of it. For of this was man's nature in want, because of the humble estate of the flesh and of death. Since then the Word, being the Image of the Father and immortal, took the form of the servant, and as man underwent for us death in His flesh, that thereby He might offer Himself for us through death to the Father; therefore also, as man, He is said because of us and for us to be highly exalted, that as by His death we all died in Christ, so again in the Christ Himself we might be highly exalted, being raised from the dead, and ascending into heaven, 'whither the forerunner Jesus is for us entered, not into the figures of the true, but into heaven itself, now to appear in the presence of God for us.' But if now for us the Christ is entered into heaven itself, though He was even before and always Lord and Framer of the heavens, for us therefore is that present exaltation written. And as He Himself, who sanctifies all, says also that He sanctifies Himself to the Father for our sakes, not that the Word may become holy, but that He Himself may in Himself sanctify all of us, in like manner we must take the present phrase, 'He highly exalted Him,' not that He Himself should be exalted, for He is the highest, but that He may become righteousness for us , and we may be exalted in Him, and that we may enter the gates of heaven, which He has also opened for us, the forerunners saying, 'Lift up your gates, O you rulers, and be lifted up, you everlasting doors, and the King of Glory shall come in.' For here also not on Him were shut the gates, as being Lord and Maker of all, but because of us is this too written, to whom the door of paradise was shut. And therefore in a human relation, because of the flesh which He bore, it is said of Him, 'Lift up your gates,' and 'shall come in,' as if a man were entering; but in a divine relation on the other hand it is said of Him, since 'the Word was God,' that He is the 'Lord' and the 'King of Glory.' Such our exaltation the Spirit foreannounced in the eighty-ninth Psalm, saying, 'And in Your righteousness shall they be exalted, for You are the glory of their strength.' And if the Son be Righteousness, then He is not exalted as being Himself in need, but it is we who are exalted in that Righteousness, which is He 1 Corinthians 1:30 .

42. And so too the words 'gave Him' are not written because of the Word Himself; for even before He became man He was worshipped, as we have said, by the Angels and the whole creation in virtue of being proper to the Father; but because of us and for us this too is written of Him. For as Christ died and was exalted as man, so, as man, is He said to take what, as God, He ever had, that even such a grant of grace might reach to us. For the Word was not impaired in receiving a body, that He should seek to receive a grace, but rather He deified that which He put on, and more than that, 'gave' it graciously to the race of man. For as He was ever worshipped as being the Word and existing in the form of God, so being what He ever was, though become man and called Jesus, He none the less has the whole creation under foot, and bending their knees to Him in this Name, and confessing that the

Word's becoming flesh, and undergoing death in flesh, has not happened against the glory of His Godhead, but 'to the glory of God the Father.' For it is the Father's glory that man, made and then lost, should be found again; and, when dead, that he should be made alive, and should become God's temple. For whereas the powers in heaven, both Angels and Archangels, were ever worshipping the Lord, as they are now worshipping Him in the Name of Jesus, this is our grace and high exaltation, that even when He became man, the Son of God is worshipped, and the heavenly powers will not be astonished at seeing all of us, who are of one body with Him , introduced into their realms. And this had not been, unless He who existed in the form of God had taken on Him a servant's form, and had humbled Himself, yielding His body to come unto death.

43. Behold then what men considered the foolishness of God because of the Cross, has become of all things most honoured. For our resurrection is stored up in it; and no longer Israel alone, but henceforth all the nations, as the Prophet has foretold, leave their idols and acknowledge

the true God, the Father of the Christ. And the illusion of demons has come to nought, and He only who is really God is worshipped in the Name of our Lord Jesus Christ. For the fact that the Lord, even when come in human body and called Jesus, was worshipped and believed to be God's Son, and that through Him the Father was known, shows, as has been said, that not the Word, considered as the Word, received this so great grace, but we. For because of our relationship to His Body we too have become God's temple, and in consequence are made God's sons, so that even in us the Lord is now worshipped, and beholders report, as the Apostle says, that God is in them of a truth. As also John says in the Gospel, 'As many as received Him, to them gave He power to become children of God John 1:12;' and in his Epistle he writes, 'By this we know that He abides in us by His Spirit which He has given us 1 John 3:24.' And this too is an evidence of His goodness towards us that, while we were exalted because that the Highest Lord is in us, and on our account grace was given to Him, because that the Lord who supplies the grace has become a man like us, He on the other hand, the Saviour, humbled Himself in taking 'our body of humiliation Philippians 3:21,' and took a servant's form, putting on that flesh which was enslaved to sin. And He indeed has gained nothing from us for His own promotion: for the Word of God is without want and full; but rather we were promoted from Him; for He is the 'Light, which lightens every man, coming into the world John 1:9.' And in vain do the Arians lay stress upon the conjunction 'wherefore,' because Paul has said, 'Wherefore, has God highly exalted Him.' For in saying this he did not imply any prize of virtue, nor promotion from advance , but the cause why the exaltation was bestowed upon us. And what is this but that He who existed in form of God, the Son of a noble Father, humbled Himself and became a servant instead of us and in our behalf? For if the Lord had not become man, we had not been redeemed from sins, not raised from the dead, but remaining dead under the earth; not exalted into heaven, but lying in Hades. Because of us then and in our behalf are the words, 'highly exalted' and 'given.'

44. This then I consider the sense of this passage, and that, a very ecclesiastical sense. However, there is another way in which one might remark upon it, giving the same sense in a parallel way; viz. that, though it does not speak of the

exaltation of the Word Himself, so far as He is Word (for He is, as was just now said, most high and like His Father), yet by reason of His becoming man it indicates His resurrection from the dead. For after saying, 'He has humbled Himself even unto death,' He immediately added, 'Wherefore He has highly exalted Him;' wishing to show, that, although as man He is said to have died, yet, as being Life, He was exalted on the resurrection; for 'He who descended, is the same also who rose again.' He descended in body, and He rose again because He was God Himself in the body. And this again is the reason why according to this meaning he brought in the conjunction 'Wherefore;' not as a reward of virtue nor of advancement, but to signify the cause why the resurrection took place; and why, while all other men from Adam down to this time have died and remained dead, He only rose in integrity from the dead. The cause is this, which He Himself has already taught us, that, being God, He has become man. For all other men, being merely born of Adam, died, and death reigned over them; but He, the Second Man, is from heaven, for 'the Word was made flesh John 1:14,' and this Man is said to be from heaven and heavenly , because the Word descended from heaven;

wherefore He was not held under death. For though He humbled Himself, yielding His own Body to come unto death, in that it was capable of death , yet He was highly exalted from earth, because He was God's Son in a body. Accordingly what is here said, 'Wherefore God also has highly exalted Him,' answers to Peter's words in the Acts, 'Whom God raised up, having loosed the bonds of death, because it was not possible that He should be holden of it Acts 2:24.' For as Paul has written, 'Since being in form of God He became man, and humbled Himself unto death, therefore God also has highly exalted Him,' so also Peter says, 'Since, being God, He became man, and signs and wonders proved Him to beholders to be God, therefore it was not possible that He should be holden of death.' To man it was not possible to succeed in this; for death belongs to man; wherefore, the Word, being God, became flesh, that, being put to death in the flesh, He might quicken all men by His own power.

45. But since He Himself is said to be 'exalted,' and God 'gave' Him, and the heretics think this a defect or affection in the essence of the Word, it becomes necessary to

explain how these words are used. He is said to be exalted from the lower parts of the earth, because death is ascribed even to Him. Both events are reckoned His, since it was His Body, and none other's, that was exalted from the dead and taken up into heaven. And again, the Body being His, and the Word not being external to it, it is natural that when the Body was exalted, He, as man, should, because of the body, be spoken of as exalted. If then He did not become man, let this not be said of Him: but if the Word became flesh, of necessity the resurrection and exaltation, as in the case of a man, must be ascribed to Him, that the death which is ascribed to Him may be a redemption of the sin of men and an abolition of death, and that the resurrection and exaltation may for His sake remain secure for us. In both respects he has said of Him, 'God has highly exalted Him,' and 'God has given to Him;' that herein moreover he may show that it is not the Father that has become flesh, but it is His Word, who has become man, and receives after the manner of men from the Father, and is exalted by Him, as has been said. And it is plain, nor would any one dispute it, that what the Father gives, He gives through. the Son. And it is marvellous and overwhelming verily; for the grace which the Son gives from the Father, that the Son Himself is said to receive; and the exaltation, which the Son bestows from the Father, with that the Son is Himself exalted. For He who is the Son of God, became Himself the Son of Man; and, as Word, He gives from the Father, for all things which the Father does and gives, He does and supplies through Him; and as the Son of Man, He Himself is said after the manner of men to receive what proceeds from Him, because His Body is none other than His, and is a natural recipient of grace, as has been said. For He received it as far as His man's nature was exalted; which exaltation was its being deified. But such an exaltation the Word Himself always had according to the Father's Godhead and perfection, which was His.

Chapter XII. Texts Explained; Secondly, Psalm XLV. 7, 8.

Whether the words 'therefore,' 'anointed,' etc., imply that the Word has been rewarded. Argued against first from the word 'fellows' or 'partakers.' He is anointed with the Spirit in His manhood to sanctify human nature.

Therefore the Spirit descended on Him in Jordan, when in the flesh. And He is said to sanctify Himself for us, and give us the gloryHe has received. The word 'wherefore' implies His divinity. 'You have loved righteousness,' etc., do not imply trial or choice.

46. Such an explanation of the Apostle's words confutes the irreligious men; and what the sacred poet says admits also the same orthodox sense, which they misinterpret, but which in the Psalmist is manifestly religious. He says then, 'Your throne, O God, is for ever and ever; a sceptre of righteousness is the sceptre of Your Kingdom. You have loved righteousness, and hated iniquity, therefore God, even Your God, has anointed You with the oil of gladness above Your fellows.' Behold, O you Arians, and acknowledge even hence the truth. The Singer speaks of us all as 'fellows' or 'partakers' of the Lord: but were He one of things which come out of nothing and of things originate, He Himself had been one of those who partake. But, since he hymned Him as the eternal God, saying, 'Your throne, O God, is for ever and ever,' and has declared that all other things partake of Him, what

conclusion must we draw, but that He is distinct from originated things, and He only the Father's veritable Word, Radiance, and Wisdom, which all things originate partake , being sanctified by Him in the Spirit ? And therefore He is here 'anointed,' not that He may become God, for He was so even before; nor that He may become King, for He had the Kingdom eternally, existing as God's Image, as the sacred Oracle shows; but in our behalf is this written, as before. For the Israelitish kings, upon their being anointed, then became kings, not being so before, as David, as Hezekiah, as Josiah, and the rest; but the Saviour on the contrary, being God, and ever ruling in the Father's Kingdom, and being Himself He that supplies the Holy Ghost, nevertheless is here said to be anointed, that, as before, being said as man to be anointed with the Spirit, He might provide for us men, not only exaltation and resurrection, but the indwelling and intimacy of the Spirit. And signifying this the Lord Himself has said by His own mouth in the Gospel according to John, 'I have sent them into the world, and for their sakes do I sanctify Myself, that they may be sanctified in the truth.' In saying this He has shown that He is not the sanctified, but the Sanctifier; for He is not sanctified by other, but Himself sanctifies

Himself, that we may be sanctified in the truth. He who sanctifies Himself is Lord of sanctification. How then does this take place? What does He mean but this? 'I, being the Father's Word, I give to Myself, when becoming man, the Spirit; and Myself, become man, do I sanctify in Him, that henceforth in Me, who am Truth (for Your Word is Truth), all may be sanctified.'

47. If then for our sake He sanctifies Himself, and does this when He has become man, it is very plain that the Spirit's descent on Him in Jordan was a descent upon us, because of His bearing our body. And it did not take place for promotion to the Word, but again for our sanctification, that we might share His anointing, and of us it might be said, 'Do you not know that you are God's Temple, and the Spirit of God dwells in you 1 Corinthians 3:16?' For when the Lord, as man, was washed in Jordan, it was we who were washed in Him and by Him. And when He received the Spirit, we it was who by Him were made recipients of It. And moreover for this reason, not as Aaron or David or the rest, was He anointed with oil, but in another way above all His fellows, 'with the oil of

gladness,' which He Himself interprets to be the Spirit, saying by the Prophet, 'The Spirit of the Lord is upon Me, because the Lord has anointed Me Isaiah 61:1;' as also the Apostle has said, 'How God anointed Him with the Holy Ghost. Acts 10:38 ' When then were these things spoken of Him but when He came in the flesh and was baptized in Jordan, and the Spirit descended on Him? And indeed the Lord Himself said, 'The Spirit shall take of Mine;' and 'I will send Him;' and to His disciples, 'Receive the Holy Ghost.' And notwithstanding, He who, as the Word and Radiance of the Father, gives to others, now is said to be sanctified, because now He has become man, and the Body that is sanctified is His. From Him then we have begun to receive the unction and the seal, John saying, 'And you have an unction from the Holy One;' and the Apostle, 'And you were sealed with the Holy Spirit of promise.' Therefore because of us and for us are these words. What advance then of promotion, and reward of virtue or generally of conduct, is proved from this in our Lord's instance? For if He was not God, and then had become God, if not being King He was preferred to the Kingdom, your reasoning would have had some faint plausibility. But if He is God and the throne of His kingdom is everlasting, in what way could God advance? Or what was there wanting to Him who was sitting on His Father's throne? And if, as the Lord Himself has said, the Spirit is His, and takes of His, and He sends It, it is not the Word, considered as the Word and Wisdom, who is anointed with the Spirit which He Himself gives, but the flesh assumed by Him which is anointed in Him and by Him ; that the sanctification coming to the Lord as man, may come to all men from Him. For not of Itself, says He, does the Spirit speak, but the Word is He who gives It to the worthy. For this is like the passage considered above; for as the Apostle has written, 'Who existing in form of God thought it not a prize to be equal with God, but emptied Himself, and took a servant's form,' so David celebrates the Lord, as the everlasting God and King, but sent to us and assuming our body which is mortal. For this is his meaning in the Psalm, 'All your garments smell of myrrh, aloes, and cassia;' and it is represented by Nicodemus and by Mary's company, when the one came bringing 'a mixture of myrrh and aloes, about an hundred pounds weight;' and the others John 19:39; Luke 24:1 'the spices which they had prepared' for the burial of the Lord's body.

48. What advancement then was it to the Immortal to have assumed the mortal? Or what promotion is it to the Everlasting to have put on the temporal? What reward can be great to the Everlasting God and King in the bosom of the Father? See ye not, that this too was done and written because of us and for us, that us who are mortal and temporal, the Lord, become man, might make immortal, and bring into the everlasting kingdom of heaven? Blush ye not, speaking lies against the divine oracles? For when our Lord Jesus Christ had been among us, we indeed were promoted, as rescued from sin; but He is the same ; nor did He alter, when He became man (to repeat what I have said), but, as has been written, 'The Word of God abides forever.' Surely as, before His becoming man, He, the Word, dispensed to the saints the Spirit as His own , so also when made man, He sanctifies all by the Spirit and says to His Disciples, 'Receive the Holy Ghost.' And He gave to Moses and the other seventy; and through Him David prayed to the Father, saying, 'Take not Your Holy Spirit from me.' On the other hand, when made man, He said, 'I will send to you the Paraclete, the Spirit of truth

John 15:26;' and He sent Him, He, the Word of God, as being faithful. Therefore 'Jesus Christ is the same yesterday, today, and for ever Hebrews 13:8,' remaining unalterable, and at once gives and receives, giving as God's Word, receiving as man. It is not the Word then, viewed as the Word, that is promoted; for He had all things and has them always; but men, who have in Him and through Him their origin of receiving them. For, when He is now said to be anointed in a human respect, we it is who in Him are anointed; since also when He is baptized, we it is who in Him are baptized. But on all these things the Saviour throws much light, when He says to the Father, 'And the glory which You gave Me, I have given to them, that they may be one, even as We are one John 17:22.' Because of us then He asked for glory, and the words occur, 'took' and 'gave' and 'highly exalted,' that we might take, and to us might be given, and we might be exalted in Him; as also for us He sanctifies Himself, that we might be sanctified in Him.

49. But if they take advantage of the word 'wherefore,' as connected with the passage in the Psalm, 'Wherefore God,

even Your God, has anointed You,' for their own purposes, let these novices in Scripture and masters in irreligion know, that, as before, the word 'wherefore' does not imply reward of virtue or conduct in the Word, but the reason why He came down to us, and of the Spirit's anointing which took place in Him for our sakes. For He says not, 'Wherefore He anointed You in order to Your being God or King or Son or Word.' for so He was before and is for ever, as has been shown; but rather, 'Since You are God and King, therefore You were anointed, since none but You could unite man to the Holy Ghost, Thou the Image of the Father, in which we were made in the beginning; for Yours is even the Spirit.' For the nature of things originate could give no warranty for this, Angels having transgressed, and men disobeyed. Wherefore there was need of God and the Word is God; that those who had become under a curse, He Himself might set free. If then He was of nothing, He would not have been the Christ or Anointed, being one among others and having fellowship as the rest. But, whereas He is God, as being Son of God, and is everlasting King, and exists as Radiance and Expression Hebrews 1:3 of the Father, therefore fitly is He the expected Christ, whom the Father announces to mankind, by revelation to His holy Prophets; that as through Him we have come to be, so also in Him all men might be redeemed from their sins, and by Him all things might be ruled. And this is the cause of the anointing which took place in Him, and of the incarnate presence of the Word , which the Psalmist foreseeing, celebrates, first His Godhead and kingdom, which is the Father's, in these tones, 'Your throne, O God, is for ever and ever; a sceptre of righteousness is the sceptre of Your Kingdom ;' then announces His descent to us thus, 'Wherefore God, even Your God, has anointed You with the oil of gladness above Your fellows. '

50. What is there to wonder at, what to disbelieve, if the Lord who gives the Spirit, is here said Himself to be anointed with the Spirit, at a time when, necessity requiring it, He did not refuse in respect of His manhood to call Himself inferior to the Spirit? For the Jews saying that He cast out devils in Beelzebub, He answered and said to them, for the exposure of their blasphemy, 'But if I through the Spirit of God cast out demons Matthew 12:28.' Behold, the Giver of the Spirit here says that He

cast out demons in the Spirit; but this is not said, except because of His flesh. For since man's nature is not equal of itself to casting out demons, but only in power of the Spirit, therefore as man He said, 'But if I through the Spirit of God cast out demons.' Of course too He signified that the blasphemy offered to the Holy Ghost is greater than that against His humanity, when He said, 'Whosoever shall speak a word against the Son of man, it shall be forgiven him;' such as were those who said, 'Is not this the carpenter's son ?' but they who blaspheme against the Holy Ghost, and ascribe the deeds of the Word to the devil, shall have inevitable punishment. This is what the Lord spoke to the Jews, as man; but to the disciples showing His Godhead and His majesty, and intimating that He was not inferior but equal to the Spirit, He gave the Spirit and said, 'Receive the Holy Ghost,' and 'I send Him,' and 'He shall glorify Me,' and 'Whatsoever He hears, that He shall speak.' As then in this place the Lord Himself, the Giver of the Spirit, does not refuse to say that through the Spirit He casts out demons, as man; in like manner He the same, the Giver of the Spirit, refused not to say, 'The Spirit of the Lord is upon Me, because He has anointed Me Isaiah 61:1,' in respect of His having become flesh, as John has said; that it might be shown in both these particulars, that we are they who need the Spirit's grace in our sanctification, and again who are unable to cast out demons without the Spirit's power. Through whom then and from whom behooved it that the Spirit should be given but through the Son, whose also the Spirit is? And when were we enabled to receive It, except when the Word became man? And, as the passage of the Apostle shows, that we had not been redeemed and highly exalted, had not He who exists in form of God taken a servant's form, so David also shows, that no otherwise should we have partaken the Spirit and been sanctified, but that the Giver of the Spirit, the Word Himself, hast spoken of Himself as anointed with the Spirit for us. And therefore have we securely received it, He being said to be anointed in the flesh; for the flesh being first sanctified in Him, and He being said, as man, to have received for its sake, we have the sequel of the Spirit grace, receiving 'out of His fullness John 1:16.'

51. Nor do the words, 'You have loved righteousness and hated iniquity,' which are added in the Psalm, show, as

again you suppose, that the Nature of the Word is alterable, but rather by their very force signify His unalterableness. For since of things originate the nature is alterable, and the one portion had transgressed and the other disobeyed, as has been said, and it is not certain how they will act, but it often happens that he who is now good afterwards alters and becomes different, so that one who was but now righteous, soon is found unrighteous, wherefore there was here also need of one unalterable, that men might have the immutability of the righteousness of the Word as an image and type for virtue. And this thought commends itself strongly to the right-minded. For since the first man Adam altered, and through sin death came into the world, therefore it became the second Adam to be unalterable; that, should the Serpent again assault, even the Serpent's deceit might be baffled, and, the Lord being unalterable and unchangeable, the Serpent might become powerless in his assault against all. For as when Adam had transgressed, his sin reached unto all men, so, when the Lord had become man and had overthrown the Serpent, that so great strength of His is to extend through all men, so that each of us may say, 'For we are not ignorant of his devices. 2 Corinthians 2:11 ' Good reason then that the Lord, who ever is in nature unalterable, loving righteousness and hating iniquity, should be anointed and Himself sent, that, He, being and remaining the same , by taking this alterable flesh, 'might condemn sin in it ,' and might secure its freedom, and its ability henceforth 'to fulfil the righteousness of the law?' in itself, so as to be able to say, 'But we are not in the flesh but in the Spirit, if so be that the Spirit of God dwells in us Romans 8:9.'

52. Vainly then, here again, O Arians, have you made this conjecture, and vainly alleged the words of Scripture; for God's Word is unalterable, and is ever in one state, not as it may happen , but as the Father is; since how is He like the Father, unless He be thus? Or how is all that is the Father's the Son's also, if He has not the unalterableness and unchangeableness of the Father ? Not as being subject to laws , and biassed to one side, does He love the one and hate the other, lest, if from fear of falling away He chooses the one, we admit that He is alterable otherwise also; but, as being God and the Father's Word, He is a just judge and lover of virtue, or rather its dispenser. Therefore being

just and holy by nature, on this account He is said to love righteousness and to hate iniquity; as much as to say, that He loves and chooses the virtuous, and rejects and hates the unrighteous. And divine Scripture says the same of the Father; 'The Righteous Lord loves righteousness; Thou hate all them that work iniquity ,' and 'The Lord loves the gates of Sion, more than all the dwellings of Jacob ;' and, 'Jacob have I loved, but Esau have I hated Malachi 1:2-3;' and in Isaiah there is the voice of God again saying, 'I the Lord love righteousness, and hate robbery of unrighteousness Isaiah 61:8.' Let them then expound those former words as these latter; for the former also are written of the Image of God: else, misinterpreting these as those, they will conceive that the Father too is alterable. But since the very hearing others say this is not without peril, we do well to think that God is said to love righteousness and to hate robbery of unrighteousness, not as if biassed to one side, and capable of the contrary, so as to select the latter and not choose the former, for this belongs to things originated, but that, as a judge, He loves and takes to Him the righteous and withdraws from the bad. It follows then to think the same concerning the Image of God also, that He loves and hates no otherwise than thus. For such must be the nature of the Image as is Its Father, though the Arians in their blindness fail to see either that image or any other truth of the divine oracles. For being forced from the conceptions or rather misconceptions of their own hearts, they fall back upon passages of divine Scripture, and here too from want of understanding, according to their wont, they discern not their meaning; but laying down their own irreligion as a sort of canon of interpretation , they wrest the whole of the divine oracles into accordance with it. And so on the bare mention of such doctrine, they deserve nothing but the reply, 'You do err, not knowing the Scriptures nor the power of God Matthew 22:29;' and if they persist in it, they must be put to silence, by the words, 'Render to' man 'the things that are' man's, 'and to God the things that are' God's.

Chapter XIII. Texts Explained; Thirdly, Hebrews I. 4.

Additional texts brought as objections; e.g. Hebrews 1:4; 7:22. Whether the word 'better' implies likeness to the

Angels; and 'made' or 'become' implies creation. Necessary to consider the circumstances under which Scripture speaks. Difference between 'better' and 'greater;' texts in proof. 'Made' or 'become' a general word. Contrast in Hebrews 1:4, between the Son and the Works in point of nature. The difference of the punishments under the two Covenants shows the difference of the natures of the Son and the Angels. 'Become' relates not to the nature of the Word, but to His manhood and office and relation towards us. Parallel passages in which the term is applied to the Eternal Father.

53. But it is written, say they, in the Proverbs, 'The Lord created me the beginning of His ways, for His Works ;' and in the Epistle to the Hebrews the Apostle says, 'Being made so much better than the Angels, as He has by inheritance obtained a more excellent Name than they.' And soon after, 'Wherefore, holy brethren, partakers of the heavenly calling, consider the Apostle and High Priest of our profession, Christ Jesus, who was faithful to Him that made Him.' And in the Acts, 'Therefore let all the house of Israel know assuredly, that God has made that same

Jesus whom you have crucified both Lord and Christ.' These passages they brought forward at every turn, mistaking their sense, under the idea that they proved that the Word of God was a creature and work and one of things originate; and thus they deceive the thoughtless, making the language of Scripture their pretence, but instead of the true sense sowing upon it the poison of their own heresy. For had they known, they would not have been irreligious against 'the Lord of glory 1 Corinthians 2:8,' nor have wrested the good words of Scripture. If then henceforward openly adopting Caiaphas's way, they have determined on judaizing, and are ignorant of the text, that verily God shall dwell upon the earth , let them not inquire into the Apostolical sayings; for this is not the manner of Jews. But if, mixing themselves up with the godless Manichees , they deny that 'the Word was made flesh,' and His Incarnate presence, then let them not bring forward the Proverbs, for this is out of place with the Manichees. But if for preferment-sake, and the lucre of avarice which follows , and the desire for good repute, they venture not on denying the text, 'The Word was made flesh,' since so it is written, either let them rightly interpret the words of Scripture, of the embodied presence of the Saviour, or, if they deny their sense, let them deny that the Lord became man at all. For it is unseemly, while confessing that 'the Word became flesh,' yet to be ashamed at what is written of Him, and on that account to corrupt the sense.

54. For it is written, 'So much better than the Angels.' let us then first examine this. Now it is right and necessary, as in all divine Scripture, so here, faithfully to expound the time of which the Apostle wrote, and the person , and the point; lest the reader, from ignorance missing either these or any similar particular, may be wide of the true sense. This understood that inquiring eunuch, when he thus besought Philip, 'I pray you, of whom does the Prophet speak this? Of himself, or of some other man Acts 8:34?' for he feared lest, expounding the lesson unsuitably to the person, he should wander from the right sense. And the disciples, wishing to learn the time of what was foretold, besought the Lord, 'Tell us,' said they, 'when shall these things be? And what is the sign of Your coming Matthew 24:3?' And again, hearing from the Saviour the events of the end, they desired to learn the time of it, that they

might be kept from error themselves, and might be able to teach others; as, for instance, when they had learned, they set right the Thessalonians , who were going wrong. When then one knows properly these points, his understanding of the faith is right and healthy; but if he mistakes any such points, immediately he falls into heresy. Thus Hymenæus and Alexander and their fellows were beside the time, when they said that the resurrection had already been; and the Galatians were after the time, in making much of circumcision now. And to miss the person was the lot of the Jews, and is still, who think that of one of themselves is said, 'Behold, the Virgin shall conceive, and bear a Son, and they shall call his Name Emmanuel, which is being interpreted, God with us Isaiah 7:14; Matthew 1:23;' and that, 'A prophet shall the Lord your God raise up to you Deuteronomy 18:15,' is spoken of one of the Prophets; and who, as to the words, 'He was led as a sheep to the slaughter Isaiah 53:7,' instead of learning from Philip, conjecture them spoken of Isaiah or some other of the former Prophets.

55. (3.) Such has been the state of mind under which Christ's enemies have fallen into their execrable heresy. For had they known the person, and the subject, and the season of the Apostle's words, they would not have expounded of Christ's divinity what belongs to His manhood, nor in their folly have committed so great an act of irreligion. Now this will be readily seen, if one expounds properly the beginning of this lection. For the Apostle says, 'God who at sundry times and various manners spoke in times past unto the fathers by the prophets, has in these last days spoken unto us by His Son Hebrews 1:1-2;' then again shortly after he says, 'when He had by Himself purged our sins, He sat down on the right hand of the Majesty on high, having become so much better than the Angels, as He has by inheritance obtained a more excellent Name than they.' It appears then that the Apostle's words make mention of that time, when God spoke unto us by His Son, and when a purging of sins took place. Now when did He speak unto us by His Son, and when did purging of sins take place? And when did He become man? When, but subsequently to the Prophets in the last days? Next, proceeding with his account of the economy in which we were concerned, and speaking of the last times,

he is naturally led to observe that not even in the former times was God silent with men, but spoke to them by the Prophets. And, whereas the prophets ministered, and the Law was spoken by Angels, while the Son too came on earth, and that in order to minister, he was forced to add, 'Become so much better than the Angels,' wishing to show that, as much as the son excels a servant, so much also the ministry of the Son is better than the ministry of servants. Contrasting then the old ministry and the new, the Apostle deals freely with the Jews, writing and saying, 'Become so much better than the Angels.' This is why throughout he uses no comparison, such as 'become greater,' or 'more honourable,' lest we should think of Him and them as one in kind, but 'better' is his word, by way of marking the difference of the Son's nature from things originated. And of this we have proof from divine Scripture; David, for instance, saying in the Psalm, 'One day in Your courts is better than a thousand :' and Solomon crying out, 'Receive my instruction and not silver, and knowledge rather than choice gold. For wisdom is better than rubies; and all the things that may be desired are not to be compared to it Proverbs 8:10-11.' Are not wisdom and stones of the earth different in essence and separate in nature? Are heavenly courts at all akin to earthly houses? Or is there any similarity between things eternal and spiritual, and things temporal and mortal? And this is what Isaiah says, 'Thus says the Lord unto the eunuchs that keep My sabbaths, and choose the things that please Me, and take hold of My Covenant; even unto them will I give in Mine house, and within My walls, a place and a name better than of sons and of daughters: I will give them an everlasting name that shall not be cut off Isaiah 56:4-5.' In like manner there is nought akin between the Son and the Angels; so that the word 'better' is not used to compare but to contrast, because of the difference of His nature from them. And therefore the Apostle also himself, when he interprets the word 'better,' places its force in nothing short of the Son's excellence over things originated, calling the one Son, the other servants; the one, as a Son with the Father, sitting on the right; and the others, as servants, standing before Him, and being sent, and fulfilling offices.

56. Scripture, in speaking thus, implies, O Arians, not that the Son is originate, but rather other than things originate,

and proper to the Father, being in His bosom. (4.) Nor does even the expression 'become,' which here occurs, show that the Son is originate, as you suppose. If indeed it were simply 'become' and no more, a case might stand for the Arians; but, whereas they are forestalled with the word 'Son' throughout the passage, showing that He is other than things originate, so again not even the word 'become' occurs absolutely , but 'better' is immediately subjoined. For the writer thought the expression immaterial, knowing that in the case of one who was confessedly a genuine Son, to say 'become' is the same with saying that He had been made, and is, 'better.' For it matters not even if we speak of what is generate, as 'become' or 'made;' but on the contrary, things originate cannot be called generate, God's handiwork as they are, except so far as after their making they partake of the generate Son, and are therefore said to have been generated also, not at all in their own nature, but because of their participation of the Son in the Spirit. And this again divine Scripture recognises; for it says in the case of things originate, 'All things came to be through Him, and without Him nothing came to be John 1:3,' and, 'In wisdom have You made them all ;' but in the case of sons which are generate, 'To Job there came to be seven sons and three daughters Job 1:2,' and, 'Abraham was an hundred years old when there came to be to him Isaac his son Genesis 21:5;' and Moses said Deuteronomy 21:15, 'If to any one there come to be sons.' Therefore since the Son is other than things originate, alone the proper offspring of the Father's essence, this plea of the Arians about the word 'become' is worth nothing.

(5.) If moreover, baffled so far, they should still violently insist that the language is that of comparison, and that comparison in consequence implies oneness of kind, so that the Son is of the nature of Angels, they will in the first place incur the disgrace of rivalling and repeating what Valentinus held, and Carpocrates, and those other heretics, of whom the former said that the Angels were one in kind with the Christ, and Carpocrates that Angels are framers of the world. Perchance it is under the instruction of these masters that they compare the Word of God with the Angels.

57. Though surely amid such speculations, they will be moved by the sacred poet, saying, 'Who is he among the gods that shall be like the Lord ,' and, 'Among the gods there is none like You, O Lord.' However, they must be answered, with the chance of their profiting by it, that comparison confessedly does belong to subjects one in kind, not to those which differ. No one, for instance, would compare God with man, or again man with brutes, nor wood with stone, because their natures are unlike; but God is beyond comparison, and man is compared to man, and wood to wood, and stone to stone. Now in such cases we should not speak of 'better,' but of 'rather' and 'more;' thus Joseph was comely rather than his brethren, and Rachel than Leah; star is not better than star, but is the rather excellent in glory; whereas in bringing together things which differ in kind, then 'better' is used to mark the difference, as has been said in the case of wisdom and jewels. Had then the Apostle said, 'by so much has the Son precedence of the Angels,' or 'by so much greater,' you would have had a plea, as if the Son were compared with the Angels; but, as it is, in saying that He is 'better,' and differs as far as Son from servants, the Apostle shows that He is other than the Angels in nature.

(6.) Moreover by saying that He it is who has 'laid the foundation of all things Hebrews 1:10,' he shows that He is other than all things originate. But if He be other and different in essence from their nature, what comparison of His essence can there be, or what likeness to them? Though, even if they have any such thoughts, Paul shall refute them, who speaks to the very point, 'For unto which of the Angels said He at any time, You are My Son, this day have I begotten You? And of the Angels He says, Who makes His Angels spirits, and His ministers a flame of fire Hebrews 1:7.'

58. Observe here, the word 'made' belongs to things originate, and he calls them things made; but to the Son he speaks not of making, nor of becoming, but of eternity and kingship, and a Framer's office, exclaiming, 'Your Throne, O God, is for ever and ever;' and, 'Thou, Lord, in the beginning hast laid the foundation of the earth, and the heavens are the works of Your hands; they shall perish, but You remain.' From which words even they, were they but willing, might perceive that the Framer is other than things framed, the former God, the latter things originate,

made out of nothing. For what has been said, 'They shall perish,' is said, not as if the creation were destined for destruction, but to express the nature of things originate by the issue to which they tend. For things which admit of perishing, though through the grace of their Maker they perish not, yet have come out of nothing, and themselves witness that they once were not. And on this account, since their nature is such, it is said of the Son, 'You remain,' to show His eternity; for not having the capacity of perishing, as things originate have, but having eternal duration, it is foreign to Him to have it said, 'He was not before His generation,' but proper to Him to be always, and to endure together with the Father. And though the Apostle had not thus written in his Epistle to the Hebrews, still his other Epistles, and the whole of Scripture, would certainly forbid their entertaining such notions concerning the Word. But since he has here expressly written it, and, as has been above shown, the Son is Offspring of the Father's essence, and He is Framer, and other things are framed by Him, and He is the Radiance and Word and Image and Wisdom of the Father, and things originate stand and serve in their place below the Triad, therefore the Son is different in kind and different in essence from things originate, and on the contrary is proper to the Father's essence and one in nature with it. And hence it is that the Son too says not, 'My Father is better than I John 14:28,' lest we should conceive Him to be foreign to His Nature, but 'greater,' not indeed in greatness, nor in time, but because of His generation from the Father Himself , nay, in saying 'greater' He again shows that He is proper to His essence.

59. (7). And the Apostle's own reason for saying, 'so much better than the Angels,' was not any wish in the first instance to compare the essence of the Word to things originate (for He cannot be compared, rather they are incommeasurable), but regarding the Word's visitation in the flesh, and the Economy which He then sustained, he wished to show that He was not like those who had gone before Him; so that, as much as He excelled in nature those who were sent afore by Him, by so much also the grace which came from and through Him was better than the ministry through Angels. For it is the function of servants, to demand the fruits and no more; but of the Son

and Master to forgive the debts and to transfer the vineyard.

(8.) Certainly what the Apostle proceeds to say shows the excellence of the Son over things originate; 'Therefore we ought to give the more earnest heed to the things which we have heard, lest at any time we should let them slip. For if the word spoken by Angels was steadfast, and every transgression and disobedience received a just recompense of reward; how shall we escape, if we neglect so great salvation; which at the first began to be spoken by the Lord, and was confirmed unto us by them that heard Him Hebrews 2:1-3.' But if the Son were in the number of things originate, He was not better than they, nor did disobedience involve increase of punishment because of Him; any more than in the Ministry of Angels there was not, according to each Angel, greater or less guilt in the transgressors, but the Law was one, and one was its vengeance on transgressors. But, whereas the Word is not in the number of originate things, but is Son of the Father, therefore, as He Himself is better and His acts better and transcendent, so also the punishment is worse. Let them contemplate then the grace which is through the Son, and let them acknowledge the witness which He gives even from His works, that He is other than things originated, and alone the very Son in the Father and the Father in Him. And the Law was spoken by Angels, and perfected no one Hebrews 7:19, needing the visitation of the Word, as Paul has said; but that visitation has perfected the work of the Father. And then, from Adam unto Moses death reigned Romans 5:14; but the presence of the Word abolished death. 2 Timothy 1:10 And no longer in Adam are we all dying 1 Corinthians 15:22; but in Christ we are all reviving. And then, from Dan to Beersheba was the Law proclaimed, and in Judæa only was God known; but now, unto all the earth has gone forth their voice, and all the earth has been filled with the knowledge of God , and the disciples have made disciples of all the nations Matthew 28:19, and now is fulfilled what is written, 'They shall be all taught of God John 6:45; Isaiah 54:13.' And then what was revealed was but a type; but now the truth has been manifested. And this again the Apostle himself describes afterwards more clearly, saying, 'By so much was Jesus made a surety of a better testament;' and again, 'But now has He obtained a more excellent ministry, by how much also He is the Mediator of a better covenant, which was established upon better promises.' And, 'For the Law made nothing perfect, but the bringing in of a better hope did.' And again he says, 'It was therefore necessary that the patterns of things in the heavens should be purified with these; but the heavenly things themselves with better sacrifices than these.' Both in the verse before us, then, and throughout, does he ascribe the word 'better' to the Lord, who is better and other than originated things. For better is the sacrifice through Him, better the hope in Him; and also the promises through Him, not merely as great compared with small, but the one differing from the other in nature, because He who conducts this economy, is 'better' than things originated.

60. (9.) Moreover the words 'He has become surety' denote the pledge in our behalf which He has provided. For as, being the 'Word,' He 'became flesh John 1:14 ' and 'become' we ascribe to the flesh, for it is originated and created, so do we here the expression 'He has become,' expounding it according to a second sense, viz. because He has become man. And let these contentious men know,

that they fail in this their perverse purpose; let them know that Paul does not signify that His essence has become, knowing, as he did, that He is Son and Wisdom and Radiance and Image of the Father; but here too he refers the word 'become' to the ministry of that covenant, in which death which once ruled is abolished. Since here also the ministry through Him has become better, in that 'what the Law could not do in that it was weak through the flesh, God sending His own Son in the likeness of sinful flesh, and for sin condemned sin in the flesh Romans 8:3,' ridding it of the trespass, in which, being continually held captive, it admitted not the Divine mind. And having rendered the flesh capable of the Word, He made us walk, no longer according to the flesh, but according to the Spirit, and say again and again, 'But we are not in the flesh but in the Spirit,' and, 'For the Son of God came into the world, not to judge the world, but to redeem all men, and that the world might be saved through Him John 3:17.' Formerly the world, as guilty, was under judgment from the Law; but now the Word has taken on Himself the judgment, and having suffered in the body for all, has bestowed salvation to all. With a view to this has John exclaimed, 'The law was given by Moses, but grace and truth came by Jesus Christ John 1:17.' Better is grace than the Law, and truth than the shadow.

61. (10.) 'Better' then, as has been said, could not have been brought to pass by any other than the Son, who sits on the right hand of the Father. And what does this denote but the Son's genuineness, and that the Godhead of the Father is the same as the Son's ? For in that the Son reigns in His Father's kingdom, is seated upon the same throne as the Father, and is contemplated in the Father's Godhead, therefore is the Word God, and whoever beholds the Son, beholds the Father; and thus there is one God. Sitting then on the right, yet He does not place His Father on the left ; but whatever is right and precious in the Father, that also the Son has, and says, 'All things that the Father has are Mine John 16:15.' Wherefore also the Son, though sitting on the right, also sees the Father on the right, though it be as become man that He says, 'I saw the Lord always before My face, for He is on My right hand, therefore I shall not fall.' This shows moreover that the Son is in the Father and the Father in the Son; for the Father being on the right, the Son is on the right; and

while the Son sits on the right of the Father, the Father is in the Son. And the Angels indeed minister ascending and descending; but concerning the Son he says, 'And let all the Angels of God worship Him Hebrews 1:6.' And when Angels minister, they say, 'I am sent unto you,' and, 'The Lord has commanded;' but the Son, though He say in human fashion, 'I am sent ,' and comes to finish the work and to minister, nevertheless says, as being Word and Image, 'I am in the Father, and the Father in Me;' and, 'He that has seen Me, has seen the Father.' and, 'The Father that abides in Me, He does the works ;' for what we behold in that Image are the Father's works.

(11.) What has been already said ought to shame those persons who are fighting against the very truth; however, if, because it is written, 'become better,' they refuse to understand 'become,' as used of the Son, as 'has been and is ;' or again as referring to the better covenant having come to be , as we have said, but consider from this expression that the Word is called originate, let them hear the same again in a concise form, since they have forgotten what has been said.

62. If the Son be in the number of the Angels, then let the word 'become' apply to Him as to them, and let Him not differ at all from them in nature; but be they either sons with Him, or be He an Angel with them; sit they one and all together on the right hand of the Father, or be the Son standing with them all as a ministering Spirit, sent forth to minister Himself as they are. But if on the other hand Paul distinguishes the Son from things originate, saying, 'To which of the Angels said He at any time, You are My Son.' and the one frames heaven and earth, but they are made by Him; and He sits with the Father, but they stand by ministering, who does not see that he has not used the word 'become' of the essence of the Word, but of the ministration come through Him? For as, being the 'Word,' He 'became flesh,' so when become man, He became by so much better in His ministry, than the ministry which came by the Angels, as Son excels servants and Framer things framed. Let them cease therefore to take the word 'become' of the substance of the Son, for He is not one of originated things; and let them acknowledge that it is indicative of His ministry and the Economy which came to pass.

(12.) But how He became better in His ministry, being better in nature than things originate, appears from what has been said before, which, I consider, is sufficient in itself to put them to shame. But if they carry on the contest, it will be proper upon their rash daring to close with them, and to oppose to them those similar expressions which are used concerning the Father Himself. This may serve to shame them to refrain their tongue from evil, or may teach them the depth of their folly. Now it is written, 'Become my strong rock and house of defense, that You may save me.' And again, 'The Lord became a defense for the oppressed ,' and the like which are found in divine Scripture. If then they apply these passages to the Son, which perhaps is nearest to the truth, then let them acknowledge that the sacred writers ask Him, as not being originate, to become to them 'a strong rock and house of defense;' and for the future let them understand 'become,' and 'He made,' and 'He created,' of His incarnate presence. For then did He become 'a strong rock and house of defense,' when He bore our sins in His own body upon the tree, and said, 'Come unto Me, all you that labour and are heavy laden, and I will give you rest Matthew 11:28.'

63. But if they refer these passages to the Father, will they, when it is here also written, 'Become' and 'He became,' venture so far as to affirm that God is originate? Yea, they will dare, as they thus argue concerning His Word; for the course of their argument carries them on to conjecture the same things concerning the Father, as they devise concerning His Word. But far be such a notion ever from the thoughts of all the faithful! For neither is the Son in the number of things originated, nor do the words of Scripture in question, 'Become,' and 'He became,' denote beginning of being, but that succour which was given to the needy. For God is always, and one and the same; but men have come to be afterwards through the Word, when the Father Himself willed it; and God is invisible and inaccessible to originated things, and especially to men upon earth. When then men in infirmity invoke Him, when in persecution they ask help, when under injuries they pray, then the Invisible, being a lover of man, shines forth upon them with His beneficence, which He exercises through and in His proper Word. And immediately the divine manifestation is made to every one according to his need, and is made to the weak health, and to the persecuted a 'refuge' and 'house of defense;' and to the

injured He says, 'While you speak I will say, Here I am Isaiah 58:9.' Whatever defense then comes to each through the Son, that each says that God has come to be to himself, since succour comes from God Himself through the Word. Moreover the usage of men recognises this, and every one will confess its propriety. Often succour comes from man to man; one has undertaken toil for the injured, as Abraham for Lot; and another has opened his home to the persecuted, as Obadiah to the sons of the prophets; and another has entertained a stranger, as Lot the Angels; and another has supplied the needy, as Job those who begged of him. And then, should one and the other of these benefited persons say, 'Such a one became an assistance to me,' and another 'and to me a refuge,' and 'to another a supply,' yet in so saying would not be speaking of the original becoming or of the essence of their benefactors, but of the beneficence coming to themselves from them; so also when the saints say concerning God, 'He became' and 'become Thou,' they do not denote any original becoming, for God is without beginning and unoriginate, but the salvation which is made to be unto men from Him.

64. This being so understood, it is parallel also respecting the Son, that whatever, and however often, is said, such as, 'He became' and 'become,' should ever have the same sense: so that as, when we hear the words in question, 'become better than the Angels' and 'He became,' we should not conceive any original becoming of the Word, nor in any way fancy from such terms that He is originate; but should understand Paul's words of His ministry and Economy when He became man. For when 'the Word became flesh and dwelt among us John 1:14 ' and came to minister and to grant salvation to all, then He became to us salvation, and became life, and became propitiation; then His economy in our behalf became much better than the Angels, and He became the Way and became the Resurrection. And as the words 'Become my strong rock' do not denote that the essence of God Himself became, but His lovingkindness, as has been said, so also here the 'having become better than the Angels,' and, 'He became,' and, 'by so much is Jesus become a better surety,' do not signify that the essence of the Word is originate (perish the thought!), but the beneficence which towards us came to be through His becoming Man; unthankful though the heretics be, and obstinate in behalf of their irreligion.

Discourse II

Chapter XIV. Texts Explained; Fourthly, Hebrews III. 2.

Introduction; the Regula Fidei counter to an Arian sense of the text; which is not supported by the word `servant,' nor by `made' which occurs in it; (how can the Judge be among the `works' which `God will bring into judgment?') nor by `faithful;' and is confuted by the immediate context, which is about Priesthood; and by the foregoing passage, which explains the word `faithful' as meaning trustworthy, as do 1 Pet. iv. fin. and other texts. On the whole made may safely be understood either of the divine generation or the human creation.

1. I did indeed think that enough had been said already against the hollow professors of Arius's madness, whether for their refutation or in the truth's behalf, to insure a cessation and repentance of their evil thoughts and words about the Saviour. They, however, for whatever reason, still do not succumb; but, as swine and dogs wallow in their

own vomit and their own mire, rather invent new expedients for their irreligion. Thus they misunderstand the passage in the Proverbs, 'The Lord has created me a beginning of His ways for His works ,' and the words of the Apostle, 'Who was faithful to Him that made Him Hebrews 3:2,' and straightway argue, that the Son of God is a work and a creature. But although they might have learned from what is said above, had they not utterly lost their power of apprehension, that the Son is not from nothing nor in the number of things originate at all, the Truth witnessing it (for, being God, He cannot be a work, and it is impious to call Him a creature, and it is of creatures and works that we say, 'out of nothing,' and 'it was not before its generation'), yet since, as if dreading to desert their own fiction, they are accustomed to allege the aforesaid passages of divine Scripture, which have a good meaning, but are by them practised on, let us proceed afresh to take up the question of the sense of these, to remind the faithful, and to show from each of these passages that they have no knowledge at all of Christianity. Were it otherwise, they would not have shut themselves up in the unbelief of the present Jews , but would have inquired and learned that, whereas 'In the beginning was the Word, and the Word was with God, and the Word was God,' in consequence, it was when at the good pleasure of the Father the Word became man, that it was said of Him, as by John, 'The Word became flesh John 1:14;' so by Peter, 'He has made Him Lord and Christ Acts 2:36 ' — as by means of Solomon in the Person of the Lord Himself, 'The Lord created me a beginning of His ways for His works Proverbs 8:22;' so by Paul, 'Become so much better than the Angels Hebrews 1:4;' and again, 'He emptied Himself, and took upon Him the form of a servant Philippians 2:7;' and again, 'Wherefore, holy brethren, partakers of the heavenly calling, consider the Apostle and High Priest of our profession, Jesus, who was faithful to Him that made Him.' For all these texts have the same force and meaning, a religious one, declarative of the divinity of the Word, even those of them which speak humanly concerning Him, as having become the Son of man. But, though this distinction is sufficient for their refutation, still, since from a misconception of the Apostle's words (to mention them first), they consider the Word of God to be one of the works, because of its being written, 'Who was faithful to Him that made Him,' I have thought it needful to silence this further argument of theirs, taking in hand , as before, their statement.

2. If then He be not a Son, let Him be called a work, and let all that is said of works be said of Him, nor let Him and Him alone be called Son, nor Word, nor Wisdom; neither let God be called Father, but only Framer and Creator of things which by Him come to be; and let the creature be Image and Expression of His framing will, and let Him, as they would have it, be without generative nature, so that there be neither Word, nor Wisdom, no, nor Image, of His proper substance. For if He be not Son , neither is He Image. But if there be not a Son, how then say you that God is a Creator? Since all things that come to be are through the Word and in Wisdom, and without This nothing can be, whereas you say He has not That in and through which He makes all things. For if the Divine Essence be not fruitful itself , but barren, as they hold, as a light that lightens not, and a dry fountain, are they not ashamed to speak of His possessing framing energy? And whereas they deny what is by nature, do they not blush to place before it what is by will ? But if He frames things

that are external to Him and before were not, by willing them to be, and becomes their Maker, much more will He first be Father of an Offspring from His proper Essence. For if they attribute to God the willing about things which are not, why recognise they not that in God which lies above the will? Now it is a something that surpasses will, that He should be by nature, and should be Father of His proper Word. If then that which comes first, which is according to nature, did not exist, as they would have it in their folly, how could that which is second come to be, which is according to will? For the Word is first, and then the creation. On the contrary the Word exists, whatever they affirm, those irreligious ones; for through Him did creation come to be, and God, as being Maker, plainly has also His framing Word, not external, but proper to Him — for this must be repeated. If He has the power of will, and His will is effective, and suffices for the consistence of the things that come to be, and His Word is effective, and a Framer, that Word must surely be the living Will of the Father, and an essential energy, and a real Word, in whom all things both consist and are excellently governed. No one can even doubt, that He who disposes is prior to the disposition and the things disposed. And thus, as I said,

God's creating is second to His begetting; for Son implies something proper to Him and truly from that blessed and everlasting Essence; but what is from His will, comes into consistence from without, and is framed through His proper Offspring who is from It.

3. As we have shown then they are guilty of great extravagance who say that the Lord is not Son of God, but a work, and it follows that we all of necessity confess that He is Son. And if He be Son, as indeed He is, and a son is confessed to be not external to his father but from him, let them not question about the terms, as I said before, which the sacred writers use of the Word Himself, viz. not 'to Him that begot Him,' but 'to Him that made Him;' for while it is confessed what His nature is, what word is used in such instances need raise no question. For terms do not disparage His Nature; rather that Nature draws to Itself those terms and changes them. For terms are not prior to essences, but essences are first, and terms second. Wherefore also when the essence is a work or creature, then the words 'He made,' and 'He became,' and 'He created,' are used of it properly, and designate the work.

But when the Essence is an Offspring and Son, then 'He made,' and 'He became,' and 'He created,' no longer properly belong to it, nor designate a work; but 'He made' we use without question for 'He begot.' Thus fathers often call the sons born of them their servants, yet without denying the genuineness of their nature; and often they affectionately call their own servants children, yet without putting out of sight their purchase of them originally; for they use the one appellation from their authority as being fathers, but in the other they speak from affection. Thus Sara called Abraham lord, though not a servant but a wife; and while to Philemon the master the Apostle joined Onesimus the servant as a brother, Bathsheba, although mother, called her son servant, saying to his father, 'Your servant Solomon 1 Kings 1:19;'— afterwards also Nathan the Prophet came in and repeated her words to David, 'Solomon your servant.' Nor did they mind calling the son a servant, for while David heard it, he recognised the 'nature,' and while they spoke it, they forgot not the 'genuineness,' praying that he might be made his father's heir, to whom they gave the name of servant; for to David he was son by nature.

4. As then, when we read this, we interpret it fairly, without accounting Solomon a servant because we hear him so called, but a son natural and genuine, so also, if, concerning the Saviour, who is confessed to be in truth the Son, and to be the Word by nature, the saints say, 'Who was faithful to Him that made Him,' or if He say of Himself, 'The Lord created me,' and, 'I am Your servant and the Son of Your handmaid ,' and the like, let not any on this account deny that He is proper to the Father and from Him; but, as in the case of Solomon and David, let them have a right idea of the Father and the Son. For if, though they hear Solomon called a servant, they acknowledge him to be a son, are they not deserving of many deaths , who, instead of preserving the same explanation in the instance of the Lord, whenever they hear 'Offspring,' and 'Word,' and 'Wisdom,' forcibly misinterpret and deny the generation, natural and genuine, of the Son from the Father; but on hearing words and terms proper to a work, immediately drop down to the notion of His being by nature a work, and deny the Word; and this, though it is possible, from His having been made man, to refer all these terms to His humanity? And are they not proved to be 'an abomination' also 'unto the

Lord,' as having 'diverse weights Proverbs 20:23 ' with them, and with this estimating those other instances, and with that blaspheming the Lord? But perhaps they grant that the word 'servant' is used under a certain understanding, but lay stress upon 'Who made' as some great support of their heresy. But this stay of theirs also is but a broken reed; for if they are aware of the style of Scripture, they must at once give sentence against themselves. For as Solomon, though a son, is called a servant, so, to repeat what was said above, although parents call the sons springing from themselves 'made' and 'created' and 'becoming,' for all this they do not deny their nature. Thus Hezekiah, as it is written in Isaiah, said in his prayer, 'From this day I will make children, who shall declare Your righteousness, O God of my salvation.' He then said, 'I will make;' but the Prophet in that very book and the Fourth of Kings, thus speaks, 'And the sons who shall come forth of you 2 Kings 20:18; Isaiah 39:7.' He uses then 'make' for 'beget,' and he calls them who were to spring from him, 'made,' and no one questions whether the term has reference to a natural offspring. Again, Eve on bearing Cain said, 'I have gotten a man from the Lord ;' thus she too used 'gotten' for 'brought forth.' For, first she saw the child, yet next she said, 'I have gotten.' Nor would any one consider, because of 'I have gotten,' that Cain was purchased from without, instead of being born of her. Again, the Patriarch Jacob said to Joseph, 'And now your two sons, Ephraim and Manasseh, which became yours in Egypt, before I came unto you into Egypt, are mine.' And Scripture says about Job, 'And there came to him seven sons and three daughters.' As Moses too has said in the Law, 'If sons become to any one,' and 'If he make a son.' Here again they speak of those who are begotten, as 'become' and 'made,' knowing that, while they are acknowledged to be sons, we need not make a question of 'they became,' or 'I have gotten,' or 'I made.' For nature and truth draw the meaning to themselves.

5. This being so, when persons ask whether the Lord is a creature or work, it is proper to ask of them this first, whether He is Son and Word and Wisdom. For if this is shown, the surmise about work and creation falls to the ground at once and is ended. For a work could never be Son and Word; nor could the Son be a work. And again, this being the state of the case, the proof is plain to all,

that the phrase, 'To Him who made Him' does not serve their heresy, but rather condemns it. For it has been shown that the expression 'He made' is applied in divine Scripture even to children genuine and natural; whence, the Lord being proved to be the Father's Son naturally and genuinely, and Word, and Wisdom, though 'He made' be used concerning Him, or 'He became,' this is not said of Him as if a work, but the saints make no question about using the expression — for instance in the case of Solomon, and Hezekiah's children. For though the fathers had begotten them from themselves, still it is written, 'I have made,' and 'I have gotten,' and 'He became.' Therefore God's enemies, in spite of their repeated allegation of such phrases, ought now, though late in the day, after what has been said, to disown their irreligious thoughts, and think of the Lord as of a true Son, Word, and Wisdom of the Father, not a work, not a creature. For if the Son be a creature, by what word then and by what wisdom was He made Himself? For all the works were made through the Word and the Wisdom, as it is written, 'In wisdom have You made them all,' and, 'All things were made by Him, and without Him was not anything made.' But if it be He who is the Word and the Wisdom, by which all things come to be, it follows that He is not in the number of works, nor in short of things originate, but the Offspring of the Father.

6. For consider how grave an error it is, to call God's Word a work. Solomon says in one place in Ecclesiastes, that 'God shall bring every work into judgment, with every secret thing, whether it be good or whether it be evil Ecclesiastes 12:14.' If then the Word be a work, do you mean that He as well as others will be brought into judgment? And what room is there for judgment, when the Judge is on trial? Who will give to the just their blessing, who to the unworthy their punishment, the Lord, as you must suppose, standing on trial with the rest? By what law shall He, the Lawgiver, Himself be judged? These things are proper to the works, to be on trial, to be blessed and to be punished by the Son. Now then fear the Judge, and let Solomon's words convince you. For if God shall bring the works one and all into judgment, but the Son is not in the number of things put on trial, but rather is Himself the Judge of works one and all, is not the proof clearer than the sun, that the Son is not a work but the

Father's Word, in whom all the works both come to be and come into judgment? Further, if the expression, 'Who was faithful,' is a difficulty to them, from the thought that 'faithful' is used of Him as of others, as if He exercises faith and so receives the reward of faith, they must proceed at this rate to find fault with Moses for saying, 'God faithful and true ,' and with St. Paul for writing, 'God is faithful, who will not suffer you to be tempted above that you are able 1 Corinthians 10:13.' But when the saints spoke thus, they were not thinking of God in a human way, but they acknowledged two senses of the word 'faithful' in Scripture, first 'believing,' then 'trustworthy,' of which the former belongs to man, the latter to God. Thus Abraham was faithful, because He believed God's word; and God faithful, for, as David says in the Psalm, 'The Lord is faithful in all His words ,' or is trustworthy, and cannot lie. Again, 'If any faithful woman have widows 1 Timothy 5:16,' she is so called for her right faith; but, 'It is a faithful saying ,' because what He has spoken has a claim on our faith, for it is true, and is not otherwise. Accordingly the words, 'Who is faithful to Him that made Him,' implies no parallel with others, nor means that by having faith He became well-pleasing; but that, being Son of the True God, He too is faithful, and ought to be believed in all He says and does, Himself remaining unalterable and not changed in His human Economy and fleshly presence.

7. Thus then we may meet these men who are shameless, and from the single expression 'He made,' may show that they err in thinking that the Word of God is a work. But further, since the drift also of the context is orthodox, showing the time and the relation to which this expression points, I ought to show from it also how the heretics lack reason; viz. by considering, as we have done above, the occasion when it was used and for what purpose. Now the Apostle is not discussing things before the creation when he thus speaks, but when 'the Word became flesh;' for thus it is written, 'Wherefore, holy brethren, partakers of the heavenly calling, consider the Apostle and High Priest of our profession Jesus, who was faithful to Him that made Him.' Now when became He 'Apostle,' but when He put on our flesh? And when became He 'High Priest of our profession,' but when, after offering Himself for us, He raised His Body from the dead, and, as now, Himself

brings near and offers to the Father those who in faith approach Him, redeeming all, and for all propitiating God? Not then as wishing to signify the Essence of the Word nor His natural generation from the Father, did the Apostle say, 'Who was faithful to Him that made Him'— (perish the thought! For the Word is not made, but makes) — but as signifying His descent to mankind and High-priesthood which did 'become'— as one may easily see from the account given of the Law and of Aaron. I mean, Aaron was not born a high-priest, but a man; and in process of time, when God willed, he became a high-priest; yet became so, not simply, nor as betokened by his ordinary garments, but putting over them the ephod, the breastplate Exodus 29:5, the robe, which the women wrought at God's command, and going in them into the holy place, he offered the sacrifice for the people; and in them, as it were, mediated between the vision of God and the sacrifices of men. Thus then the Lord also, 'In the beginning was the Word, and the Word was with God, and the Word was God;' but when the Father willed that ransoms should be paid for all and to all, grace should be given, then truly the Word, as Aaron his robe, so did He take earthly flesh, having Mary for the Mother of His

Body as if virgin earth , that, as a High Priest, having He as others an offering, He might offer Himself to the Father, and cleanse us all from sins in His own blood, and might rise from the dead.

8. For what happened of old was a shadow of this; and what the Saviour did on His coming, this Aaron shadowed out according to the Law. As then Aaron was the same and did not change by putting on the high-priestly dress , but remaining the same was only robed, so that, had any one seen him offering, and had said, 'Lo, Aaron has this day become high-priest,' he had not implied that he then had been born man, for man he was even before he became high-priest, but that he had been made high-priest in his ministry, on putting on the garments made and prepared for the high-priesthood; in the same way it is possible in the Lord's instance also to understand aright, that He did not become other than Himself on taking the flesh, but, being the same as before, He was robed in it; and the expressions 'He became' and 'He was made,' must not be understood as if the Word, considered as the Word , were made, but that the Word, being Framer of all,

afterwards was made High Priest, by putting on a body which was originate and made, and such as He can offer for us; wherefore He is said to be made. If then indeed the Lord did not become man, that is a point for the Arians to battle; but if the 'Word became flesh,' what ought to have been said concerning Him when become man, but 'Who was faithful to Him that made Him?' for as it is proper to the Word to have it said of Him, 'In the beginning was the Word,' so it is proper to man to 'become' and to be 'made.' Who then, on seeing the Lord as a man walking about, and yet appearing to be God from His works, would not have asked, Who made Him man? And who again, on such a question, would not have answered, that the Father made Him man, and sent Him to us as High Priest? And this meaning, and time, and character, the Apostle himself, the writer of the words, 'Who is faithful to Him that made Him,' will best make plain to us, if we attend to what goes before them. For there is one train of thought, and the lection is all about One and the Same. He writes then in the Epistle to the Hebrews thus; 'Forasmuch then as the children are partakers of flesh and blood, He also Himself likewise took part of the same; that through death He might destroy him that had the power of death, that is, the devil; and deliver them who through fear of death were all their lifetime subject to bondage. For verily He took not on Him the nature of Angels; but He took on Him the seed of Abraham. Wherefore in all things it behooved Him to be made like His brethren, that He might be a merciful and faithful High Priest in things pertaining to God, to make reconciliation for the sins of the people. For in that He Himself has suffered being tempted, He is able to succour them that are tempted. Wherefore, holy brethren, partakers of a heavenly calling, consider the Apostle and High Priest of our profession, Jesus; who was faithful to Him that made Him. '

9. Who can read this whole passage without condemning the Arians, and admiring the blessed Apostle, who has spoken well? For when was Christ 'made,' when became He 'Apostle,' except when, like us, He 'took part in flesh and blood.' And when became He 'a merciful and faithful High Priest,' except when 'in all things He was made like His brethren.' And then was He 'made like,' when He became man, having put upon Him our flesh. Wherefore

Paul was writing concerning the Word's human Economy, when he said, 'Who was faithful to Him that made Him,' and not concerning His Essence. Have not therefore any more the madness to say that the Word of God is a work; whereas He is Son by nature Only-begotten, and then had 'brethren,' when He took on Him flesh like ours; which moreover, by Himself offering Himself, He was named and became 'merciful and faithful,'— merciful, because in mercy to us He offered Himself for us, and faithful, not as sharing faith with us, nor as having faith in any one as we have, but as deserving to receive faith in all He says and does, and as offering a faithful sacrifice, one which remains and does not come to nought. For those which were offered according to the Law, had not this faithfulness, passing away with the day and needing a further cleansing; but the Saviour's sacrifice, taking place once, has perfected everything, and has become faithful as remaining forever. And Aaron had successors, and in a word the priesthood under the Law exchanged its first ministers as time and death went on; but the Lord having a high priesthood without transition and without succession, has become a 'faithful High Priest,' as continuing for ever; and faithful too by promise, that He may hear and not mislead those who come to Him. This may be also learned from the Epistle of the great Peter, who says, 'Let them that suffer according to the will of God, commit their souls to a faithful Creator 1 Peter 4:19.' For He is faithful as not changing, but abiding ever, and rendering what He has promised.

10. Now the so-called gods of the Greeks, unworthy the name, are faithful neither in their essence nor in their promises; for the same are not everywhere, nay, the local deities come to nought in course of time, and undergo a natural dissolution; wherefore the Word cries out against them, that 'faith is not strong in them,' but they are 'waters that fail,' and 'there is no faith in them.' But the God of all, being one really and indeed and true, is faithful, who is ever the same, and says, 'See now, that I, even I am He,' and I 'change not ;' and therefore His Son is 'faithful,' being ever the same and unchanging, deceiving neither in His essence nor in His promise — as again says the Apostle writing to the Thessalonians, 'Faithful is He who calls you, who also will do it 1 Thessalonians 5:24;' for in doing what He promises, 'He is faithful to His

words.' And he thus writes to the Hebrews as to the word's meaning 'unchangeable;' 'If we believe not, yet He abides faithful; He cannot deny Himself 2 Timothy 2:13.' Therefore reasonably the Apostle, discoursing concerning the bodily presence of the Word, says, an 'Apostle and faithful to Him that made Him,' showing us that, even when made man, 'Jesus Christ' is 'the same yesterday, and today, and for ever Hebrews 13:8 ' is unchangeable. And as the Apostle makes mention in his Epistle of His being made man when mentioning His High Priesthood, so too he kept no long silence about His Godhead, but rather mentions it immediately, furnishing to us a safeguard on every side, and most of all when he speaks of His humility, that we may immediately know His loftiness and His majesty which is the Father's. For instance, he says, 'Moses as a servant, but Christ as a Son Hebrews 3:5-6;' and the former 'faithful in his house,' and the latter 'over the house,' as having Himself built it, and being its Lord and Framer, and as God sanctifying it. For Moses, a man by nature, became faithful, in believing God who spoke to Him by His Word; but the Word was not as one of things originate in a body, nor as creature in creature, but as God in flesh , and Framer of all and Builder in that which was built by Him. And men are clothed in flesh in order to be and to subsist; but the Word of God was made man in order to sanctify the flesh, and, though He was Lord, was in the form of a servant; for the whole creature is the Word's servant, which by Him came to be, and was made.

11. Hence it holds that the Apostle's expression, 'He made,' does not prove that the Word is made, but that body, which He took like ours; and in consequence He is called our brother, as having become man. But if it has been shown, that, even though the word 'made' be referred to the Very Word, it is used for 'begot,' what further perverse expedient will they be able to fall upon, now that the present discussion has cleared up the word in every point of view, and shown that the Son is not a work, but in Essence indeed the Father's offspring, while in the Economy, according to the good pleasure of the Father, He was on our behalf made, and consists as man? For this reason then it is said by the Apostle, 'Who was faithful to Him that made Him;' and in the Proverbs, even creation is spoken of. For so long as we are confessing that He became man, there is no question about saying, as was

observed before, whether 'He became,' or 'He has been made,' or 'created,' or 'formed,' or 'servant,' or 'son of an handmaid,' or 'son of man,' or 'was constituted,' or 'took His journey,' or 'bridegroom,' or 'brother's son,' or 'brother.' All these terms happen to be proper to man's constitution; and such as these do not designate the Essence of the Word, but that He has become man.

Chapter XV. Texts Explained; Fifthly, Acts II. 36.

The Regula Fidei must be observed; madeapplies to our Lord's manhood; and to His manifestation; and to His office relative to us; and is relative to the Jews. Parallel instance in Genesis 27:29, 37. The context contradicts the Arianinterpretation.

11 (continued). The same is the meaning of the passage in the Acts which they also allege, that in which Peter says, that 'He has made both Lord and Christ that same Jesus whom you have crucified.' For here too it is not written, 'He made for Himself a Son,' or 'He made Himself a Word,' that they should have such notions. If then it has

not escaped their memory, that they speak concerning the Son of God, let them make search whether it is anywhere written, 'God made Himself a Son,' or 'He created for Himself a Word.' or again, whether it is anywhere written in plain terms, 'The Word is a work or creation.' and then let them proceed to make their case, the insensate men, that here too they may receive their answer. But if they can produce nothing of the kind, and only catch at such stray expressions as 'He made' and 'He has been made,' I fear lest, from hearing, 'In the beginning God made the heaven and the earth,' and 'He made the sun and the moon,' and 'He made the sea,' they should come in time to call the Word the heaven, and the Light which took place on the first day, and the earth, and each particular thing that has been made, so as to end in resembling the Stoics, as they are called, the one drawing out their God into all things, the other ranking God's Word with each work in particular; which they have well near done already, saying that He is one of His works.

12. But here they must have the same answer as before, and first be told that the Word is a Son, as has been said

above , and not a work, and that such terms are not to be understood of His Godhead, but the reason and manner of them investigated. To persons who so inquire, the human Economy will plainly present itself, which He undertook for our sake. For Peter, after saying, 'He has made Lord and Christ,' straightway added, 'this Jesus whom you crucified;' which makes it plain to any one, even, if so be, to them, provided they attend to the context, that not the Essence of the Word, but He according to His manhood is said to have been made. For what was crucified but the body? And how could be signified what was bodily in the Word, except by saying 'He made?' Especially has that phrase, 'He made,' a meaning consistent with orthodoxy; in that he has not said, as I observed before, 'He made Him Word,' but 'He made Him Lord,' nor that in general terms , but 'towards' us, and 'in the midst of' us, as much as to say, 'He manifested Him.' And this Peter himself, when he began this primary teaching, carefully expressed, when he said to them, 'You men of Israel, hear these words: Jesus of Nazareth, a man manifested of God towards you by miracles, and wonders, and signs, which God did by Him in the midst of you, as you yourselves know Acts 2:22.' Consequently the term which he uses in the end, 'made', this He has explained in the beginning by 'manifested,' for by the signs and wonders which the Lord did, He was manifested to be not merely man, but God in a body and Lord also, the Christ. Such also is the passage in the Gospel according to John, 'Therefore the more did the Jews persecute Him, because He not only broke the Sabbath, but said also that God was His own Father, making Himself equal with God.' For the Lord did not then fashion Himself to be God, nor indeed is a made God conceivable, but He manifested it by the works, saying, 'Though you believe not Me, believe My works, that you may know that I am in the Father, and the Father in Me.' Thus then the Father has 'made' Him Lord and King in the midst of us, and towards us who were once disobedient; and it is plain that He who is now displayed as Lord and King, does not then begin to be King and Lord, but begins to show His Lordship, and to extend it even over the disobedient.

13. If then they suppose that the Saviour was not Lord and King, even before He became man and endured the Cross, but then began to be Lord, let them know that they

are openly reviving the statements of the Samosatene. But if, as we have quoted and declared above, He is Lord and King everlasting, seeing that Abraham worships Him as Lord, and Moses says, 'Then the Lord rained upon Sodom and upon Gomorrha brimstone and fire from the Lord out of heaven Genesis 19:24;' and David in the Psalms, 'The Lord said to my Lord, Sit on My right hand ;' and, 'Your Throne, O God, is for ever and ever; a sceptre of righteousness is the sceptre of Your Kingdom ;' and, 'Your Kingdom is an everlasting Kingdom ;' it is plain that even before He became man, He was King and Lord everlasting, being Image and Word of the Father. And the Word being everlasting Lord and King, it is very plain again that Peter said not that the Essence of the Son was made, but spoke of His Lordship over us, which 'became' when He became man, and, redeeming all by the Cross, became Lord of all and King. But if they continue the argument on the ground of its being written, 'He made,' not willing that 'He made' should be taken in the sense of 'He manifested,' either from want of apprehension, or from their Christ-opposing purpose, let them attend to another sound exposition of Peter's words. For he who becomes Lord of others, comes into the possession of beings already in existence; but if the Lord is Framer of all and everlasting King, and when He became man, then gained possession of us, here too is a way in which Peter's language evidently does not signify that the Essence of the Word is a work, but the after-subjection of all things, and the Saviour's Lordship which came to be over all. And this coincides with what we said before ; for as we then introduced the words, 'Become my God and defense,' and 'the Lord became a refuge for the oppressed ,' and it stood to reason that these expressions do not show that God is originate, but that His beneficence 'becomes' towards each individual, the same sense has the expression of Peter also.

14. For the Son of God indeed, being Himself the Word, is Lord of all; but we once were subject from the first to the slavery of corruption and the curse of the Law, then by degrees fashioning for ourselves things that were not, we served, as says the blessed Apostle, 'them which by nature are no Gods Galatians 4:8,' and, ignorant of the true God, we preferred things that were not to the truth; but afterwards, as the ancient people when oppressed in Egypt groaned, so, when we too had the Law 'engrafted James

1:21 ' in us, and according to the unutterable sighings Romans 8:26 of the Spirit made our intercession, 'O Lord our God, take possession of us ,' then, as 'He became for a house of refuge' and a 'God and defense,' so also He became our Lord. Nor did He then begin to be, but we began to have Him for our Lord. For upon this, God being good and Father of the Lord, in pity, and desiring to be known by all, makes His own Son put on Him a human body and become man, and be called Jesus, that in this body offering Himself for all, He might deliver all from false worship and corruption, and might Himself become of all Lord and King. His becoming therefore in this way Lord and King, this it is that Peter means by, 'He has made Him Lord,' and 'has sent Christ.' as much as to say, that the Father in making Him man (for to be made belongs to man), did not simply make Him man, but has made Him in order to His being Lord of all men, and to His hallowing all through the Anointing. For though the Word existing in the form of God took a servant's form, yet the assumption of the flesh did not make a servant of the Word, who was by nature Lord; but rather, not only was it that emancipation of all humanity which takes place by the Word, but that very Word who was by nature Lord, and was then made man, has by means of a servant's form been made Lord of all and Christ, that is, in order to hallow all by the Spirit. And as God, when 'becoming a God and defense,' and saying, 'I will be a God to them,' does not then become God more than before, nor then begins to become God, but, what He ever is, that He then becomes to those who need Him, when it pleases Him, so Christ also being by nature Lord and King everlasting, does not become Lord more than He was at the time He is sent forth, nor then begins to be Lord and King, but what He is ever, that He then is made according to the flesh; and, having redeemed all, He becomes thereby again Lord of quick and dead. For Him henceforth do all things serve, and this is David's meaning in the Psalm, 'The Lord said to my Lord, Sit on My right hand, until I make Your enemies Your footstool.' For it was fitting that the redemption should take place through none other than Him who is the Lord by nature, lest, though created by the Son, we should name another Lord, and fall into the Arian and Greek folly, serving the creature beyond the all-creating God.

15. This, at least according to my nothingness, is the meaning of this passage; moreover, a true and a good meaning have these words of Peter as regards the Jews. For Jews, astray from the truth, expect indeed the Christ as coming, but do not reckon that He undergoes a passion, saying what they understand not; 'We know that, when the Christ comes, He abides for ever, and how do You say, that He must be lifted up?' Next they suppose Him, not the Word coming in flesh, but a mere man, as were all the kings. The Lord then, admonishing Cleopas and the other, taught them that the Christ must first suffer; and the rest of the Jews that God had come among them, saying, 'If He called them gods to whom the word of God came, and the Scripture cannot be broken, say ye of Him whom the Father has sanctified and sent into the world, Thou blaspheme, because I said, I am the Son of God John 10:36?'

16. Peter then, having learned this from the Saviour, in both points set the Jews right, saying, O Jews, the divine Scriptures announce that Christ comes, and you consider Him a mere man as one of David's descendants, whereas

what is written of Him shows Him to be not such as you say, but rather announces Him as Lord and God, and immortal, and dispenser of life. For Moses has said, 'You shall see your Life hanging before your eyes.' And David in the hundred and ninth Psalm, 'The Lord said to My Lord, Sit on My right hand, till I make Your enemies Your footstool;' and in the fifteenth, 'You shall not leave my soul in hades, neither shall Thou suffer Your Holy One to see corruption.' Now that these passages have not David for their scope he himself witnesses, avowing that He who was coming was His own Lord. Nay you yourselves know that He is dead, and His remains are with you. That the Christ then must be such as the Scriptures say, you will plainly confess yourselves. For those announcements come from God, and in them falsehood cannot be. If then ye can state that such a one has come before, and can prove him God from the signs and wonders which he did, you have reason for maintaining the contest, but if you are not able to prove His coming, but are expecting such an one still, recognise the true season from Daniel, for his words relate to the present time. But if this present season be that which was of old, afore-announced, and you have seen what has taken place among us, be sure that this Jesus, whom you crucified, this is the expected Christ. For David and all the Prophets died, and the sepulchres of all are with you, but that Resurrection which has now taken place, has shown that the scope of these passages is Jesus. For the crucifixion is denoted by 'You shall see your Life hanging,' and the wound in the side by the spear answers to 'He was led as a sheep to the slaughter Isaiah 53:7,' and the resurrection, nay more, the rising of the ancient dead from out their sepulchres (for these most of you have seen), this is, 'You shall not leave My soul in hades,' and 'He swallowed up death in strength Isaiah 25:8,' and again, 'God will wipe away.' For the signs which actually took place show that He who was in a body was God, and also the Life and Lord of death. For it became the Christ, when giving life to others, Himself not to be detained by death; but this could not have happened, had He, as you suppose, been a mere man. But in truth He is the Son of God, for men are all subject to death. Let no one therefore doubt, but the whole house of Israel know assuredly that this Jesus, whom you saw in shape a man, doing signs and such works, as no one ever yet had done, is Himself the Christ and Lord of all. For though made man, and called Jesus, as we said before, He received no loss by that human passion, but rather, in being made man, He is manifested as Lord of quick and dead. For since, as the Apostle said, 'in the wisdom of God the world by wisdom knew not God, it pleased God by the foolishness of preaching to save them that believe 1 Corinthians 1:21.' And so, since we men would not acknowledge God through His Word, nor serve the Word of God our natural Master, it pleased God to show in man His own Lordship, and so to draw all men to Himself. But to do this by a mere man beseemed not ; lest, having man for our Lord, we should become worshippers of man. Therefore the Word Himself became flesh, and the Father called His Name Jesus, and so 'made' Him Lord and Christ, as much as to say, 'He made Him to rule and to reign;' that while in the Name of Jesus, whom you crucified, every knee bows, we may acknowledge as Lord and King both the Son and through Him the Father.

17. The Jews then, most of them , hearing this, came to themselves and immediately acknowledged the Christ, as it is written in the Acts. But, the Ario-maniacs on the contrary choose to remain Jews, and to contend with

Peter; so let us proceed to place before them some parallel phrases; perhaps it may have some effect upon them, to find what the usage is of divine Scripture. Now that Christ is everlasting Lord and King, has become plain by what has gone before, nor is there a man to doubt about it; for being Son of God, He must be like Him, and being like, He is certainly both Lord and King, for He says Himself, 'He that has seen Me, has seen the Father.' On the other hand, that Peter's mere words, 'He has made Him both Lord and Christ,' do not imply the Son to be a creature, may be seen from Isaac's blessing, though this illustration is but a faint one for our subject. Now he said to Jacob, 'Become thou lord over your brother;' and to Esau, 'Behold, I have made him your lord.' Now though the word 'made' had implied Jacob's essence and the coming into being, even then it would not be right in them as much as to imagine the same of the Word of God, for the Son of God is no creature as Jacob was; besides, they might inquire and so rid themselves of that extravagance. But if they do not understand it of his essence nor of his coming into being, though Jacob was by nature creature and work, is not their madness worse than the Devil's, if what they dare not ascribe in consequence of a like phrase even to things by nature originate, that they attach to the Son of God, saying that He is a creature? For Isaac said 'Become' and 'I have made,' signifying neither the coming into being nor the essence of Jacob (for after thirty years and more from his birth he said this); but his authority over his brother, which came to pass subsequently.

18. Much more then did Peter say this without meaning that the Essence of the Word was a work; for he knew Him to be God's Son, confessing, 'You are the Christ, the Son of the Living God Matthew 16:16;' but he meant His Kingdom and Lordship which was formed and came to be according to grace, and was relatively to us. For while saying this, he was not silent about the Son of God's everlasting Godhead which is the Father's; but He had said already, that He had poured the Spirit on us; now to give the Spirit with authority, is not in the power of creature or work, but the Spirit is God's Gift. For the creatures are hallowed by the Holy Spirit; but the Son, in that He is not hallowed by the Spirit, but on the contrary Himself the Giver of it to all , is therefore no creature, but true Son of the Father. And yet He who gives the Spirit,

the same is said also to be made; that is, to be made among us Lord because of His manhood, while giving the Spirit because He is God's Word. For He ever was and is, as Son, so also Lord and Sovereign of all, being like in all things to the Father, and having all that is the Father's as He Himself has said.

Chapter XVI. Introductory to Proverbs VIII. 22, that the Son is Not a Creature.

Arianformula, a creature but not as one of the creatures; but each creature is unlike all other creatures; and no creature can create. The Word then differs from all creatures in that in which they, though otherwise differing, all agree together, as creatures; viz. in being an efficient cause; in being the one medium or instrumental agent in creation; moreover in being the revealer of the Father; and in being the object of worship.

18. (continued). Now in the next place let us consider the passage in the Proverbs, 'The Lord created me a beginning of His ways for His works ;' although in showing that the

Word is no work, it has been also shown that He is no creature. For it is the same to say work or creature, so that the proof that He is no work is a proof also that He is no creature. Whereas one may marvel at these men, thus devising excuses to be irreligious, and nothing daunted at the refutations which meet them upon every point. For first they set about deceiving the simple by their questions, 'Did He who is make from that which was not one that was not or one that was?' and, 'Had you a son before begetting him?' And when this had been proved worthless, next they invented the question, 'Is the Unoriginate one or two?' Then, when in this they had been confuted, straightway they formed another, 'Has He free-will and an alterable nature?' But being forced to give up this, next they set about saying, 'Being made so much better than the Angels;' and when the truth exposed this pretence, now again, collecting them all together, they think to recommend their heresy by 'work' and 'creature.' For they mean those very things over again, and are true to their own perverseness, putting into various shapes and turning to and fro the same errors, if so be to deceive some by that variousness. Although then abundant proof has been given above of this their reckless expedient, yet, since they make all places sound with this passage from the Proverbs, and to many who are ignorant of the faith of Christians, seem to say somewhat, it is necessary to examine separately, 'He created' as well as 'Who was faithful to Him that made Him ;' that, as in all others, so in this text also, they may be proved to have got no further than a fantasy.

19. And first let us see the answers, which they returned to Alexander of blessed memory, in the outset, while their heresy was in course of formation. They wrote thus: 'He is a creature, but not as one of the creatures; a work, but not as one of the works; an offspring, but not as one of the offsprings.' Let every one consider the profligacy and craft of this heresy; for knowing the bitterness of its own malignity, it makes an effort to trick itself out with fair words, and says, what indeed it means, that He is a creature, yet thinks to be able to screen itself by adding, 'but not as one of the creatures.' However, in thus writing, they rather convict themselves of irreligion; for if, in your opinion, He is simply a creature, why add the pretence, 'but not as one of the creatures?' And if He is simply a

work, how 'not as one of the works?' In which we may see the poison of the heresy. For by saying, 'offspring, but not as one of the offsprings,' they reckon many sons, and one of these they pronounce to be the Lord; so that according to them He is no more Only begotten, but one out of many brethren, and is called offspring and son. What use then is this pretence of saying that He is a creature and not a creature? For though you shall say, Not as 'one of the creatures,' I will prove this sophism of yours to be foolish. For still ye pronounce Him to be one of the creatures; and whatever a man might say of the other creatures, such ye hold concerning the Son, you truly 'fools and blind Matthew 23:19.' For is any one of the creatures just what another is , that you should predicate this of the Son as some prerogative ? And all the visible creation was made in six days:— in the first, the light which He called day; in the second the firmament; in the third, gathering together the waters, He bared the dry land, and brought out the various fruits that are in it; and in the fourth, He made the sun and the moon and all the host of the stars; and on the fifth, He created the race of living things in the sea, and of birds in the air; and on the sixth, He made the quadrupeds on the earth, and at length man. And 'the invisible things of Him from the creation of the world are clearly seen, being understood by the things that are made Romans 1:20;' and neither the light is as the night, nor the sun as the moon; nor the irrational as rational man; nor the Angels as the Thrones, nor the Thrones as the Authorities, yet they are all creatures, but each of the things made according to its kind exists and remains in its own essence, as it was made.

20. Let the Word then be excepted from the works, and as Creator be restored to the Father, and be confessed to be Son by nature; or if simply He be a creature, then let Him be assigned the same condition as the rest one with another, and let them as well as He be said every one of them to be 'a creature but not as one of the creatures, offspring or work, but not as one of the works or offsprings.' For you say that an offspring is the same as a work, writing 'generated or made.' For though the Son excel the rest on a comparison, still a creature He is nevertheless, as they are; since in those which are by nature creatures one may find some excelling others. Star, for instance, differs from star in glory, and the rest have all of

them their mutual differences when compared together; yet it follows not for all this that some are lords, and others servants to the superior, nor that some are efficient causes, others by them come into being, but all have a nature which comes to be and is created, confessing in their own selves their Framer: as David says in the Psalms, 'The heavens declare the glory of God, and the firmament shows His handy work;' and as Zorobabel the wise says, 'All the earth calls upon the Truth, and the heaven blesses it: all works shake and tremble at it Ezra 4:36.' But if the whole earth hymns the Framer and the Truth, and blesses, and fears it, and its Framer is the Word, and He Himself says, 'I am the Truth John 14:6,' it follows that the Word is not a creature, but alone proper to the Father, in whom all things are disposed, and He is celebrated by all, as Framer; for 'I was by Him disposing;' and 'My Father works hitherto, and I work John 5:17.' And the word 'hitherto' shows His eternal existence in the Father as the Word; for it is proper to the Word to work the Father's works and not to be external to Him.

21. But if what the Father works, that the Son works also , and what the Son creates, that is the creation of the Father, and yet the Son be the Father's work or creature, then either He will work His own self, and will be His own creator (since what the Father works is the Son's work also), which is absurd and impossible; or, in that He creates and works the things of the Father, He Himself is not a work nor a creature; for else being Himself an efficient cause , He may cause that to be in the case of things caused, which He Himself has become, or rather He may have no power to cause at all. For how, if, as you hold, He has come of nothing, is He able to frame things that are nothing into being? Or if He, a creature, withal frames a creature, the same will be conceivable in the case of every creature, viz. the power to frame others. And if this pleases you, what is the need of the Word, seeing that things inferior can be brought to be by things superior? Or at all events, every thing that is brought to be could have heard in the beginning God's words, 'Become' and 'be made,' and so would have been framed. But this is not so written, nor could it be. For none of things which are brought to be is an efficient cause, but all things were made through the Word: who would not have wrought all

things, were He Himself in the number of the creatures. For neither would the Angels be able to frame, since they too are creatures, though Valentinus, and Marcion, and Basilides think so, and you are their copyists; nor will the sun, as being a creature, ever make what is not into what is; nor will man fashion man, nor stone devise stone, nor wood give growth to wood. But God is He who fashions man in the womb, and fixes the mountains, and makes wood grow; whereas man, as being capable of science, puts together and arranges that material, and works things that are, as he has learned; and is satisfied if they are but brought to be, and being conscious of what his nature is, if he needs anything, knows to ask it of God.

22. If then God also wrought and compounded out of materials, this indeed is a gentile thought, according to which God is an artificer and not a Maker, but yet even in that case let the Word work the materials, at the bidding and in the service of God. But if He calls into existence things which existed not by His proper Word, then the Word is not in the number of things non-existing and called; or we have to seek another Word , through whom

He too was called; for by the Word the things which were not have come to be. And if through Him He creates and makes, He is not Himself of things created and made; but rather He is the Word of the Creator God and is known from the Father's works which He Himself works, to be 'in the Father and the Father in Him,' and 'He that has seen Him has seen the Father ,' because the Son's Essence is proper to the Father, and He in all points like Him. How then does He create through Him, unless it be His Word and His Wisdom? And how can He be Word and Wisdom, unless He be the proper offspring of His Essence , and did not come to be, as others, out of nothing? And whereas all things are from nothing, and are creatures, and the Son, as they say, is one of the creatures too and of things which once were not, how does He alone reveal the Father, and none else but He know the Father? For could He, a work, possibly know the Father, then must the Father be also known by all according to the proportion of the measures of each: for all of them are works as He is. But if it be impossible for things originate either to see or to know, for the sight and the knowledge of Him surpasses all (since God Himself says, 'No one shall see My face and live '), yet the Son has declared, 'No one knows the Father, save the Son Matthew 11:27,' therefore the Word is different from all things originate, in that He alone knows and alone sees the Father, as He says, 'Not that any one has seen the Father, save He that is from the Father,' and 'no one knows the Father save the Son ,' though Arius think otherwise. How then did He alone know, except that He alone was proper to Him? And how proper, if He were a creature, and not a true Son from Him? (For one must not mind saying often the same thing for religion's sake.) Therefore it is irreligious to think that the Son is one of all things; and blasphemous and unmeaning to call Him 'a creature, but not as one of the creatures, and a work, but not as one of the works, an offspring, but not as one of the offsprings.' for how not as one of these, if, as they say, He was not before His generation ? For it is proper to the creatures and works not to be before their origination, and to subsist out of nothing, even though they excel other creatures in glory; for this difference of one with another will be found in all creatures, which appears in those which are visible.

23. Moreover if, as the heretics hold, the Son were creature or work, but not as one of the creatures, because of His excelling them in glory, it were natural that Scripture should describe and display Him by a comparison in His favour with the other works; for instance, that it should say that He is greater than Archangels, and more honourable than the Thrones, and both brighter than sun and moon, and greater than the heavens. But he is not in fact thus referred to; but the Father shows Him to be His own proper and only Son, saying, 'You are My Son,' and 'This is My beloved Son, in whom I am well pleased.' Accordingly the Angels ministered unto Him, as being one beyond themselves; and they worship Him, not as being greater in glory, but as being some one beyond all the creatures, and beyond themselves, and alone the Father's proper Son according to essence. For if He was worshipped as excelling them in glory, each of things subservient ought to worship what excels itself. But this is not the case; for creature does not worship creature, but servant Lord, and creature God. Thus Peter the Apostle hinders Cornelius who would worship him, saying, 'I myself also am a man Acts 10:26.' And an Angel, when John would worship him in the Apocalypse, hinders him,

saying, 'See thou do it not; for I am your fellow-servant, and of your brethren the Prophets, and of them that keep the sayings of this book: worship God Revelation 22:9.' Therefore to God alone appertains worship, and this the very Angels know, that though they excel other beings in glory, yet they are all creatures and not to be worshipped, but worship the Lord. Thus Manoah, the father of Samson, wishing to offer sacrifice to the Angel, was thereupon hindered by him, saying, 'Offer not to me, but to God.' On the other hand, the Lord is worshipped even by the Angels; for it is written, 'Let all the Angels of God worship Him Hebrews 1:6;' and by all the Gentiles, as Isaiah says, 'The labour of Egypt and merchandize of Ethiopia and of the Sabeans, men of stature, shall come over unto you, and they shall be your servants;' and then, 'they shall fall down unto you, and shall make supplication unto you, saying, Surely God is in you, and there is none else, there is no God Isaiah 45:14.' And He accepts His disciples' worship, and certifies them who He is, saying, 'Call ye Me not Lord and Master? And you say well, for so I am.' And when Thomas said to Him, 'My Lord and my God,' He allows his words, or rather accepts him instead of hindering him. For He is, as the other Prophets declare, and David says in the Psalm, 'the Lord of hosts, the Lord of Sabaoth,' which is interpreted, 'the Lord of Armies,' and God True and Almighty, though the Arians burst at the tidings.

24. But He had not been thus worshipped, nor been thus spoken of, were He a creature merely. But now since He is not a creature, but the proper offspring of the Essence of that God who is worshipped, and His Son by nature, therefore He is worshipped and is believed to be God, and is Lord of armies, and in authority, and Almighty, as the Father is; for He has said Himself, 'All things that the Father has, are Mine John 16:15.' For it is proper to the Son, to have the things of the Father, and to be such that the Father is seen in Him, and that through Him all things were made, and that the salvation of all comes to pass and consists in Him.

Chapter XVII. Introduction to Proverbs VIII. 22 Continued.

Absurdity of supposing a Son or Word created in order to the creation of other creatures; as to the creation being unable to bear God's immediate hand, God condescends to the lowest. Moreover, if the Son a creature, He too could not bear God's hand, and an infiniteseries of media will be necessary. Objected, that, as Moseswho led out the Israelites was a man, so our Lord; but Moseswas not the Agent in creation:— again, that unity is found in created ministrations, but all such ministrations are defective and dependent:— again, that He learned to create, yet could God's Wisdom need teaching? And why should He learn, if the Father works hitherto? If the Son was created to create us, He is for our sake, not we for His

24. (continued). And here it were well to ask them also this question , for a still clearer refutation of their heresy — Wherefore, when all things are creatures, and all are brought into consistence from nothing, and the Son Himself, according to you, is creature and work, and once

was not, wherefore has He made 'all things through Him' alone, 'and without Him was made not one thing John 1:3?' or why is it, when 'all things' are spoken of, that no one thinks the Son is signified in the number, but only things originate; whereas when Scripture speaks of the Word, it does not understand Him as being in the number of 'all,' but places Him with the Father, as Him in whom Providence and salvation for 'all' are wrought and effected by the Father, though all things surely might at the same command have come to be, at which He was brought into being by God alone? For God is not wearied by commanding , nor is His strength unequal to the making of all things, that He should alone create the only Son , and need His ministry and aid for the framing of the rest. For He lets nothing stand over, which He wills to be done; but He willed only , and all things subsisted, and no one 'has resisted His will Romans 9:19.' Why then were not all things brought into being by God alone at that same command, at which the Son came into being? Or let them tell us, why did all things through Him come to be, who was Himself but originate? How void of reason! However, they say concerning Him, that 'God willing to create originate nature, when He saw that it could not endure the untempered hand of the Father, and to be created by Him, makes and creates first and alone one only, and calls Him Son and Word, that, through Him as a medium, all things might thereupon be brought to be.' This they not only have said, but they have dared to put it into writing, namely, Eusebius, Arius, and Asterius who sacrificed.

25. Is not this a full proof of that irreligion, with which they have drugged themselves with much madness, till they blush not to be intoxicate against the truth? For if they shall assign the toil of making all things as the reason why God made the Son only, the whole creation will cry out against them as saying unworthy things of God; and Isaiah too who has said in Scripture, 'The Everlasting God, the Lord, the Creator of the ends of the earth, faints not, neither is weary: there is no searching of His understanding Isaiah 40:28.' And if God made the Son alone, as not deigning to make the rest, but committed them to the Son as an assistant, this on the other hand is unworthy of God, for in Him there is no pride. Nay the Lord reproves the thought, when He says, 'Are not two sparrows sold for a farthing?' and 'one of them shall not

fall on the ground without your Father which is in heaven.' And again, 'Take no thought for your life, what you shall eat, nor yet for your body, what you shall put on. Is not the life more than meat, and the body than raiment? Behold the fowls of the air, for they sow not, neither do they reap, nor gather into barns; yet your heavenly Father feeds them; are you not much better than they? Which of you by taking thought, can add one cubit unto his stature? And why take ye thought for raiment? Consider the lilies of the field, how they grow; they toil not, neither do they spin: and yet I say unto you, that even Solomon in all his glory was not arrayed like one of these. Wherefore if God so clothe the grass of the field which today is, and tomorrow is cast into the oven, shall He not much more clothe you, O you of little faith?' If then it be not unworthy of God to exercise His Providence, even down to things so small, a hair of the head, and a sparrow, and the grass of the field, also it was not unworthy of Him to make them. For what things are the subjects of His Providence, of those He is Maker through His proper Word. Nay a worse absurdity lies before the men who thus speak; for they distinguish between the creatures and the framing; and consider the latter the work of the Father, the creatures the work of the Son; whereas either all things must be brought to be by the Father with the Son, or if all that is originate comes to be through the Son, we must not call Him one of the originated things.

26. Next, their folly may be exposed thus:— if even the Word be of originated nature, how, whereas this nature is too feeble to be God's own handywork, could He alone of all endure to be made by the unoriginate and unmitigated Essence of God, as you say? For it follows either that, if He could endure it, all could endure it, or, it being endurable by none, it was not endurable by the Word, for you say that He is one of originate things. And again, if because originate nature could not endure to be God's own handywork, there arose need of a mediator , it must follow, that, the Word being originate and a creature, there is need of medium in His framing also, since He too is of that originate nature which endures not to be made of God, but needs a medium. But if some being as a medium be found for Him, then again a fresh mediator is needed for that second, and thus tracing back and following out, we shall invent a vast crowd of accumulating mediators;

and thus it will be impossible that the creation should subsist, as ever wanting a mediator, and that medium not coming into being without another mediator; for all of them will be of that originate nature which endures not to be made of God alone, as you say. How abundant is that folly, which obliges them to hold that what has already come into being, admits not of coming! Or perhaps they opine that they have not even come to be, as still seeking their mediator; for, on the ground of their so irreligious and futile notion, what is would not have subsistence, for want of the medium.

27. But again they allege this:— 'Behold, through Moses too did He lead the people from Egypt, and through him He gave the Law, yet he was a man; so that it is possible for like to be brought into being by like.' They should veil their face when they say this, to save their much shame. For Moses was not sent to frame the world, nor to call into being things which were not, or to fashion men like himself, but only to be the minister of words to the people, and to King Pharaoh. And this is a very different thing, for to minister is of things originate as of servants, but to

frame and to create is of God alone, and of His proper Word and His Wisdom. Wherefore, in the matter of framing, we shall find none but God's Word; for 'all things are made in Wisdom,' and 'without the Word was made not one thing.' But as regards ministrations there are, not one only, but man out of their whole number, whomever the Lord will send. For there are many Archangels, many Thrones, and Authorities, and Dominions, thousands of thousands, and myriads of myriads, standing before Him , ministering and ready to be sent. And many Prophets, and twelve Apostles, and Paul. And Moses himself was not alone, but Aaron with him, and next other seventy were filled with the Holy Ghost. And Moses was succeeded by Joshua the Son of Nun, and he by the Judges, and they not by one, but by a number of Kings. If then the Son were a creature and one of things originate, there must have been many such sons, that God might have many such ministers, just as there is a multitude of those others. But if this is not to be seen, but while the creatures are many, the Word is one, any one will collect from this, that the Son differs from all, and is not on a level with the creatures, but proper to the Father. Hence there are not many Words, but one only Word of the one Father, and one

Image of the one God. 'But behold,' they say, 'there is one sun only, and one earth.' Let them maintain, senseless as they are, that there is one water and one fire, and then they may be told that everything that is brought to be, is one in its own essence; but for the ministry and service committed to it, by itself it is not adequate nor sufficient alone. For God said, 'Let there be lights in the firmament of heaven, to give light upon the earth and to divide the day from the night; and let them be for signs and for seasons and for days and years.' And then he says, 'And God made two great lights, the greater light to rule the day, and the lesser light to rule the night: He made the stars also. And God set them in the firmament of the heaven, to give light upon the earth, and to rule over the day and over the night.'

28. Behold there are many lights, and not the sun only, nor the moon only, but each is one in essence, and yet the service of all is one and common; and what each lacks, is supplied by the other, and the office of lighting is performed by all. Thus the sun has authority to shine throughout the day and no more; and the moon through

the night; and the stars together with them accomplish the seasons and years, and become for signs, each according to the need that calls for it. Thus too the earth is not for all things, but for the fruits only, and to be a ground to tread on for the living things that inhabit it. And the firmament is to divide between waters and waters, and to be a place to set the stars in. So also fire and water, with other things, have been brought into being to be the constituent parts of bodies; and in short no one thing is alone, but all things that are made, as if members of each other, make up as it were one body, namely, the world. If then they thus conceive of the Son, let all men throw stones at them, considering the Word to be a part of this universe, and a part insufficient without the rest for the service committed to Him. But if this be manifestly irreligious, let them acknowledge that the Word is not in the number of things originate, but the sole and proper Word of the Father, and their Framer. 'But,' say they, 'though He is a creature and of things originate; yet as from a master and artificer has He learned to frame, and thus ministered to God who taught Him.' For thus the Sophist Asterius, on the strength of having learned to deny the Lord, has dared to write, not observing the absurdity which follows. For if framing be a thing to be taught, let them beware lest they say that God Himself be a Framer not by nature but by science, so as to admit of His losing the power. Besides, if the Wisdom of God attained to frame by teaching, how is He still Wisdom, when He needs to learn? And what was He before He learned? For it was not Wisdom, if it needed teaching; it was surely but some empty thing, and not essential Wisdom , but from advancement it had the name of Wisdom, and will be only so long Wisdom as it can keep what it has learned. For what has accrued not by any nature, but from learning, admits of being one time unlearned. But to speak thus of the Word of God, is not the part of Christians but of Greeks.

29. For if the power of framing accrues to anyone from teaching, these insensate men are ascribing jealousy and weakness to God — jealousy, in that He has not taught many how to frame, so that there may be around Him, as Archangels and Angels many, so framers many; and weakness, in that He could not make by Himself, but needed a fellow-worker, or under-worker; and that, though it has been already shown that created nature admits of

being made by God alone, since they consider the Son to be of such a nature and so made. But God is deficient in nothing: perish the thought! For He has said Himself, 'I am full Isaiah 1:11.' Nor did the Word become Framer of all from teaching; but being the Image and Wisdom of the Father, He does the things of the Father. Nor has He made the Son for the making of things created; for behold, though the Son exists, still the Father is seen to work, as the Lord Himself says, 'My Father works hitherto and I work John 5:17.' If however, as you say, the Son came into being for the purpose of making the things after Him, and yet the Father is seen to work even after the Son, you must hold even in this light the making of such a Son to be superfluous. Besides, why, when He would create us, does He seek for a mediator at all, as if His will did not suffice to constitute whatever seemed good to Him? Yet the Scriptures say, 'He has done whatsoever pleased Him ,' and 'Who has resisted His will Romans 9:19?' And if His mere will is sufficient for the framing of all things, you make the office of a mediator superfluous; for your instance of Moses, and the sun and the moon has been shown not to hold. And here again is an argument to silence you. You say that God, willing the creation of originated nature, and deliberating concerning it, designs and creates the Son, that through Him He may frame us; now, if so, consider how great an irreligion you have dared to utter.

30. First, the Son appears rather to have been for us brought to be, than we for Him; for we were not created for Him, but He is made for us ; so that He owes thanks to us, not we to Him, as the woman to the man. 'For the man,' says Scripture, 'was not created for the woman, but the woman for the man.' Therefore, as 'the man is the image and glory of God, and the woman the glory of the man 1 Corinthians 11:7, 9,' so we are made God's image and to His glory; but the Son is our image, and exists for our glory. And we were brought into being that we might be; but God's Word was made, as you must hold, not that He might be ; but as an instrument for our need, so that not we from Him, but He is constituted from our need. Are not men who even conceive such thoughts, more than insensate? For if for us the Word was made, He has not precedence of us with God; for He did not take counsel about us having Him within Him, but having us in

Himself, counselled, as they say, concerning His own Word. But if so, perchance the Father had not even a will for the Son at all; for not as having a will for Him, did He create Him, but with a will for us, He formed Him for our sake; for He designed Him after designing us; so that, according to these irreligious men, henceforth the Son, who was made as an instrument, is superfluous, now that they are made for whom He was created. But if the Son alone was made by God alone, because He could endure it, but we, because we could not, were made by the Word, why does He not first take counsel about the Word, who could endure His making, instead of taking counsel about us? Or why does He not make more of Him who was strong, than of us who were weak? Or why making Him first, does He not counsel about Him first? Or why counselling about us first, does He not make us first, His will being sufficient for the constitution of all things? But He creates Him first, yet counsels first about us; and He wills us before the Mediator; and when He wills to create us, and counsels about us, He calls us creatures; but Him, whom He frames for us, He calls Son and proper Heir. But we, for whose sake He made Him, ought rather to be called sons; or certainly He, who is His Son, is rather the object of His previous thoughts and of His will, for whom He makes all us. Such the sickness, such the vomit of the heretics.

Chapter XVIII. Introduction to Proverbs VIII. 22 Continued.

Contrast between the Father's operations immediately and naturally in the Son, instrumentally by the creatures; Scripture terms illustrative of this. Explanation of these illustrations; which should be interpreted by the doctrine of the Church; perverse sense put on them by the Arians, refuted. Mystery of Divine Generation. Contrast between God's Word and man's word drawn out at length. Asterius betrayed into holding two Unoriginates; his inconsistency. Baptism how by the Son as well as by the Father. On the Baptism of heretics. Why Arian worse than other heresies.

31. But the sentiment of Truth in this matter must not be hidden, but must have high utterance. For the Word of God was not made for us, but rather we for Him, and 'in Him all things were created Colossians 1:16.' Nor for that

we were weak, was He strong and made by the Father alone, that He might frame us by means of Him as an instrument; perish the thought! It is not so. For though it had seemed good to God not to make things originate, still had the Word been no less with God, and the Father in Him. At the same time, things originate could not without the Word be brought to be; hence they were made through Him — and reasonably. For since the Word is the Son of God by nature proper to His essence, and is from Him, and in Him , as He said Himself, the creatures could not have come to be, except through Him. For as the light enlightens all things by its radiance, and without its radiance nothing would be illuminated, so also the Father, as by a hand , in the Word wrought all things, and without Him makes nothing. For instance, God said, as Moses relates, 'Let there be light,' and 'Let the waters be gathered together,' and 'let the dry land appear,' and 'Let Us make man ;' as also Holy David in the Psalm, 'He spoke and they were made; He commanded and they were created.' And He spoke , not that, as in the case of men, some under-worker might hear, and learning the will of Him who spoke might go away and do it; for this is what is proper to creatures, but it is unseemly so to think or speak of the Word. For the Word of God is Framer and Maker, and He is the Father's Will. Hence it is that divine Scripture says not that one heard and answered, as to the manner or nature of the things which He wished made; but God only said, 'Let it become,' and he adds, 'And it became;' for what He thought good and counselled, that immediately the Word began to do and to finish. For when God commands others, whether the Angels, or converses with Moses, or commands Abraham, then the hearer answers; and the one says, 'Whereby shall I know Genesis 15:8?' and the other, 'Send some one else Exodus 4:13;' and again, 'If they ask me, what is His Name, what shall I say to them ?' and the Angel said to Zacharias, 'Thus says the Lord ;' and he asked the Lord, 'O Lord of hosts, how long will You not have mercy on Jerusalem.' and waits to hear good words and comfortable. For each of these has the Mediator Word, and the Wisdom of God which makes known the will of the Father. But when that Word Himself works and creates, then there is no questioning and answer, for the Father is in Him and the Word in the Father; but it suffices to will, and the work is done; so that the word 'He said' is a token of the will for our sake, and 'It was so,' denotes the work which is done through the Word and the Wisdom, in which Wisdom also is the Will of the Father. And 'God said' is explained in 'the Word,' for, he says, 'You have made all things in Wisdom;' and 'By the Word of the Lord were the heavens made fast.' and 'There is one Lord Jesus Christ, by whom are all things, and we by Him.'

32. It is plain from this that the Arians are not fighting with us about their heresy; but while they pretend us, their real fight is against the Godhead Itself. For if the voice were ours which says, 'This it My Son ,' small were our complaint of them; but if it is the Father's voice, and the disciples heard it, and the Son too says of Himself, 'Before all the mountains He begot me ,' are they not fighting against God, as the giants in story, having their tongue, as the Psalmist says, a sharp sword for irreligion? For they neither feared the voice of the Father, nor reverenced the Saviour's words, nor trusted the Saints, one of whom writes, 'Who being the Brightness of His glory and the Expression of His subsistence,' and 'Christ the power of God and the Wisdom of God ;' and another says in the Psalm, 'With You is the well of life, and in Your Light

shall we see light,' and 'You made all things in Wisdom ;' and the Prophets say, 'And the Word of the Lord came to me Jeremiah 2:1;' and John, 'In the beginning was the Word.' and Luke, 'As they delivered them unto us which from the beginning were eye-witnesses and ministers of the Word John 1:1; Luke 1:2;' and as David again says, 'He sent His Word and healed them.' All these passages proscribe in every light the Arian heresy, and signify the eternity of the Word, and that He is not foreign but proper to the Father's Essence. For when saw any one light without radiance? Or who dares to say that the expression can be different from the subsistence? Or has not a man himself lost his mind who even entertains the thought that God was ever without Reason and without Wisdom? For such illustrations and such images has Scripture proposed, that, considering the inability of human nature to comprehend God, we might be able to form ideas even from these however poorly and dimly, and as far as is attainable. And as the creation contains abundant matter for the knowledge of the being of a God and a Providence ('for by the greatness and beauty of the creatures proportionably the Maker of them is seen Wisdom 13:5 '), and we learn from them without asking for voices, but hearing the Scriptures we believe, and surveying the very order and the harmony of all things, we acknowledge that He is Maker and Lord and God of all, and apprehend His marvellous Providence and governance over all things; so in like manner about the Son's Godhead, what has been above said is sufficient, and it becomes superfluous, or rather it is very mad to dispute about it, or to ask in an heretical way, How can the Son be from eternity? Or how can He be from the Father's Essence, yet not a part? Since what is said to be of another, is a part of him; and what is divided, is not whole.

33. These are the evil sophistries of the heterodox; yet, though we have already shown their shallowness, the exact sense of these passages themselves and the force of these illustrations will serve to show the baseless nature of their loathsome tenet. For we see that reason is ever, and is from him and proper to his essence, whose reason it is, and does not admit a before and an after. So again we see that the radiance from the sun is proper to it, and the sun's essence is not divided or impaired; but its essence is whole and its radiance perfect and whole , yet without impairing the

essence of light, but as a true offspring from it. We understand in like manner that the Son is begotten not from without but from the Father, and while the Father remains whole, the Expression of His Subsistence is ever, and preserves the Father's likeness and unvarying Image, so that he who sees Him, sees in Him the Subsistence too, of which He is the Expression. And from the operation of the Expression we understand the true Godhead of the Subsistence, as the Saviour Himself teaches when He says, 'The Father who dwells in Me, He does the works John 14:10 ' which I do; and 'I and the Father are one,' and 'I in the Father and the Father in Me John 10:30.' Therefore let this Christ — opposing heresy attempt first to divide the examples found in things originate, and say, 'Once the sun was without his radiance,' or, 'Radiance is not proper to the essence of light,' or 'It is indeed proper, but it is a part of light by division; and then let it divide Reason, and pronounce that it is foreign to mind, or that once it was not, or that it was not proper to its essence, or that it is by division a part of mind.' And so of His Expression and the Light and the Power, let it do violence to these as in the case of Reason and Radiance; and instead let it imagine what it will. But if such extravagance be impossible for them, are they not greatly beside themselves, presumptuously intruding into what is higher than things originate and their own nature, and essaying impossibilities ?

34. For if in the case of these originate and irrational things offsprings are found which are not parts of the essences from which they are, nor subsist with passion, nor impair the essences of their originals, are they not mad again in seeking and conjecturing parts and passions in the instance of the immaterial and true God, and ascribing divisions to Him who is beyond passion and change, thereby to perplex the ears of the simple and to pervert them from the Truth? For who hears of a son but conceives of that which is proper to the father's essence? Who heard, in his first catechising , that God has a Son and has made all things by His proper Word, but understood it in that sense in which we now mean it? Who on the rise of this odious heresy of the Arians, was not at once startled at what he heard, as strange , and a second sowing, besides that Word which had been sown from the beginning? For what is sown in every soul from

the beginning is that God has a Son, the Word, the Wisdom, the Power, that is, His Image and Radiance; from which it at once follows that He is always; that He is from the Father; that He is like; that He is the eternal offspring of His essence; and there is no idea involved in these of creature or work. But when the man who is an enemy, while men slept, made a second sowing, of 'He is a creature,' and 'There was once when He was not,' and 'How can it be?' thenceforth the wicked heresy of Christ's enemies rose as tares, and immediately, as bereft of every right thought, they meddle like robbers, and venture to say, 'How can the Son always exist with the Father.' for men come of men and are sons, after a time; and the father is thirty years old, when the son begins to be, being begotten; and in short of every son of man, it is true that he was not before his generation. And again they whisper, 'How can the Son be Word, or the Word be God's Image? For the word of men is composed of syllables, and only signifies the speaker's will, and then is over and is lost.'

35. They then afresh, as if forgetting the proofs which have been already urged against them, 'pierce themselves

through ' with these bonds of irreligion, and thus argue. But the word of truth confutes them as follows:— if they were disputing concerning any man, then let them exercise reason in this human way, both concerning His Word and His Son; but if of God who created man, no longer let them entertain human thoughts, but others which are above human nature. For such as he that begets, such of necessity is the offspring; and such as is the Word's Father, such must be also His Word. Now man, begotten in time, in time also himself begets the child; and whereas from nothing he came to be, therefore his word also is over and continues not. But God is not as man, as Scripture has said; but is existing and is ever; therefore also His Word is existing and is everlastingly with the Father, as radiance of light. And man's word is composed of syllables, and neither lives nor operates anything, but is only significant of the speaker's intention, and does but go forth and go by, no more to appear, since it was not at all before it was spoken; wherefore the word of man neither lives nor operates anything, nor in short is man. And this happens to it, as I said before, because man who begets it, has his nature out of nothing. But God's Word is not merely pronounced, as one may say, nor a sound of accents, nor by

His Son is meant His command ; but as radiance of light, so is He perfect offspring from perfect. Hence He is God also, as being God's Image; for 'the Word was God John 1:1 ' says Scripture. And man's words avail not for operation; hence man works not by means of words but of hands, for they have being, and man's word subsists not. But the 'Word of God,' as the Apostle says, 'is living and powerful and sharper than any two-edged sword, piercing even to the dividing asunder of soul and spirit, and of the joints and marrow, and is a discerner of the thoughts and intents of the heart. Neither is there any creature that is not manifest in His sight; but all things are naked and opened unto the eyes of Him with whom we have to do. Hebrews 4:12-13 ' He is then Framer of all, 'and without Him was made not one thing John 1:3,' nor can anything be made without Him.

36. Nor must we ask why the Word of God is not such as our word, considering God is not such as we, as has been before said; nor again is it right to seek how the word is from God, or how He is God's radiance, or how God begets, and what is the manner of His begetting. For a

man must be beside himself to venture on such points; since a thing ineffable and proper to God's nature, and known to Him alone and to the Son, this he demands to be explained in words. It is all one as if they sought where God is, and how God is, and of what nature the Father is. But as to ask such questions is irreligious, and argues an ignorance of God, so it is not holy to venture such questions concerning the generation of the Son of God, nor to measure God and His Wisdom by our own nature and infirmity. Nor is a person at liberty on that account to swerve in his thoughts from the truth, nor, if any one is perplexed in such inquiries, ought he to disbelieve what is written. For it is better in perplexity to be silent and believe, than to disbelieve on account of the perplexity: for he who is perplexed may in some way obtain mercy, because, though he has questioned, he has yet kept quiet; but when a man is led by his perplexity into forming for himself doctrines which beseem not, and utters what is unworthy of God, such daring recurs a sentence without mercy. For in such perplexities divine Scripture is able to afford him some relief, so as to take rightly what is written, and to dwell upon our word as an illustration; that as it is proper to us and is from us, and not a work external to us, so also God's Word is proper to Him and from Him, and is not a work; and yet is not like the word of man, or else we must suppose God to be man. For observe, many and various are men's words which pass away day by day; because those that come before others continue not, but vanish. Now this happens because their authors are men, and have seasons which pass away, and ideas which are successive; and what strikes them first and second, that they utter; so that they have many words, and yet after them all nothing at all remaining; for the speaker ceases, and his word immediately is spent. But God's Word is one and the same, and, as it is written, 'The Word of God endures for ever ,' not changed, not before or after other, but existing the same always. For it was fitting, whereas God is One, that His Image should be One also, and His Word One and One His Wisdom.

37. Wherefore I am in wonder how, whereas God is One, these men introduce, after their private notions, many images and wisdoms and words , and say that the Father's proper and natural Word is other than the Son, by whom He even made the Son and that He who is really Son is

but notionally called Word, as vine, and way, and door, and tree of life; and that He is called Wisdom also in name, the proper and true Wisdom of the Father, which coexist ingenerately with Him, being other than the Son, by which He even made the Son, and named Him Wisdom as partaking of it. This they have not confined to words, but Arius composed in his Thalia, and the Sophist Asterius wrote, what we have stated above, as follows: 'Blessed Paul said not that he preached Christ, the Power of God or the Wisdom of God,' but without the addition of the article, 'God's power' and 'God's wisdom 1 Corinthians 1:24,' thus preaching that the proper Power of God Himself which is natural to Him, and co-existent in Him ingenerately, is something besides, generative indeed of Christ, and creative of the whole world, concerning which he teaches in his Epistle to the Romans thus —'The invisible things of Him from the creation of the world are clearly seen, being understood by the things that are made, even His eternal Power and Godhead Romans 1:20.' For as no one would say that the Godhead there mentioned was Christ, but the Father Himself, so, as I think, 'His eternal Power and Godhead also is not the Only Begotten Son, but the Father who begot Him.' And he teaches that there is another power and wisdom of God, manifested through Christ. And shortly after the same Asterius says, 'However His eternal power and wisdom, which truth argues to be without beginning and ingenerate, the same must surely be one. For there are many wisdoms which are one by one created by Him, of whom Christ is the first-born and only-begotten; all however equally depend on their Possessor. And all the powers are rightly called His who created and uses them: — as the Prophet says that the locust, which came to be a divine punishment of human sins, was called by God Himself not only a power, but a great power; and blessed David in most of the Psalms invites, not the Angels alone, but the Powers to praise God.'

38. Now are they not worthy of all hatred for merely uttering this? For if, as they hold, He is Son, not because He is begotten of the Father and proper to His Essence, but that He is called Word only because of things rational, and Wisdom because of things gifted with wisdom, and Power because of things gifted with power, surely He must be named a Son because of those who are

made sons: and perhaps because there are things existing, He has even His existence, in our notions only. And then after all what is He? For He is none of these Himself, if they are but His names: and He has but a semblance of being, and is decorated with these names from us. Rather this is some recklessness of the devil, or worse, if they are not unwilling that they should truly subsist themselves, but think that God's Word is but in name. Is not this portentous, to say that Wisdom coexists with the Father, yet not to say that this is the Christ, but that there are many created powers and wisdoms, of which one is the Lord whom they go on to compare to the caterpillar and locust? And are they not profligate, who, when they hear us say that the Word coexists with the Father, immediately murmur out, 'Are you not speaking of two Unoriginates?' yet in speaking themselves of 'His Unoriginate Wisdom,' do not see that they have already incurred themselves the charge which they so rashly urge against us? Moreover, what folly is there in that thought of theirs, that the Unoriginate Wisdom coexisting with God is God Himself! For what coexists does not coexist with itself, but with some one else, as the Evangelists say of the Lord, that He was together with His disciples; for He was not together with Himself, but with His disciples — unless indeed they would say that God is of a compound nature, having wisdom a constituent or complement of His Essence, unoriginate as well as Himself, which moreover they pretend to be the framer of the world, that so they may deprive the Son of the framing of it. For there is nothing they would not maintain, sooner than hold the truth concerning the Lord.

39. For where at all have they found in divine Scripture, or from whom have they heard, that there is another Word and another Wisdom besides this Son, that they should frame to themselves such a doctrine? True, indeed, it is written, 'Are not My words like fire, and like a hammer that breaks the rock in pieces Jeremiah 23:29?' and in the Proverbs, 'I will make known My words unto you Proverbs 1:23;' but these are precepts and commands, which God has spoken to the saints through His proper and only true Word, concerning which the Psalmist said, 'I have refrained my feet from every evil way, that I may keep Your words.' Such words accordingly the Saviour signifies to be distinct from Himself, when He says in His own

person, 'The words which I have spoken unto you John 6:63.' For certainly such words are not offsprings or sons, nor are there so many words that frame the world, nor so many images of the One God, nor so many who have become men for us, nor as if from many such there were one who has become flesh, as John says; but as being the only Word of God was He preached by John, 'The Word was made flesh,' and 'all things were made by Him.' Wherefore of Him alone, our Lord Jesus Christ, and of His oneness with the Father, are written and set forth the testimonies, both of the Father signifying that the Son is One, and of the saints, aware of this and saying that the Word is One, and that He is Only-Begotten. And His works also are set forth; for all things, visible and invisible, have been brought to be through Him, and 'without Him was made not one thing.' But concerning another or any one else they have not a thought, nor frame to themselves words or wisdoms, of which neither name nor deed are signified by Scripture, but are named by these only. For it is their invention and Christ-opposing surmise, and they make the most of the name of the Word and the Wisdom; and framing to themselves others, they deny the true Word of God, and the real and only Wisdom of the

Father, and thereby, miserable men, rival the Manichees. For they too, when they behold the works of God, deny Him the only and true God, and frame to themselves another, whom they can show neither by work, nor in any testimony drawn from the divine oracles.

40. Therefore, if neither in the divine oracles is found another wisdom besides this Son, nor from the fathers have we heard of any such, yet they have confessed and written of the Wisdom coexisting with the Father unoriginately, proper to Him, and the Framer of the world, this must be the Son who even according to them is eternally coexistent with the Father. For He is Framer of all, as it is written, 'In Wisdom have You made them all.' Nay, Asterius himself, as if forgetting what he wrote before, afterwards, in Caiaphas's fashion, involuntarily, when urging the Greeks, instead of naming many wisdoms, or the caterpillar, confesses but one, in these words —'God the Word is one, but many are the things rational; and one is the essence and nature of Wisdom, but many are the things wise and beautiful.' And soon afterwards he says again:— 'Who are they whom they

honour with the title of God's children? For they will not say that they too are words, nor maintain that there are many wisdoms. For it is not possible, whereas the Word is one, and Wisdom has been set forth as one, to dispense to the multitude of children the Essence of the Word, and to bestow on them the appellation of Wisdom.' It is not then at all wonderful, that the Arians should battle with the truth, when they have collisions with their own principles and conflict with each other, at one time saying that there are many wisdoms, at another maintaining one; at one time classing wisdom with the caterpillar, at another saying that it coexists with the Father and is proper to Him; now that the Father alone is unoriginate, and then again that His Wisdom and His Power are unoriginate also. And they battle with us for saying that the Word of God is ever, yet forget their own doctrines, and say themselves that Wisdom coexists with God unoriginately. So dizzied are they in all these matters, denying the true Wisdom, and inventing one which is not, as the Manichees who make to themselves another God, after denying Him that is.

41. But let the other heresies and the Manichees also know that the Father of the Christ is One, and is Lord and Maker of the creation through His proper Word. And let the Ario-maniacs know in particular, that the Word of God is One, being the only Son proper and genuine from His Essence, and having with His Father the oneness of Godhead indivisible, as we said many times, being taught it by the Saviour Himself. Since, were it not so, wherefore through Him does the Father create, and in Him reveal Himself to whom He will, and illuminate them? Or why too in the baptismal consecration is the Son named together with the Father? For if they say that the Father is not all-sufficient, then their answer is irreligious, but if He be, for this it is right to say, what is the need of the Son for framing the worlds, or for the holy laver? For what fellowship is there between creature and Creator? Or why is a thing made classed with the Maker in the consecration of all of us? Or why, as you hold, is faith in one Creator and in one creature delivered to us? For if it was that we might be joined to the Godhead, what need of the creature? But if that we might be united to the Son a creature, superfluous, according to you, is this naming of the Son in Baptism, for God who made Him a Son is able

to make us sons also. Besides, if the Son be a creature, the nature of rational creatures being one, no help will come to creatures from a creature , since all need grace from God. We said a few words just now on the fitness that all things should be made by Him; but since the course of the discussion has led us also to mention holy Baptism, it is necessary to state, as I think and believe, that the Son is named with the Father, not as if the Father were not all-sufficient, not without meaning, and by accident; but, since He is God's Word and own Wisdom, and being His Radiance, is ever with the Father, therefore it is impossible, if the Father bestows grace, that He should not give it in the Son, for the Son is in the Father as the radiance in the light. For, not as if in need, but as a Father in His own Wisdom has God founded the earth, and made all things in the Word which is from Him, and in the Son confirms the Holy Laver. For where the Father is, there is the Son, and where the light, there the radiance; and as what the Father works, He works through the Son , and the Lord Himself says, 'What I see the Father do, that do I also;' so also when baptism is given, whom the Father baptizes, him the Son baptizes; and whom the Son baptizes, he is consecrated in the Holy Ghost. And again as when the sun shines, one might say that the radiance illuminates, for the light is one and indivisible, nor can be detached, so where the Father is or is named, there plainly is the Son also; and is the Father named in Baptism? Then must the Son be named with Him.

42. Therefore, when He made His promise to the saints, He thus spoke; 'I and the Father will come, and make Our abode in him;' and again, 'that, as I and Thou are One, so they may be one in Us.' And the grace given is one, given from the Father in the Son, as Paul writes in every Epistle, 'Grace unto you, and peace from God our Father and the Lord Jesus Christ.' For the light must be with the ray, and the radiance must be contemplated together with its own light. Whence the Jews, as denying the Son as well as they, have not the Father either; for, as having left the 'Fountain of Wisdom Baruch 3:12,' as Baruch reproaches them, they put from them the Wisdom springing from it, our Lord Jesus Christ (for 'Christ,' says the Apostle, is 'God's power and God's wisdom 1 Corinthians 1:24),' when they said, 'We have no king but Cæsar John 19:15.' The Jews then have the penal award of their denial; for their city as well

as their reasoning came to nought. And these too hazard the fullness of the mystery, I mean Baptism; for if the consecration is given to us into the Name of Father and Son, and they do not confess a true Father, because they deny what is from Him and like His Essence, and deny also the true Son, and name another of their own framing as created out of nothing, is not the rite administered by them altogether empty and unprofitable, making a show, but in reality being no help towards religion? For the Arians do not baptize into Father and Son, but into Creator and creature, and into Maker and work. And as a creature is other than the Son, so the Baptism, which is supposed to be given by them, is other than the truth, though they pretend to name the Name of the Father and the Son, because of the words of Scripture, For not he who simply says, 'O Lord,' gives Baptism; but he who with the Name has also the right faith. On this account therefore our Saviour also did not simply command to baptize, but first says, 'Teach;' then thus: 'Baptize into the Name of Father, and Son, and Holy Ghost;' that the right faith might follow upon learning, and together with faith might come the consecration of Baptism.

43. There are many other heresies too, which use the words only, but not in a right sense, as I have said, nor with sound faith, and in consequence the water which they administer is unprofitable, as deficient in piety, so that he who is sprinkled by them is rather polluted by irreligion than redeemed. So Gentiles also, though the name of God is on their lips, incur the charge of Atheism, because they know not the real and very God, the Father of our Lord Jesus Christ. So Manichees and Phrygians, and the disciples of the Samosatene, though using the Names, nevertheless are heretics, and the Arians follow in the same course, though they read the words of Scripture, and use the Names, yet they too mock those who receive the rite from them, being more irreligious than the other heresies, and advancing beyond them, and making them seem innocent by their own recklessness of speech. For these other heresies lie against the truth in some certain respect, either erring concerning the Lord's Body, as if He did not take flesh of Mary, or as if He has not died at all, nor become man, but only appeared, and was not truly, and seemed to have a body when He had not, and seemed to have the shape of man, as visions in a dream; but the Arians are without disguise irreligious against the Father

Himself. For hearing from the Scriptures that His Godhead is represented in the Son as in an image, they blaspheme, saying, that it is a creature, and everywhere concerning that Image, they carry about with them the phrase, 'He was not,' as mud in a wallet , and spit it forth as serpents their venom. Then, whereas their doctrine is nauseous to all men, immediately, as a support against its fall, they prop up the heresy with human patronage, that the simple, at the sight or even by the fear may overlook the mischief of their perversity. Right indeed is it to pity their dupes; well is it to weep over them, for that they sacrifice their own interest for that immediate phantasy which pleasures furnish, and forfeit their future hope. In thinking to be baptized into the name of one who exists not, they will receive nothing; and ranking themselves with a creature, from the creation they will have no help, and believing in one unlike and foreign to the Father in essence, to the Father they will not be joined, not having His own Son by nature, who is from Him, who is in the Father, and in whom the Father is, as He Himself has said; but being led astray by them, the wretched men henceforth remain destitute and stripped of the Godhead. For this phantasy of earthly goods will not follow them upon their death; nor when they see the Lord whom they have denied, sitting on His Father's throne, and judging quick and dead, will they be able to call to their help any one of those who have now deceived them; for they shall see them also at the judgment-seat, repenting for their deeds of sin and irreligion.

Chapter XIX. Texts Explained; Sixthly, Proverbs VIII. 22.

Proverbs are of a figurative nature, and must be interpreted as such. We must interpret them, and in particular this passage, by the Regula Fidei. 'He created me' not equivalent to 'I am a creature.' Wisdom a creature so far forth as Its human body. Again, if He is a creature, it is as 'a beginning of ways,' an office which, though not an attribute, is a consequence, of a higher and divine nature. And it is 'for the works,' which implied the works existed, and therefore much more He, before He was created. Also 'the Lord' not the Father 'created' Him, which implies the creation was that of a servant.

44. We have gone through thus much before the passage in the Proverbs, resisting the insensate fables which their hearts have invented, that they may know that the Son of God ought not to be called a creature, and may learn lightly to read what admits in truth of a right explanation. For it is written, 'The Lord created me a beginning of His ways, for His works ;' since, however, these are proverbs, and it is expressed in the way of proverbs, we must not expound them nakedly in their first sense, but we must inquire into the person, and thus religiously put the sense on it. For what is said in proverbs, is not said plainly, but is put forth latently, as the Lord Himself has taught us in the Gospel according to John, saying, 'These things have I spoken unto you in proverbs, but the time comes when I shall no more speak unto you in proverbs, but openly John 16:25.' Therefore it is necessary to unfold the sense of what is said, and to seek it as something hidden, and not nakedly to expound as if the meaning were spoken 'plainly,' lest by a false interpretation we wander from the truth. If then what is written be about Angel, or any other of things originate, as concerning one of us who are works, let it be said, 'created me;' but if it be the Wisdom of God, in whom all things originate have been framed, that

speaks concerning Itself, what ought we to understand but that 'He created' means nothing contrary to 'He begot.' Nor, as forgetting that It is Creator and Framer, or ignorant of the difference between the Creator and the creatures, does It number Itself among the creatures; but It signifies a certain sense, as in proverbs, not 'plainly,' but latent; which It inspired the saints to use in prophecy, while soon after It does Itself give the meaning of 'He created' in other but parallel expressions, saying, 'Wisdom made herself a house Proverbs 9:1.' Now it is plain that our body is Wisdom's house, which It took on Itself to become man; hence consistently does John say, 'The Word was made flesh John 1:14;' and by Solomon Wisdom says of Itself with cautious exactness, not 'I am a creature,' but only 'The Lord created me a beginning of His ways for His works,' yet not 'created me that I might have being,' nor 'because I have a creature's beginning and origin.'

45. For in this passage, not as signifying the Essence of His Godhead, nor His own everlasting and genuine generation from the Father, has the Word spoken by Solomon, but on the other hand His manhood and

Economy towards us. And, as I said before, He has not said 'I am a creature,' or 'I became a creature,' but only 'He created.' For the creatures, having a created essence, are originate, and are said to be created, and of course the creature is created: but this mere term 'He created' does not necessarily signify the essence or the generation, but indicates something else as coming to pass in Him of whom it speaks, and not simply that He who is said to be created, is at once in His Nature and Essence a creature. And this difference divine Scripture recognises, saying concerning the creatures, 'The earth is full of Your creation,' and 'the creation itself groans together and travails together ;' and in the Apocalypse it says, 'And the third part of the creatures in the sea died which had life;' as also Paul says, 'Every creature of God is good, and nothing is to be refused if it be received with thanksgiving ;' and in the book of Wisdom it is written, 'Having ordained man through Your wisdom, that he should have dominion over the creatures which You have made Wisdom 9:2.' And these, being creatures, are also said to be created, as we may further hear from the Lord, who says, 'He who created them, made them male and female ;' and from Moses in the Song, who writes, 'Ask now of the days that are past, which were before you since the day that God created man upon the earth, and from the one side of heaven unto the other Deuteronomy 4:32.' And Paul in Colossians, 'Who is the Image of the Invisible God, the Firstborn of every creature, for in Him were all things created that are in heaven, and that are on earth, visible and invisible, whether they be thrones, or dominions, or principalities, or powers; all things were created through Him, and for Him, and He is before all. '

46. That to be called creatures, then, and to be created belongs to things which have by nature a created essence, these passages are sufficient to remind us, though Scripture is full of the like; on the other hand that the single word 'He created' does not simply denote the essence and mode of generation, David shows in the Psalm, 'This shall be written for another generation, and the people that is created shall praise the Lord ;' and again, 'Create in me a clean heart, O God ;' and Paul in Ephesians says, 'Having abolished the law of commandments contained in ordinances, for to create in Himself of two one new man Ephesians 2:15;' and again,

'Put on the new man, which after God is created in righteousness and true holiness.' For neither David spoke of any people created in essence, nor prayed to have another heart than that he had, but meant renovation according to God and renewal; nor did Paul signify two persons created in essence in the Lord, nor again did he counsel us to put on any other man; but he called the life according to virtue the 'man after God,' and by the 'created' in Christ he meant the two people who are renewed in Him. Such too is the language of the book of Jeremiah; 'The Lord created a new salvation for a planting, in which salvation men shall walk to and fro ;' and in thus speaking, he does not mean any essence of a creature, but prophesies of the renewal of salvation among men, which has taken place in Christ for us. Such then being the difference between 'the creatures' and the single word 'He created,' if you find anywhere in divine Scripture the Lord called 'creature,' produce it and fight; but if it is nowhere written that He is a creature, only He Himself says about Himself in the Proverbs, 'The Lord created me,' shame upon you, both on the ground of the distinction aforesaid and for that the diction is like that of proverbs; and accordingly let 'He created' be understood, not of His being a creature, but of that human nature which became His, for to this belongs creation. Indeed is it not evidently unfair in you, when David and Paul say 'He created,' then indeed not to understand it of the essence and the generation, but the renewal; yet, when the Lord says 'He created' to number His essence with the creatures? And again when Scripture says, 'Wisdom built her a house, she set it upon seven pillars Proverbs 9:1,' to understand 'house' allegorically, but to take 'He created' as it stands, and to fasten on it the idea of creature? And neither His being Framer of all has had any weight with you, nor have you feared His being the sole and proper Offspring of the Father, but recklessly, as if you had enlisted against Him, do ye fight, and think less of Him than of men.

47. For the very passage proves that it is only an invention of your own to call the Lord creature. For the Lord, knowing His own Essence to be the Only-begotten Wisdom and Offspring of the Father, and other than things originate and natural creatures, says in love to man, 'The Lord created me a beginning of His ways,' as if to say, 'My Father has prepared for Me a body, and has

created Me for men in behalf of their salvation.' For, as when John says, 'The Word was made flesh John 1:14,' we do not conceive the whole Word Himself to be flesh , but to have put on flesh and become man, and on hearing, 'Christ has become a curse for us,' and 'He has made Him sin for us who knew no sin ,' we do not simply conceive this, that whole Christ has become curse and sin, but that He has taken on Him the curse which lay against us (as the Apostle has said, 'Has redeemed us from the curse,' and 'has carried,' as Isaiah has said, 'our sins,' and as Peter has written, 'has borne them in the body on the wood '); so, if it is said in the Proverbs 'He created,' we must not conceive that the whole Word is in nature a creature, but that He put on the created body and that God created Him for our sakes, preparing for Him the created body, as it is written, for us, that in Him we might be capable of being renewed and deified. What then deceived you, O senseless, to call the Creator a creature? Or whence did you purchase for you this new thought, to parade it ? For the Proverbs say 'He created,' but they call not the Son creature, but Offspring; and, according to the distinction in Scripture aforesaid of 'He created' and 'creature,' they acknowledge, what is by nature proper to the Son, that He is the Only-begotten Wisdom and Framer of the creatures, and when they say 'He created,' they say it not in respect of His Essence, but signify that He was becoming a beginning of many ways; so that 'He created' is in contrast to 'Offspring,' and His being called the 'Beginning of ways ' to His being the Only-begotten Word.

48. For if He is Offspring, how call ye Him creature? For no one says that He begets what He creates, nor calls His proper offspring creatures; and again, if He is Only-begotten, how becomes He 'beginning of the ways?' for of necessity, if He was created a beginning of all things, He is no longer alone, as having those who came into being after Him. For Reuben, when he became a beginning of the children , was not only-begotten, but in time indeed first, but in nature and relationship one among those who came after him. Therefore if the Word also is 'a beginning of the ways,' He must be such as the ways are, and the ways must be such as the Word, though in point of time He be created first of them. For the beginning or initiative of a city is such as the other parts of the city are, and the

members too being joined to it, make the city whole and one, as the many members of one body; nor does one part of it make, and another come to be, and is subject to the former, but all the city equally has its government and constitution from its maker. If then the Lord is in such sense created as a 'beginning' of all things, it would follow that He and all other things together make up the unity of the creation, and He neither differs from all others, though He become the 'beginning' of all, nor is He Lord of them, though older in point of time; but He has the same manner of framing and the same Lord as the rest. Nay, if He be a creature, as you hold, how can He be created sole and first at all, so as to be beginning of all? When it is plain from what has been said, that among the creatures not any is of a constant nature and of prior formation, but each has its origination with all the rest, however it may excel others in glory. For as to the separate stars or the great lights, not this appeared first, and that second, but in one day and by the same command, they were all called into being. And such was the original formation of the quadrupeds, and of birds, and fishes, and cattle, and plants; thus too has the race made after God's Image come to be, namely men; for though Adam only was formed out of earth, yet in him was involved the succession of the whole race.

49. And from the visible creation, we clearly discern that His invisible things also, 'being perceived by the things that are made Romans 1:20,' are not independent of each other; for it was not first one and then another, but all at once were constituted after their kind. For the Apostle did not number individually, so as to say 'whether Angel, or Throne, or Dominion, or Authority,' but he mentions together all according to their kind, 'whether Angels, or Archangels, or Principalities :' for in this way is the origination of the creatures. If then, as I have said, the Word were creature He must have been brought into being, not first of them, but with all the other Powers, though in glory He excel the rest ever so much. For so we find it to be in their case, that at once they came to be, with neither first nor second, and they differ from each other in glory, some on the right of the throne, some all around, and some on the left, but one and all praising and standing in service before the Lord. Therefore if the Word be creature He would not be first or beginning of the rest;

yet if He be before all, as indeed He is, and is Himself alone First and Son, it does not follow that He is beginning of all things as to His Essence, for what is the beginning of all is in the number of all. And if He is not such a beginning, then neither is He a creature, but it is very plain that He differs in essence and nature from the creatures, and is other than they, and is Likeness and Image of the sole and true God, being Himself sole also. Hence He is not classed with creatures in Scripture, but David rebukes those who dare even to think of Him as such, saying, 'Who among the gods is like the Lord?' and 'Who is like the Lord among the sons of God.' and Baruch, 'This is our God, and another shall not be reckoned with Him Baruch 3:35.' For the One creates, and the rest are created; and the One is the own Word and Wisdom of the Father's Essence, and through this Word things which came to be, which before existed not, were made.

50. Your famous assertion then, that the Son is a creature, is not true, but is your fantasy only; nay Solomon convicts you of having many times slandered him. For he has not

called Him creature, but God's Offspring and Wisdom, saying, 'God in Wisdom established the earth,' and 'Wisdom built her an house.' And the very passage in question proves your irreligious spirit; for it is written, 'The Lord created me a beginning of His ways for His works.' Therefore if He is before all things, yet says 'He created me' (not 'that I might make the works,' but) 'for the works,' unless 'He created' relates to something later than Himself, He will seem later than the works, finding them on His creation already in existence before Him, for the sake of which He is also brought into being. And if so, how is He before all things notwithstanding? And how were all things made through Him and consist in Him? For behold, you say that the works consisted before Him, for which He is created and sent. But it is not so; perish the thought! false is the supposition of the heretics. For the Word of God is not creature but Creator; and says in the manner of proverbs, 'He created me' when He put on created flesh. And something besides may be understood from the passage itself; for, being Son and having God for His Father, for He is His proper Offspring, yet here He names the Father Lord; not that He was servant, but because He took the servant's form. For it became Him, on the one hand being the Word from the Father, to call God Father: for this is proper to son towards father; on the other, having come to finish the work, and taken a servant's form, to name the Father Lord. And this difference He Himself has taught by an apt distinction, saying in the Gospels, 'I thank You, O Father,' and then, 'Lord of heaven and earth Matthew 11:25.' For He calls God His Father, but of the creatures He names Him Lord; as showing clearly from these words, that, when He put on the creature , then it was He called the Father Lord. For in the prayer of David the Holy Spirit marks the same distinction, saying in the Psalms, 'Give Your strength unto Your Child, and help the Son of Your handmaid.' For the natural and true child of God is one, and the sons of the handmaid, that is, of the nature of things originate, are other. Wherefore the One, as Son, has the Father's might; but the rest are in need of salvation.

51. (But if, because He was called child, they idly talk, let them know that both Isaac was named Abraham's child, and the son of the Shunamite was called young child.) Reasonably then, we being servants, when He became as

we, He too calls the Father Lord, as we do; and this He has so done from love to man, that we too, being servants by nature, and receiving the Spirit of the Son, might have confidence to call Him by grace Father, who is by nature our Lord. But as we, in calling the Lord Father, do not deny our servitude by nature (for we are His works, and it is 'He that has made us, and not we ourselves '), so when the Son, on taking the servant's form, says, 'The Lord created me a beginning of His ways,' let them not deny the eternity of His Godhead, and that 'in the beginning was the Word,' and 'all things were made by Him,' and 'in Him all things were created. '

Chapter XX. Texts Explained; Sixthly, Proverbs VIII. 22 Continued.

Our Lord is said to be created 'for the works,' i.e. with a particular purpose, which no mere creatures are ever said to be. Parallel of Isaiah 49:5, etc. When His manhood is spoken of, a reason for it is added; not so when His Divine Nature; Texts in proof.

51 (continued). For the passage in the Proverbs, as I have said before, signifies, not the Essence, but the manhood of the Word; for if He says that He was created 'for the works,' He shows His intention of signifying, not His Essence, but the Economy which took place 'for His works,' which comes second to being. For things which are in formation and creation are made specially that they may be and exist , and next they have to do whatever the Word bids them, as may be seen in the case of all things. For Adam was created, not that He might work, but that first he might be man; for it was after this that he received the command to work. And Noah was created, not because of the ark, but that first he might exist and be a man; for after this he received commandment to prepare the ark. And the like will be found in every case on inquiring into it — thus the great Moses first was made a man, and next was entrusted with the government of the people. Therefore here too we must suppose the like; for you see, that the Word is not created into existence, but, 'In the beginning was the Word,' and He is afterwards sent 'for the works' and the Economy towards them. For before the works were made, the Son was ever, nor was there yet need that He should be created; but when the works were

created and need arose afterwards of the Economy for their restoration, then it was that the Word took upon Himself this condescension and assimilation to the works; which He has shown us by the word 'He created.' And through the Prophet Isaiah willing to signify the like, He says again: 'And now thus says the Lord, who formed me from the womb to be His servant, to gather together Jacob unto Him and Israel, I shall be brought together and be glorified before the Lord.'

52. See here too, He is formed, not into existence, but in order to gather together the tribes, which were in existence before He was formed. For as in the former passage stands 'He created,' so in this 'He formed;' and as there 'for the works,' so here 'to gather together;' so that in every point of view it appears that 'He created' and 'He formed' are said after 'the Word was.' For as before His forming the tribes existed, for whose sake He was formed, so does it appear that the works exist, for which He was created. And when 'in the beginning was the Word,' not yet were the works, as I have said before; but when the works were made and the need required, then 'He created' was said;

and as if some son, when the servants were lost, and in the hands of the enemy by their own carelessness, and need was urgent, were sent by his father to succour and recover them, and on setting out were to put over him the like dress with them, and should fashion himself as they, lest the capturers, recognising him as the master, should take to flight and prevent his descending to those who were hidden under the earth by them; and then were any one to inquire of him, why he did so, were to make answer, 'My Father thus formed and prepared me for his works,' while in thus speaking, he neither implies that he is a servant nor one of the works, nor speaks of the beginning of His origination, but of the subsequent charge given him over the works — in the same way the Lord also, having put over Him our flesh, and 'being found in fashion as a man,' if He were questioned by those who saw Him thus and marvelled, would say, 'The Lord created Me the beginning of His ways for His works,' and 'He formed Me to gather together Israel.' This again the Spirit foretells in the Psalms, saying, 'You set Him over the works of Your hands Hebrews 2:7;' which elsewhere the Lord signified of Himself, 'I am set as King by Him upon His holy hill of Sion.' And as, when He shone in the body upon Sion, He had not His beginning of existence or of reign, but being God's Word and everlasting King, He vouchsafed that His kingdom should shine in a human way in Sion, that redeeming them and us from the sin which reigned in them, He might bring them under His Father's Kingdom, so, on being set 'for the works,' He is not set for things which did not yet exist, but for such as already were and needed restoration.

53. 'He created' then and 'He formed' and 'He set,' having the same meaning, do not denote the beginning of His being, or of His essence as created, but His beneficent renovation which came to pass for us. Accordingly, though He thus speaks, yet He taught also that He Himself existed before this, when He said, 'Before Abraham came to be, I am John 8:58;' and 'when He prepared the heavens, I was present with Him;' and 'I was with Him disposing things.' And as He Himself was before Abraham came to be, and Israel had come into being after Abraham, and plainly He exists first and is formed afterwards, and His forming signifies not His beginning of being but His taking manhood, wherein also He collects

together the tribes of Israel; so, as 'being always with the Father,' He Himself is Framer of the creation, and His works are evidently later than Himself, and 'He created' signifies, not His beginning of being, but the Economy which took place for the works, which He effected in the flesh. For it became Him, being other than the works, nay rather their Framer, to take upon Himself their renovation, that, whereas He is created for us, all things may be now created in Him. For when He said 'He created,' He immediately added the reason, naming 'the works,' that His creation for the works might signify His becoming man for their renovation. And this is usual with divine Scripture ; for when it signifies the fleshly origination of the Son, it adds also the cause for which He became man; but when he speaks or His servants declare anything of His Godhead, all is said in simple diction, and with an absolute sense, and without reason being added. For He is the Father's Radiance; and as the Father is, but not for any reason, neither must we seek the reason of that Radiance. Thus it is written, 'In the beginning was the Word, and the Word was with God, and the Word was God John 1:1;' and the wherefore it assigns not ; but when 'the Word was made flesh John 1:14,' then it adds the reason why, saying, 'And dwelt among us.' And again the Apostle saying, 'Who being in the form of God,' has not introduced the reason, till 'He took on Him the form of a servant;' for then he continues, 'He humbled Himself unto death, even the death of the cross Philippians 2:6-8;' for it was for this that He both became flesh and took the form of a servant.

54. And the Lord Himself has spoken many things in proverbs; but when giving us notices about Himself, He has spoken absolutely ; 'I in the Father and the Father in Me,' and 'I and the Father are one,' and, 'He that has seen Me, has seen the Father,' and 'I am the Light of the world,' and, 'I am the Truth ;' not setting down in every case the reason, nor the wherefore, lest He should seem second to those things for which He was made. For that reason would needs take precedence of Him, without which not even He Himself had come into being. Paul, for instance, 'separated an Apostle for the Gospel, which the Lord had promised afore by the Prophets Romans 1:1-2,' was thereby made subordinate to the Gospel, of which he was made minister, and John, being chosen to prepare the

Lord's way, was made subordinate to the Lord; but the Lord, not being made subordinate to any reason why He should be Word, save only that He is the Father's Offspring and Only-begotten Wisdom, when He becomes man, then assigns the reason why He is about to take flesh. For the need of man preceded His becoming man, apart from which He had not put on flesh. And what the need was for which He became man, He Himself thus signifies, 'I came down from heaven, not to do My own will, but the will of Him that sent Me. And this is the will of Him which has sent Me, that of all which He has given Me, I should lose nothing, but should raise it up again at the last day. And this is the will of My Father, that every one which sees the Son and believes in Him may have everlasting life, and I will raise him up at the last day.' And again; 'I have come a light into the world, that whosoever believes in Me, should not abide in darkness.' And again he says; 'To this end was I born, and for this cause came I into the world, that I should bear witness unto the truth.' And John has written: 'For this was manifested the Son of God, that He might destroy the works of the devil 1 John 3:8.'

55. To give a witness then, and for our sakes to undergo death, to raise man up and destroy the works of the devil, the Saviour came, and this is the reason of His incarnate presence. For otherwise a resurrection had not been, unless there had been death; and how had death been, unless He had had a mortal body? This the Apostle, learning from Him, thus sets forth, 'Forasmuch then as the children are partakers of flesh and blood, He also Himself likewise took part of the same; that through death He might bring to nought him that had the power of death, that is, the devil, and deliver them who through fear of death were all their lifetime subject to bondage Hebrews 2:14-15.' And, 'Since by man came death, by man came also the resurrection of the dead 1 Corinthians 15:21.' And again, 'For what the Law could not do, in that it was weak through the flesh, God, sending His own Son in the likeness of sinful flesh, and for sin, condemned sin in the flesh; that the ordinance of the Law might be fulfilled in us, who walk not after the flesh but after the Spirit Romans 8:3-4.' And John says, 'For God sent not His Son into the world to condemn the world, but that the world through Him might be saved John 3:17.' And again, the Saviour has spoken in His own person, 'For judgment am

I come into this world, that they who see not might see, and that they which see might become blind.' Not for Himself then, but for our salvation, and to abolish death, and to condemn sin, and to give sight to the blind, and to raise up all from the dead, has He come; but if not for Himself, but for us, by consequence not for Himself but for us is He created. But if not for Himself is He created, but for us, then He is not Himself a creature, but, as having put on our flesh, He uses such language. And that this is the sense of the Scriptures, we may learn from the Apostle, who says in Ephesians, 'Having broken down the middle wall of partition between us, having abolished in His flesh the enmity, even the law of commandments contained in ordinances, to create in Himself of two one new man, so making peace Ephesians 2:14-15.' But if in Him the two are created, and these are in His body, reasonably then, bearing the two in Himself, He is as if Himself created; for those who were created in Himself He made one, and He was in them, as they. And thus, the two being created in Him, He may say suitably, 'The Lord created me.' For as by receiving our infirmities, He is said to be infirm Himself, though not Himself infirm, for He is the Power of God, and He became sin for us and a curse, though not having sinned Himself, but because He Himself bare our sins and our curse, so , by creating us in Him, let Him say, 'He created me for the works,' though not Himself a creature.

56. For if, as they hold, the Essence of the Word being of created nature, therefore He says, 'The Lord created me,' being a creature, He was not created for us; but if He was not created for us, we are not created in Him; and, if not created in Him, we have Him not in ourselves but externally; as, for instance, as receiving instruction from Him as from a teacher. And it being so with us, sin has not lost its reign over the flesh, being inherent and not cast out of it. But the Apostle opposes such a doctrine a little before, when he says, 'For we are His workmanship, created in Christ Jesus Ephesians 2:10;' and if in Christ we are created, then it is not He who is created, but we in Him; and thus the words 'He created' are for our sake. For because of our need, the Word, though being Creator, endured words which are used of creatures; which are not proper to Him, as being the Word, but are ours who are created in Him. And as, since the Father is always, so is

His Word, and always being, always says 'I was daily His delight, rejoicing always before Him Proverbs 8:30,' and 'I am in the Father and the Father in Me John 14:10;' so, when for our need He became man, consistently does He use language, as ourselves, 'The Lord has created Me,' that, by His dwelling in the flesh, sin might perfectly be expelled from the flesh, and we might have a free mind. For what ought He, when made man, to say? 'In the beginning I was man?' this were neither suitable to Him nor true; and as it beseemed not to say this, so it is natural and proper in the case of man to say, 'He created' and 'He made' Him. On this account then the reason of 'He created' is added, namely, the need of the works; and where the reason is added, surely the reason rightly explains the lection. Thus here, when He says 'He created,' He sets down the cause, 'the works;' on the other hand, when He signifies absolutely the generation from the Father, straightway He adds, 'Before all the hills He begets me Proverbs 8:25;' but He does not add the 'wherefore,' as in the case of 'He created,' saying, 'for the works,' but absolutely, 'He begets me,' as in the text, 'In the beginning was the Word John 1:1.' For, though no works had been created, still 'the Word' of God 'was,' and 'the Word was

God.' And His becoming man would not have taken place, had not the need of men become a cause. The Son then is not a creature.

Chapter XXI. Texts Explained; Sixthly, Proverbs VIII. 22, Continued.

Our Lord not said in Scripture to be 'created,' or the works to be 'begotten.' 'In the beginning' means in the case of the works 'from the beginning.' Scripture passages explained. We are made by God first, begotten next; creatures by nature, sons by grace. Christ begotten first, made or created afterwards. Sense of 'First-born of the dead;' of 'First-born among many brethren;' of 'First-born of all creation,' contrasted with 'Only-begotten.' Further interpretation of 'beginning of ways,' and 'for the works.' Why a creature could not redeem; why redemption was necessary at all. Texts which contrast the Word and the works.

57. For had He been a creature, He had not said, 'He begets me,' for the creatures are from without, and are

works of the Maker; but the Offspring is not from without nor a work, but from the Father, and proper to His Essence. Wherefore they are creatures; this God's Word and Only-begotten Son. For instance, Moses did not say of the creation, 'In the beginning He begot,' nor 'In the beginning was,' but 'In the beginning God created the heaven and the earth Genesis 1:1.' Nor did David say in the Psalm, 'Your hands have begotten me,' but 'made me and fashioned me ,' everywhere applying the word 'made' to the creatures. But to the Son contrariwise; for he has not said 'I made,' but 'I begot ,' and 'He begets me,' and 'My heart uttered a good Word.' And in the instance of the creation, 'In the beginning He made;' but in the instance of the Son, 'In the beginning was the Word John 1:1.' And there is this difference, that the creatures are made upon the beginning, and have a beginning of existence connected with an interval; wherefore also what is said of them, 'In the beginning He made,' is as much as saying of them, 'From the beginning He made:'— as the Lord, knowing that which He had made, taught, when He silenced the Pharisees, with the words, 'He which made them from the beginning, made them male and female Matthew 19:4;' for from some beginning, when they were not yet, were originate things brought into being and created. This too the Holy Spirit has signified in the Psalms, saying, 'Thou, Lord, at the beginning hast laid the foundation of the earth ;' and again, 'O think upon Your congregation which You have purchased from the beginning ;' now it is plain that what takes place at the beginning, has a beginning of creation, and that from some beginning God purchased His congregation. And that 'In the beginning He made,' from his saying 'made,' means 'began to make,' Moses himself shows by saying, after the completion of all things, 'And God blessed the seventh day and sanctified it, because that in it He had rested from all His work which God began to make Genesis 2:3.' Therefore the creatures began to be made; but the Word of God, not having beginning of being, certainly did not begin to be, nor begin to come to be, but was ever. And the works have their beginning in their making, and their beginning precedes their coming to be; but the Word, not being of things which come to be, rather comes to be Himself the Framer of those which have a beginning. And the being of things originate is measured by their becoming , and from some beginning does God begin to make them through the Word, that it may be known that they were not before their origination; but the Word has His being, in no other beginning than the Father, whom they allow to be without beginning, so that He too exists without beginning in the Father, being His Offspring, not His creature.

58. Thus does divine Scripture recognise the difference between the Offspring and things made, and show that the Offspring is a Son, not begun from any beginning, but eternal; but that the thing made, as an external work of the Maker, began to come into being. John therefore delivering divine doctrine about the Son, and knowing the difference of the phrases, said not, 'In the beginning has become' or 'been made,' but 'In the beginning was the Word.' that we might understand 'Offspring' by 'was,' and not account of Him by intervals, but believe the Son always and eternally to exist. And with these proofs, how, O Arians, misunderstanding the passage in Deuteronomy, did you venture a fresh act of irreligion against the Lord, saying that 'He is a work,' or 'creature,' or indeed 'offspring?' for offspring and work you take to mean the same thing; but here too you shall be shown to be as

unlearned as you are irreligious. Your first passage is this, 'Is not He your Father that bought you? Did He not make you and create you ?' And shortly after in the same Song he says, 'You deserted God Who begot you, and forgot God Who nourished you.' Now the meaning conveyed in these passages is very remarkable; for he says not first 'He begot,' lest that term should be taken as indiscriminate with 'He made,' and these men should have a pretence for saying, 'Moses tells us indeed that God said from the beginning, Let Us make man Genesis 1:26,' but he soon after says himself, 'God that begot you you deserted,' as if the terms were indifferent; for offspring and work are the same. But after the words 'bought' and 'made,' he has added last of all 'begot,' that the sentence might carry its own interpretation; for in the word 'made' he accurately denotes what belongs to men by nature, to be works and things made; but in the word 'begot' he shows God's lovingkindness exercised towards men after He had created them. And since they have proved ungrateful upon this, thereupon Moses reproaches them, saying first, 'Do ye thus requite the Lord.' and then adds, 'Is not He your Father that bought you? Did He not make you and create you Deuteronomy 32:6?' And next he says, 'They sacrificed unto devils, not to God, to gods whom they knew not. New gods and strange came up, whom your fathers knew not; the God that begot you you deserted. '

59. For God not only created them to be men, but called them to be sons, as having begotten them. For the term 'begot' is here as elsewhere expressive of a Son, as He says by the Prophet, 'I begot sons and exalted them;' and generally, when Scripture wishes to signify a son, it does so, not by the term 'created,' but undoubtedly by that of 'begot.' And this John seems to say, 'He gave to them power to become children of God, even to them that believe in His Name; which were begotten not of blood, nor of the will of the flesh, nor of the will of man, but of God John 1:12-13.' And here too the cautious distinction is well kept up, for first he says 'become,' because they are not called sons by nature but by adoption; then he says 'were begotten,' because they too had received at any rate the name of son. But the People, as says the Prophet, 'despised' their Benefactor. But this is God's kindness to man, that of whom He is Maker, of them according to grace He afterwards becomes Father also; becomes, that is,

when men, His creatures, receive into their hearts, as the Apostle says, 'the Spirit of His Son, crying, Abba, Father.' And these are they who, having received the Word, gained power from Him to become sons of God; for they could not become sons, being by nature creatures, otherwise than by receiving the Spirit of the natural and true Son. Wherefore, that this might be, 'The Word became flesh,' that He might make man capable of Godhead. This same meaning may be gained also from the Prophet Malachi, who says, 'Hath not One God created us? Have we not all one Father Malachi 2:10?' for first he puts 'created,' next 'Father,' to show, as the other writers, that from the beginning we were creatures by nature, and God is our Creator through the Word; but afterwards we were made sons, and thenceforward God the Creator becomes our Father also. Therefore 'Father' is proper to the Son; and not 'creature,' but 'Son' is proper to the Father. Accordingly this passage also proves, that we are not sons by nature, but the Son who is in us; and again, that God is not our Father by nature, but of that Word in us, in whom and because of whom we 'cry, Abba, Father Galatians 4:6.' And so in like manner, the Father calls them sons in whomsoever He sees His own Son, and says, 'I begot.'

since begetting is significant of a Son, and making is indicative of the works. And thus it is that we are not begotten first, but made; for it is written, 'Let Us make man Genesis 1:26;' but afterwards, on receiving the grace of the Spirit, we are said thenceforth to be begotten also; just as the great Moses in his Song with an apposite meaning says first 'He bought,' and afterwards 'He begot.' lest, hearing 'He begot,' they might forget their own original nature; but that they might know that from the beginning they are creatures, but when according to grace they are said to be begotten, as sons, still no less than before are men works according to nature.

60. And that creature and offspring are not the same, but differ from each other in nature and the signification of the words, the Lord Himself shows even in the Proverbs. For having said, 'The Lord created me a beginning of His ways;' He has added, 'But before all the hills He begot me.' If then the Word were by nature and in His Essence a creature, and there were no difference between offspring and creature, He would not have added, 'He begot me,' but had been satisfied with 'He created,' as if that term

implied 'He begot.' but, as it is, after saying, 'He created me a beginning of His ways for His works,' He has added, not simply 'begot me,' but with the connection of the conjunction 'But,' as guarding thereby the term 'created,' when he says, 'But before all the hills He begot me.' For 'begot me' succeeding in such close connection to 'created me,' makes the meaning one, and shows that 'created' is said with an object, but that 'begot me' is prior to 'created me.' For as, if He had said the reverse, 'The Lord begot me,' and went on, 'But before the hills He created me,' 'created' would certainly precede 'begot,' so having said first 'created,' and then added 'But before all the hills He begot me,' He necessarily shows that 'begot' preceded 'created.' For in saying, 'Before all He begot me,' He intimates that He is other than all things; it having been shown to be true in an earlier part of this book, that no one creature was made before another, but all things originate subsisted at once together upon one and the same command. Therefore neither do the words which follow 'created,' also follow 'begot me;' but in the case of 'created' is added 'beginning of ways,' but of 'begot me,' He says not, 'He begot me as a beginning,' but 'before all He begot me.' But He who is before all is not a beginning of all, but is other than all ; but if other than all (in which 'all' the beginning of all is included), it follows that He is other than the creatures; and it becomes a clear point, that the Word, being other than all things and before all, afterwards is created 'a beginning of the ways for works,' because He became man, that, as the Apostle has said, He who is the 'Beginning' and 'First-born from the dead, in all things might have the preeminence Colossians 1:18.'

61. Such then being the difference between 'created' and 'begot me,' and between 'beginning of ways' and 'before all,' God, being first Creator, next, as has been said, becomes Father of men, because of His Word dwelling in them. But in the case of the Word the reverse; for God, being His Father by nature, becomes afterwards both His Creator and Maker, when the Word puts on that flesh which was created and made, and becomes man. For, as men, receiving the Spirit of the Son, become children through Him, so the Word of God, when He Himself puts on the flesh of man, then is said both to be created and to have been made. If then we are by nature sons, then is He by nature creature and work; but if we become sons

by adoption and grace, then has the Word also, when in grace towards us He became man, said, 'The Lord created me.' And in the next place, when He put on a created nature and became like us in body, reasonably was He therefore called both our Brother and 'First-born.' For though it was after us that He was made man for us, and our brother by similitude of body, still He is therefore called and is the 'First-born' of us, because, all men being lost, according to the transgression of Adam, His flesh before all others was saved and liberated, as being the Word's body ; and henceforth we, becoming incorporate with It, are saved after Its pattern. For in It the Lord becomes our guide to the Kingdom of Heaven and to His own Father, saying, 'I am the way' and 'the door ,' and 'through Me all must enter.' Whence also is He said to be 'First-born from the dead Revelation 1:5,' not that He died before us, for we had died first; but because having undergone death for us and abolished it, He was the first to rise, as man, for our sakes raising His own Body. Henceforth He having risen, we too from Him and because of Him rise in due course from the dead.

62. But if He is also called 'First-born of the creation ,' still this is not as if He were levelled to the creatures, and only first of them in point of time (for how should that be, since He is 'Only-begotten?'), but it is because of the Word's condescension to the creatures, according to which He has become the 'Brother' of 'many.' For the term 'Only-begotten' is used where there are no brethren, but 'First-born ' because of brethren. Accordingly it is nowhere written in the Scriptures, 'the first-born of God,' nor 'the creature of God;' but 'Only-begotten' and 'Son' and 'Word' and 'Wisdom,' refer to Him as proper to the Father. Thus, 'We have seen His glory, the glory as of the Only-begotten of the Father John 1:14;' and 'God sent His Only-begotten Son 1 John 4:9;' and 'O Lord, Your Word endures for ever ;' and 'In the beginning was the Word, and the Word was with God;' and 'Christ the Power of God and the Wisdom of God 1 Corinthians 1:24;' and 'This is My beloved Son.' and 'You are the Christ, the Son of the Living God.' But 'first-born' implied the descent to the creation ; for of it has He been called first-born; and 'He created' implies His grace towards the works, for for them is He created. If then He is Only-begotten, as indeed He is, 'First-born' needs some

explanation; but if He be really First-born, then He is not Only-begotten. For the same cannot be both Only-begotten and First-born, except in different relations;—that is, Only-begotten, because of His generation from the Father, as has been said; and First-born, because of His condescension to the creation and His making the many His brethren. Certainly, those two terms being inconsistent with each other, one should say that the attribute of being Only-begotten has justly the preference in the instance of the Word, in that there is no other Word, or other Wisdom, but He alone is very Son of the Father. Moreover, as was before said, not in connection with any reason, but absolutely it is said of Him, 'The Only-begotten Son which is in the bosom of the Father John 1:18;' but the word 'First-born' has again the creation as a reason in connection with it, which Paul proceeds to say, 'for in Him all things were created Colossians 1:16.' But if all the creatures were created in Him, He is other than the creatures, and is not a creature, but the Creator of the creatures.

63. Not then because He was from the Father was He called 'First-born,' but because in Him the creation came to be; and as before the creation He was the Son, through whom was the creation, so also before He was called the First-born of the whole creation, not the less was the Word Himself with God and the Word was God. But this also not understanding, these irreligious men go about saying, 'If He is First-born of all creation, it is plain that He too is one of the creation.' Senseless men! If He is simply 'First-born of the whole creation,' then He is other than the whole creation; for he says not, 'He is First-born above the rest of the creatures,' lest He be reckoned to be as one of the creatures, but it is written, 'of the whole creation,' that He may appear other than the creation. Reuben, for instance, is not said to be first-born of all the children of Jacob , but of Jacob himself and his brethren; lest he should be thought to be some other beside the children of Jacob. Nay, even concerning the Lord Himself the Apostle says not, 'that He may become First-born of all,' lest He be thought to bear a body other than ours, but 'among many brethren Romans 8:29,' because of the likeness of the flesh. If then the Word also were one of the creatures, Scripture would have said of Him also that He

was First-born of other creatures; but in fact, the saints saying that He is 'First-born of the whole creation Colossians 1:15,' the Son of God is plainly shown to be other than the whole creation and not a creature. For if He is a creature, He will be First-born of Himself. How then is it possible, O Arians, for Him to be before and after Himself? Next, if He is a creature, and the whole creation through Him came to be, and in Him consists, how can He both create the creation and be one of the things which consist in Him? Since then such a notion is in itself unseemly, it is proved against them by the truth, that He is called 'First-born among many brethren?' because of the relationship of the flesh, and 'First-born from the dead,' because the resurrection of the dead is from Him and after Him; and 'First-born of the whole creation,' because of the Father's love to man, which brought it to pass that in His Word not only 'all things consist ,' but the creation itself, of which the Apostle speaks, 'waiting for the manifestation of the sons of God, shall be delivered' one time 'from the bondage of corruption into the glorious liberty of the children of God.' Of this creation thus delivered, the Lord will be First-born, both of it and of all those who are made children, that by His being called first, those that come after Him may abide, as depending on the Word as a beginning.

64. And I think that the irreligious men themselves will be shamed from such a thought; for if the case stands not as we have said, but they will rule it that He is 'First-born of the whole creation' as in essence— a creature among creatures, let them reflect that they will be conceiving Him as brother and fellow of the things without reason and life. For of the whole creation these also are parts; and the 'First-born' must be first indeed in point of time but only thus, and in kind and similitude must be the same with all. How then can they say this without exceeding all measures of irreligion? Or who will endure them, if this is their language? Or who can but hate them even imagining such things? For it is evident to all, that neither for Himself, as being a creature, nor as having any connection according to essence with the whole creation, has He been called 'First-born' of it: but because the Word, when at the beginning He framed the creatures, condescended to things originate, that it might be possible for them to come to be. For they could not have endured His nature,

which was untempered splendour, even that of the Father, unless condescending by the Father's love for man He had supported them and taken hold of them and brought them into existence ; and next, because, by this condescension of the Word, the creation too is made a son through Him, that He might be in all respects 'First-born' of it, as has been said, both in creating, and also in being brought for the sake of all into this very world. For so it is written, 'When He brings the First-born into the world, He says, Let all the Angels of God worship Him Hebrews 1:6.' Let Christ's enemies hear and tear themselves to pieces, because His coming into the world is what makes Him called 'First-born' of all; and thus the Son is the Father's 'Only-begotten,' because He alone is from Him, and He is the 'First-born of creation,' because of this adoption of all as sons. And as He is First-born among brethren and rose from the dead 'the first fruits of them that slept 1 Corinthians 15:20;' so, since it became Him 'in all things to have the preeminence Colossians 1:18,' therefore He is created 'a beginning of ways,' that we, walking along it and entering through Him who says, 'I am the Way' and 'the Door,' and partaking of the knowledge of the Father, may also hear the words, 'Blessed are the undefiled in the Way,' and 'Blessed are the pure in heart, for they shall see God.'

65. And thus since the truth declares that the Word is not by nature a creature, it is fitting now to say, in what sense He is 'beginning of ways.' For when the first way, which was through Adam, was lost, and in place of paradise we deviated unto death, and heard the words, 'Dust you are, and unto dust Genesis 3:19 shall you return,' therefore the Word of God, who loves man, puts on Him created flesh at the Father's will , that whereas the first man had made it dead through the transgression, He Himself might quicken it in the blood of His own body , and might open 'for us a way new and living,' as the Apostle says, 'through the veil, that is to say, His flesh Hebrews 10:20;' which he signifies elsewhere thus, 'Wherefore, if any man be in Christ, he is a new creation; old things are passed away, behold all things have become new 2 Corinthians 5:17.' But if a new creation has come to pass, some one must be first of this creation; now a man, made of earth only, such as we have become from the transgression, he could not be. For in the first creation, men had become unfaithful, and through them that first creation had been lost; and

there was need of some one else to renew the first creation, and preserve the new which had come to be. Therefore from love to man none other than the Lord, the 'beginning' of the new creation, is created as 'the Way,' and consistently says, 'The Lord created me a beginning of ways for His works;' that man might walk no longer according to that first creation, but there being as it were a beginning of a new creation, and with the Christ 'a beginning of its ways,' we might follow Him henceforth, who says to us, 'I am the Way:'— as the blessed Apostle teaches in Colossians, saying, 'He is the Head of the body, the Church, who is the Beginning, the First-born from the dead, that in all things He might have the preeminence.'

66. For if, as has been said, because of the resurrection from the dead He is called a beginning, and then a resurrection took place when He, bearing our flesh, had given Himself to death for us, it is evident that His words, 'He created me a beginning of ways,' is indicative not of His essence, but of His bodily presence. For to the body death was proper; and in like manner to the bodily presence are the words proper, 'The Lord created me a

beginning of His ways.' For since the Saviour was thus created according to the flesh, and had become a beginning of things new created, and had our first fruits, viz. that human flesh which He took to Himself, therefore after Him, as is fit, is created also the people to come, David saying, 'Let this be written for another generation, and the people that shall be created shall praise the Lord.' And again in the twenty-first Psalm, 'The generation to come shall declare unto the Lord, and they shall declare His righteousness, unto a people that shall be born whom the Lord made.' For we shall no more hear, 'In the day that you eat thereof, you shall surely die Genesis 2:17,' but 'Where I am, there ye' shall 'be also;' so that we may say, 'We are His workmanship, created unto good works John 14:3; Ephesians 2:10.' And again, since God's work, that is, man, though created perfect, has become wanting through the transgression, and dead by sin, and it was unbecoming that the work of God should remain imperfect (wherefore all the saints were praying concerning this, for instance in the hundred and thirty-seventh Psalm, saying, 'Lord, You shall requite for me; despise not then the works of Your hands '); therefore the perfect Word of God puts around Him an imperfect body, and is said to be created 'for the works;' that, paying the debt in our stead, He might, by Himself, perfect what was wanting to man. Now immortality was wanting to him, and the way to paradise. This then is what the Saviour says, 'I glorified You on the earth, I perfected the work which You have given Me to do John 17:4;' and again, 'The works which the Father has given Me to perfect, the same works that I do, bear witness of Me;' but 'the works ' He here says that the Father had given Him to perfect, are those for which He is created, saying in the Proverbs, 'The Lord created me a beginning of His ways, for His works;' for it is all one to say, 'The Father has given me the works,' and 'The Lord created me for the works.'

67. When then received He the works to perfect, O God's enemies? For from this also 'He created' will be understood. If you say, 'At the beginning when He brought them into being out of what was not,' it is an untruth; for they were not yet made; whereas He appears to speak as taking what was already in being. Nor is it pious to refer to the time which preceded the Word's becoming flesh, lest His coming should thereupon seem

superfluous, since for the sake of these works that coming took place. Therefore it remains for us to say that when He has become man, then He took the works. For then He perfected them, by healing our wounds and vouchsafing to us the resurrection from the dead. But if, when the Word became flesh, then were given to Him the works, plainly when He became man, then also is He created for the works. Not of His essence then is 'He created' indicative, as has many times been said, but of His bodily generation. For then, because the works had become imperfect and mutilated from the transgression, He is said in respect to the body to be created; that by perfecting them and making them whole, He might present the Church unto the Father, as the Apostle says, 'not having spot or wrinkle or any such thing, but holy and without blemish Ephesians 5:27.' Mankind then is perfected in Him and restored, as it was made at the beginning, nay, with greater grace. For, on rising from the dead, we shall no longer fear death, but shall ever reign in Christ in the heavens. And this has been done, since the own Word of God Himself, who is from the Father, has put on the flesh, and become man. For if, being a creature, He had become man, man had remained just what he was, not joined to God; for how had a work been joined to the Creator by a work ? Or what succour had come from like to like, when one as well as other needed it ? And how, were the Word a creature, had He power to undo God's sentence, and to remit sin, whereas it is written in the Prophets, that this is God's doing? For 'who is a God like You, that pardons iniquity, and passes by transgression Micah 7:18?' For whereas God has said, 'Dust you are, and unto dust shall you return Genesis 3:19,' men have become mortal; how then could things originate undo sin? But the Lord is He who has undone it, as He says Himself, 'Unless the Son shall make you free ;' and the Son, who made free, has shown in truth that He is no creature, nor one of things originate, but the proper Word and Image of the Father's Essence, who at the beginning sentenced, and alone remits sins. For since it is said in the Word, 'Dust you are, and unto dust you shall return,' suitably through the Word Himself and in Him the freedom and the undoing of the condemnation has come to pass.

68. 'Yet,' they say, 'though the Saviour were a creature, God was able to speak the word only and undo the curse.' And so another will tell them in like manner, 'Without His coming among us at all, God was able just to speak and undo the curse.' but we must consider what was expedient for mankind, and not what simply is possible with God. He could have destroyed, before the Ark of Noah, the then transgressors; but He did it after the ark. He could too, without Moses, have spoken the word only and have brought the people out of Egypt; but it profited to do it through Moses. And God was able without the judges to save His people; but it was profitable for the people that for a season judges should be raised up to them. The Saviour too might have come among us from the beginning, or on His coming might not have been delivered to Pilate; but He came 'at the fullness of the ages Galatians 4:4,' and when sought for said, 'I am He John 18:5.' For what He does, that is profitable for men, and was not fitting in any other way; and what is profitable and fitting, for that He provides. Accordingly He came, not 'that He might be ministered unto, but that He might minister ,' and might work our salvation. Certainly He was able to speak the Law from heaven, but He saw that it was

expedient to men for Him to speak from Sinai; and that He has done, that it might be possible for Moses to go up, and for them hearing the word near them the rather to believe. Moreover, the good reason of what He did may be seen thus; if God had but spoken, because it was in His power, and so the curse had been undone, the power had been shown of Him who gave the word, but man had become such as Adam was before the transgression, having received grace from without , and not having it united to the body; (for he was such when he was placed in Paradise) nay, perhaps had become worse, because he had learned to transgress. Such then being his condition, had he been seduced by the serpent, there had been fresh need for God to give command and undo the curse; and thus the need had become interminable , and men had remained under guilt not less than before, as being enslaved to sin; and, ever sinning, would have ever needed one to pardon them, and had never become free, being in themselves flesh, and ever worsted by the Law because of the infirmity of the flesh.

69. Again, if the Son were a creature, man had remained mortal as before, not being joined to God; for a creature had not joined creatures to God, as seeking itself one to join it ; nor would a portion of the creation have been the creation's salvation, as needing salvation itself. To provide against this also, He sends His own Son, and He becomes Son of Man, by taking created flesh; that, since all were under sentence of death, He, being other than them all, might Himself for all offer to death His own body; and that henceforth, as if all had died through Him, the word of that sentence might be accomplished (for 'all died 2 Corinthians 5:14 ' in Christ), and all through Him might thereupon become free from sin and from the curse which came upon it, and might truly abide for ever, risen from the dead and clothed in immortality and incorruption. For the Word being clothed in the flesh, as has many times been explained, every bite of the serpent began to be utterly staunched from out it; and whatever evil sprung from the motions of the flesh, to be cut away, and with these death also was abolished, the companion of sin, as the Lord Himself says , 'The prince of this world comes, and finds nothing in Me;' and 'For this end was He manifested,' as John has written, 'that He might destroy

the works of the devil 1 John 3:8.' And these being destroyed from the flesh, we all were thus liberated by the kinship of the flesh, and for the future were joined, even we, to the Word. And being joined to God, no longer do we abide upon earth; but, as He Himself has said, where He is, there shall we be also; and henceforward we shall fear no longer the serpent, for he was brought to nought when he was assailed by the Saviour in the flesh, and heard Him say, 'Get behind Me, Satan Matthew 16:23,' and thus he is cast out of paradise into the eternal fire. Nor shall we have to watch against woman beguiling us, for 'in the resurrection they neither marry nor are given in marriage, but are as the Angels Mark 12:25;' and in Christ Jesus it shall be 'a new creation,' and 'neither male nor female, but all and in all Christ ;' and where Christ is, what fear, what danger can still happen?

70. But this would not have come to pass, had the Word been a creature; for with a creature, the devil, himself a creature, would have ever continued the battle, and man, being between the two, had been ever in peril of death, having none in whom and through whom he might be

joined to God and delivered from all fear. Whence the truth shows us that the Word is not of things originate, but rather Himself their Framer. For therefore did He assume the body originate and human, that having renewed it as its Framer, He might deify it in Himself, and thus might introduce us all into the kingdom of heaven after His likeness. For man had not been deified if joined to a creature, or unless the Son were very God; nor had man been brought into the Father's presence, unless He had been His natural and true Word who had put on the body. And as we had not been delivered from sin and the curse, unless it had been by nature human flesh, which the Word put on (for we should have had nothing common with what was foreign), so also the man had not been deified, unless the Word who became flesh had been by nature from the Father and true and proper to Him. For therefore the union was of this kind, that He might unite what is man by nature to Him who is in the nature of the Godhead, and his salvation and deification might be sure. Therefore let those who deny that the Son is from the Father by nature and proper to His Essence, deny also that He took true human flesh of Mary Ever-Virgin ; for in neither case had it been of profit to us men, whether the

Word were not true and naturally Son of God, or the flesh not true which He assumed. But surely He took true flesh, though Valentinus rave; yea the Word was by nature Very God, though Ario-maniacs rave ; and in that flesh has come to pass the beginning of our new creation, He being created man for our sake, and having made for us that new way, as has been said.

71. The Word then is neither creature nor work; for creature, thing made, work, are all one; and were He creature and thing made, He would also be work. Accordingly He has not said, 'He created Me a work,' nor 'He made Me with the works,' lest He should appear to be in nature and essence a creature; nor, 'He created Me to make works,' lest, on the other hand, according to the perverseness of the irreligious, He should seem as an instrument made for our sake. Nor again has He declared, 'He created Me before the works,' lest, as He really is before all, as an Offspring, so, if created also before the works, He should give 'Offspring' and 'He created' the same meaning. But He has said with exact discrimination , 'for the works;' as much as to say, 'The Father has made

Me, into flesh, that I might be man,' which again shows that He is not a work but an offspring. For as he who comes into a house, is not part of the house, but is other than the house, so He who is created for the works, must be by nature other than the works. But if otherwise, as you hold, O Arians, the Word of God be a work, by what Hand and Wisdom did He Himself come into being? For all things that came to be, came by the Hand and Wisdom of God, who Himself says, 'My hand has made all these things Isaiah 66:2;' and David says in the Psalm, 'And You, Lord, in the beginning hast laid the foundations of the earth, and the heavens are the work of Your hands ;' and again, in the hundred and forty-second Psalm, 'I do remember the time past, I muse upon all Your works, yea I exercise myself in the works of Your hands.' Therefore if by the Hand of God the works are wrought, and it is written that 'all things were made through the Word,' and 'without Him was not made one thing John 1:3,' and again, 'One Lord Jesus, through whom are all things 1 Corinthians 8:9,' and 'in Him all things consist Colossians 1:17,' it is very plain that the Son cannot be a work, but He is the Hand of God and the Wisdom. This knowing, the martyrs in Babylon, Ananias, Azarias, and Misael, arraign the Arian irreligion. For when they say, 'O all you works of the Lord, bless ye the Lord,' they recount things in heaven, things on earth, and the whole creation, as works; but the Son they name not. For they say not, 'Bless, O Word, and praise, O Wisdom;' to show that all other things are both praising and are works; but the Word is not a work nor of those that praise, but is praised with the Father and worshipped and confessed as God , being His Word and Wisdom, and of the works the Framer. This too the Spirit has declared in the Psalms with a most apposite distinction, 'the Word of the Lord is true, and all His works are faithful ;' as in another Psalm too He says, 'O Lord, how manifold are Your works! In Wisdom have You made them all. '

72. But if the Word were a work, then certainly He as others had been made in Wisdom; nor would Scripture distinguish Him from the works, nor while it named them works, preach Him as Word and own Wisdom of God. But, as it is, distinguishing Him from the works, He shows that Wisdom is Framer of the works, and not a work. This distinction Paul also observes, writing to the

Hebrews, 'The Word of God is quick and powerful, and sharper than any two-edged sword, reaching even to the dividing of soul and spirit, joints and marrow, and a discerner of the thoughts and intents of the heart, neither is there any creature hidden before Him, but all things are naked and open unto the eyes of Him with whom is our account Hebrews 4:12-13.' For behold he calls things originate 'creature;' but the Son he recognises as the Word of God, as if He were other than the creatures. And again saying, 'All things are naked and open to the eyes of Him with whom is our account,' he signifies that He is other than all of them. For hence it is that He judges, but each of all things originate is bound to give account to Him. And so also, when the whole creation is groaning together with us in order to be set free from the bondage of corruption, the Son is thereby shown to be other than the creatures. For if He were creature, He too would be one of those who groan, and would need one who should bring adoption and deliverance to Himself as well as others. But if the whole creation groans together, for the sake of freedom from the bondage of corruption, whereas the Son is not of those that groan nor of those who need freedom, but He it is who gives sonship and freedom to all, saying to the Jews of His time , 'The servant remains not in the house for ever, but the Son remains for ever; if then the Son shall make you free, you shall be free indeed John 8:35-36;' it is clearer than the light from these considerations also, that the Word of God is not a creature but true Son, and by nature genuine, of the Father. Concerning then 'The Lord has created me a beginning of the ways,' this is sufficient, as I think, though in few words, to afford matter to the learned to frame more ample refutations of the Arian heresy.

Chapter XXII. Texts Explained; Sixthly, the Context of Proverbs VIII. 22 Vz. 22-30.

The Son reveals the Father, first by the works, then by the Incarnation.

But since the heretics, reading the next verse, take a perverse view of that also, because it is written, 'He founded me before the world Proverbs 8:23,' namely, that this is said of the Godhead of the Word and not of His incarnate Presence , it is necessary, explaining this verse also, to show their error.

73. It is written, 'The Lord in Wisdom founded the earth Proverbs 3:19;' if then by Wisdom the earth is founded, how can He who founds be founded? Nay, this too is said after the manner of proverbs, and we must in like manner investigate its sense; that we may know that, while by Wisdom the Father frames and founds the earth to be firm and steadfast, Wisdom Itself is founded for us, that It may become beginning and foundation of our new creation and renewal. Accordingly here as before, He says not, 'Before the world He has made me Word or Son,' lest there should be as it were a beginning of His making. For this we must seek before all things, whether He is Son, 'and on this point specially search the Scriptures;' for this it was, when the Apostles were questioned, that Peter answered, saying, 'You are the Christ, the Son of the Living God Matthew 16:16.' This also the father of the Arian heresy asked as one of his first questions; 'If Thou be the Son of God Matthew 4:3;' for he knew that this is the truth and the sovereign principle of our faith; and that, if He were Himself the Son, the tyranny of the devil would have its end; but if He were a creature, He too was one of those descended from that Adam whom he deceived, and he had no cause for anxiety. For the same

reason the Jews of the day were angered, because the Lord said that He was Son of God, and that God was His proper Father. For had He called Himself one of the creatures, or said, 'I am a work,' they had not been startled at the intelligence, nor thought such words blasphemy, knowing, as they did, that even Angels had come among their fathers; but since He called Himself Son, they perceived that such was not the note of a creature, but of Godhead and of the Father's nature. The Arians then ought, even in imitation of their own father the devil, to take some special pains on this point; and if He has said, 'He founded me to be Word or Son,' then to think as they do; but if He has not so spoken, not to invent for themselves what is not.

74. For He says not, 'Before the world He founded me as Word or Son,' but simply, 'He founded me,' to show again, as I have said, that not for His own sake but for those who are built upon Him does He here also speak, after the way of proverbs. For this knowing, the Apostle also writes, 'Other foundation can no man lay than that is laid, which is Jesus Christ; but let every man take heed how he builds

thereupon.' And it must be that the foundation should be such as the things built on it, that they may admit of being well compacted together. Being then the Word, He has not, as Word, any such as Himself, who may be compacted with Him; for He is Only-begotten; but having become man, He has the like of Him, those namely the likeness of whose flesh He has put on. Therefore according to His manhood He is founded, that we, as precious stones, may admit of building upon Him, and may become a temple of the Holy Ghost who dwells in us. And as He is a foundation, and we stones built upon Him, so again He is a Vine and we knit to Him as branches — not according to the Essence of the Godhead; for this surely is impossible; but according to His manhood, for the branches must be like the vine, since we are like Him according to the flesh. Moreover, since the heretics have such human notions, we may suitably confute them with human resemblances contained in the very matter they urge. Thus He says not, 'He made me a foundation,' lest He might seem to be made and to have a beginning of being, and they might thence find a shameless occasion of irreligion; but, 'He founded me.' Now what is founded is founded for the sake of the stones which are raised upon it; it is not a random process, but a stone is first transported from the mountain and set down in the depth of the earth. And while a stone is in the mountain, it is not yet founded; but when need demands, and it is transported, and laid in the depth of the earth, then immediately if the stone could speak, it would say, 'He now founded me, who brought me hither from the mountain.' Therefore the Lord also did not when founded take a beginning of existence; for He was the Word before that; but when He put on our body, which He severed and took from Mary, then He says 'He has founded me;' as much as to say, 'Me, being the Word, He has enveloped in a body of earth.' For so He is founded for our sakes, taking on Him what is ours , that we, as incorporated and compacted and bound together in Him through the likeness of the flesh, may attain unto a perfect man, and abide immortal and incorruptible.

75. Nor let the words 'before the world' and 'before He made the earth' and 'before the mountains were settled' disturb any one; for they very well accord with 'founded' and 'created;' for here again allusion is made to the

Economy according to the flesh. For though the grace which came to us from the Saviour appeared, as the Apostle says, just now, and has come when He sojourned among us; yet this grace had been prepared even before we came into being, nay, before the foundation of the world, and the reason why is kindly and wonderful. It beseemed not that God should counsel concerning us afterwards, lest He should appear ignorant of our fate. The God of all then — creating us by His own Word, and knowing our destinies better than we, and foreseeing that, being made 'good Genesis 1:31,' we should in the event be transgressors of the commandment, and be thrust out of paradise for disobedience — being loving and kind, prepared beforehand in His own Word, by whom also He created us , the Economy of our salvation; that though by the serpent's deceit we fell from Him, we might not remain quite dead, but having in the Word the redemption and salvation which was afore prepared for us, we might rise again and abide immortal, what time He should have been created for us 'a beginning of the ways,' and He who was the 'First-born of creation' should become 'first-born' of the 'brethren,' and again should rise 'first-fruits of the dead.' This Paul the blessed Apostle teaches in his writings; for, as interpreting the words of the Proverbs 'before the world' and 'before the earth was,' he thus speaks to Timothy ; 'Be partaker of the afflictions of the Gospel according to the power of God, who has saved us and called us with a holy calling, not according to our works, but according to His own purpose and grace, which was given us in Christ Jesus before the world began, but is now made manifest by the appearing of our Saviour Jesus Christ, who has abolished death, and brought to light life 2 Timothy 1:8-10.' And to the Ephesians; 'Blessed be God even the Father of our Lord Jesus Christ, who has blessed us with all spiritual blessing in heavenly places in Christ Jesus, according as He has chosen us in Him before the foundation of the world, that we should be holy and without blame before Him in love, having predestinated us to the adoption of children by Jesus Christ to Himself Ephesians 1:3-5.'

76. How then has He chosen us, before we came into existence, but that, as he says himself, in Him we were represented beforehand? And how at all, before men were created, did He predestinate us unto adoption, but that the

Son Himself was 'founded before the world,' taking on Him that economy which was for our sake? Or how, as the Apostle goes on to say, have we 'an inheritance being predestinated,' but that the Lord Himself was founded 'before the world,' inasmuch as He had a purpose, for our sakes, to take on Him through the flesh all that inheritance of judgment which lay against us, and we henceforth were made sons in Him? And how did we receive it 'before the world was,' when we were not yet in being, but afterwards in time, but that in Christ was stored the grace which has reached us? Wherefore also in the Judgment, when every one shall receive according to his conduct, He says, 'Come, you blessed of My Father, inherit the kingdom prepared for you from the foundation of the world Matthew 25:34.' How then, or in whom, was it prepared before we came to be, save in the Lord who 'before the world' was founded for this purpose; that we, as built upon Him, might partake, as well-compacted stones, the life and grace which is from Him? And this took place, as naturally suggests itself to the religious mind, that, as I said, we, rising after our brief death, may be capable of an eternal life, of which we had not been capable , men as we are, formed of earth, but that 'before the world' there had been prepared for us in Christ the hope of life and salvation. Therefore reason is there that the Word, on coming into our flesh, and being created in it as 'a beginning of ways for His works,' is laid as a foundation according as the Father's will was in Him before the world, as has been said, and before land was, and before the mountains were settled, and before the fountains burst forth; that, though the earth and the mountains and the shapes of visible nature pass away in the fullness of the present age, we on the contrary may not grow old after their pattern, but may be able to live after them, having the spiritual life and blessing which before these things have been prepared for us in the Word Himself according to election. For thus we shall be capable of a life not temporary, but ever afterwards abide and live in Christ; since even before this our life had been founded and prepared in Christ Jesus.

77. Nor in any other way was it fitting that our life should be founded, but in the Lord who is before the ages, and through whom the ages were brought to be; that, since it was in Him, we too might be able to inherit that

everlasting life. For God is good; and being good always, He willed this, as knowing that our weak nature needed the succour and salvation which is from Him. And as a wise architect, proposing to build a house, consults also about repairing it, should it at any time become dilapidated after building, and, as counselling about this, makes preparation and gives to the workmen materials for a repair; and thus the means of the repair are provided before the house; in the same way prior to us is the repair of our salvation founded in Christ, that in Him we might even be new-created. And the will and the purpose were made ready 'before the world,' but have taken effect when the need required, and the Saviour came among us. For the Lord Himself will stand us in place of all things in the heavens, when He receives us into everlasting life. This then suffices to prove that the Word of God is not a creature, but that the sense of the passage is right. But since that passage, when scrutinized, has a right sense in every point of view, it may be well to state what it is; perhaps many words may bring these senseless men to shame. Now here I must recur to what has been said before, for what I have to say relates to the same proverb and the same Wisdom. The Word has not called Himself a creature by nature, but has said in proverbs, 'The Lord created me;' and He plainly indicates a sense not spoken 'plainly' but latent , such as we shall be able to find by taking away the veil from the proverb. For who, on hearing from the Framing Wisdom, 'The Lord created me a beginning of His ways,' does not at once question the meaning, reflecting how that creative Wisdom can be created? Who on hearing the Only-begotten Son of God say, that He was created 'a beginning of ways,' does not investigate the sense, wondering how the Only-begotten Son can become a Beginning of many others? For it is a dark saying ; but 'a man of understanding,' says he, 'shall understand a proverb and the interpretation, the words of the wise and their dark sayings Proverbs 1:5-6.'

78. Now the Only-begotten and very Wisdom of God is Creator and Framer of all things; for 'in Wisdom have You made them all ,' he says, and 'the earth is full of Your creation.' But that what came into being might not only be, but be good , it pleased God that His own Wisdom should condescend to the creatures, so as to introduce an impress and semblance of Its Image on all in common and

on each, that what was made might be manifestly wise works and worthy of God. For as of the Son of God, considered as the Word, our word is an image, so of the same Son considered as Wisdom is the wisdom which is implanted in us an image; in which wisdom we, having the power of knowledge and thought, become recipients of the All-framing Wisdom; and through It we are able to know Its Father. 'For he who has the Son,' says He, 'has the Father also;' and 'he that receives Me, receives Him that sent Me.' Such an impress then of Wisdom being created in us, and being in all the works, with reason does the true and framing Wisdom take to Itself what belongs to its own impress, and say, 'The Lord created me for His works;' for what the wisdom in us says, that the Lord Himself speaks as if it were His own; and, whereas He is not Himself created, being Creator, yet because of the image of Him created in the works, He says this as if of Himself. And as the Lord Himself has said, 'He that receives you, receives Me Matthew 10:40,' because His impress is in us, so, though He be not among the creatures, yet because His image and impress is created in the works, He says, as if in His own person, 'The Lord created me a beginning of His ways for His works.' And therefore has this impress of Wisdom in the works been brought into being, that, as I said before, the world might recognise in it its own Creator the Word, and through Him the Father. And this is what Paul said, 'Because that which may be known of God is manifest in them, for God has showed it unto them: for the invisible things of Him from the creation of the world are clearly seen, being understood by the things that are made Romans 1:19-20.' But if so, the Word is not a creature in essence ; but the wisdom which is in us and so called, is spoken of in this passage in the Proverbs.

79. But if this too fails to persuade them, let them tell us themselves, whether there is any wisdom in the creatures or not ? If not how is it that the Apostle complains, 'For after that in the Wisdom of God the world by wisdom knew not God 1 Corinthians 1:21?' or how is it if there is no wisdom, that a 'multitude of wise men ' are found in Scripture? For 'a wise man fears and departs from evil Proverbs 14:16;' and 'through wisdom is a house built ;' and the Preacher says, 'A man's wisdom makes his face to shine;' and he blames those who are headstrong thus, 'Say

not thou, what is the cause that the former days were better than these? For thou dost not inquire in wisdom concerning this.' But if, as the Son of Sirach says, 'He poured her out upon all His works; she is with all flesh according to His gift, and He has given her to them that love Him Sirach 1:9-10,' and this outpouring is a note, not of the Essence of the Very Wisdom and Only-begotten, but of that wisdom which is imaged in the world, how is it incredible that the All-framing and true Wisdom Itself, whose impress is the wisdom and knowledge poured out in the world, should say, as I have already explained, as if of Itself, 'The Lord created me for His works?' For the wisdom in the world is not creative, but is that which is created in the works, according to which 'the heavens declare the glory of God, and the firmament shows His handywork.' This if men have within them, they will acknowledge the true Wisdom of God; and will know that they are made really after God's Image. And, as some son of a king, when the father wished to build a city, might cause his own name to be printed upon each of the works that were rising, both to give security to them of the works remaining, by reason of the show of his name on everything, and also to make them remember him and his father from the name, and having finished the city might be asked concerning it, how it was made, and then would answer, 'It is made securely, for according to the will of my father, I am imaged in each work, for my name was made in the works;' but saying this, he does not signify that his own essence is created, but the impress of himself by means of his name; in the same manner, to apply the illustration, to those who admire the wisdom in the creatures, the true Wisdom makes answer, 'The Lord created me for the works,' for my impress is in them; and I have thus condescended for the framing of all things.

80. Moreover, that the Son should be speaking of the impress that is within us as if it were Himself, should not startle any one, considering (for we must not shrink from repetition) that, when Saul was persecuting the Church, in which was His impress and image, He said, as if He were Himself under persecution, 'Saul, why do you persecute Me Acts 9:4?' Therefore (as has been said), as, supposing the impress itself of Wisdom which is in the works had said, 'The Lord created me for the works,' no one would have been startled, so, if He, the True and

Framing Wisdom, the Only-begotten Word of God, should use what belongs to His image as about Himself, namely, 'The Lord created me for the works,' let no one, overlooking the wisdom created in the world and in the works, think that 'He created' is said of the Substance of the Very Wisdom, lest, diluting the wine with water, he be judged a defrauder of the truth. For It is Creative and Framer; but Its impress is created in the works, as the copy of the image. And He says, 'Beginning of ways,' since such wisdom becomes a sort of beginning. and, as it were, rudiments of the knowledge of God; for a man entering, as it were, upon this way first, and keeping it in the fear of God (as Solomon says, 'The fear of the Lord is the beginning of wisdom'), then advancing upwards in his thoughts and perceiving the Framing Wisdom which is in the creation, will perceive in It also Its Father, as the Lord Himself has said, 'He that has seen Me, has seen the Father,' and as John writes, 'He who acknowledges the Son, has the Father also.' And He says, 'Before the world He founded me,' since in Its impress the works remain settled and eternal. Then, lest any, hearing concerning the wisdom thus created in the works, should think the true Wisdom, God's Son, to be by nature a creature, He has found it necessary to add, 'Before the mountains, and before the earth, and before the waters, and before all hills He begets me,' that in saying, 'before every creature' (for He includes all the creation under these heads), He may show that He is not created together with the works according to Essence. For if He was created 'for the works,' yet is before them, it follows that He is in being before He was created. He is not then a creature by nature and essence, but as He Himself has added, an Offspring. But in what differs a creature from an offspring, and how it is distinct by nature, has been shown in what has gone before.

81. But since He proceeds to say, 'When He prepared the heaven, I was present with Him ,' we ought to know that He says not this as if without Wisdom the Father prepared the heaven or the clouds above (for there is no room to doubt that all things are created in Wisdom, and without It was made not even one John 1:3 thing); but this is what He says, 'All things took place in Me and through Me, and when there was need that Wisdom should be created in the works, in My Essence indeed I was with the

303

Father, but by a condescension to things originate, I was disposing over the works My own impress, so that the whole world as being in one body, might not be at variance but in concord with itself.' All those then who with an upright understanding, according to the wisdom given unto them, come to contemplate the creatures, are able to say for themselves, 'By Your appointment all things continue ;' but they who make light of this must be told, 'Professing themselves to be wise, they became fools;' for 'that which may be known of God is manifest in them; for God has revealed it unto them; for the invisible things of Him from the creation of the world are clearly seen, being perceived by the things that are made, even His eternal Power and Godhead, so that they are without excuse. Because that when they knew God, they glorified Him not as God, but served the creature more than the Creator of all, who is blessed forever. Amen.' And they will surely be shamed at hearing, 'For, after that in the wisdom of God (in the mode we have explained above), the world by wisdom knew not God, it pleased God by the foolishness of the preaching to save them that believe 1 Corinthians 1:21.' For no longer, as in the former times, God has willed to be known by an image and shadow of wisdom, that namely which is in the creatures, but He has made the true Wisdom Itself to take flesh, and to become man, and to undergo the death of the cross; that by the faith in Him, henceforth all that believe may obtain salvation. However, it is the same Wisdom of God, which through Its own Image in the creatures (whence also It is said to be created), first manifested Itself, and through Itself Its own Father; and afterwards, being Itself the Word, has 'become flesh John 1:14,' as John says, and after abolishing death and saving our race, still more revealed Himself and through Him His own Father, saying, 'Grant unto them that they may know You the only true God, and Jesus Christ whom You have sent.'

82. Hence the whole earth is filled with the knowledge of Him; for the knowledge of Father through Son and of Son from Father is one and the same, and the Father delights in Him, and in the same joy the Son rejoices in the Father, saying, 'I was by Him, daily His delight, rejoicing always before Him Proverbs 8:30.' And this again proves that the Son is not foreign, but proper to the Father's Essence. For behold, not because of us has He

come to be, as the irreligious men say, nor is He out of nothing (for not from without did God procure for Himself a cause of rejoicing), but the words denote what is His own and like. When then was it, when the Father rejoiced not? But if He ever rejoiced, He was ever, in whom He rejoiced. And in whom does the Father rejoice, except as seeing Himself in His own Image, which is His Word? And though in sons of men also He had delight, on finishing the world, as it is written in these same Proverbs Proverbs 8:31, yet this too has a consistent sense. For even thus He had delight, not because joy was added to Him, but again on seeing the works made after His own Image; so that even this rejoicing of God is on account of His Image. And how too has the Son delight, except as seeing Himself in the Father? For this is the same as saying, 'He that has seen Me, has seen the Father,' and 'I am in the Father and the Father in Me John 14:9-10.' Vain then is your vaunt as is on all sides shown, O Christ's enemies, and vainly did ye parade and circulate everywhere your text, 'The Lord created me a beginning of His ways,' perverting its sense, and publishing, not Solomon's meaning, but your own comment. For behold your sense is proved to be but a fantasy; but the passage in the Proverbs, as well as all that is above said, proves that the Son is not a creature in nature and essence, but the proper Offspring of the Father, true Wisdom and Word, by whom 'all things were made,' and 'without Him was made not one thing. John 1:3 '

Discourse III

Chapter XXIII. Texts Explained; Seventhly, John XIV. 10.

The doctrine of the coinherence. The Father and the Son Each whole and perfect God. They are in Each Other, because their Essence is One and the Same. They are Each Perfect and have One Essence, because the Second Person is the Son of the First. Asterius's evasive explanation of the text under review; refuted. Since the Son has all that the Father has, He is His Image; and the Father is the One God, because the Son is in the Father.

1. The Ario-maniacs, as it appears, having once made up their minds to transgress and revolt from the Truth, are strenuous in appropriating the words of Scripture, 'When the impious comes into a depth of evils, he despises ;' for refutation does not stop them, nor perplexity abash them; but, as having 'a whore's forehead,' they 'refuse to be ashamed Jeremiah 3:3 ' before all men in their irreligion. For whereas the passages which they alleged, 'The Lord

created me ,' and 'Made better than the Angels ,' and 'First-born ,' and 'Faithful to Him that made Him ' have a right sense , and inculcate religiousness towards Christ, so it is that these men still, as if bedewed with the serpent's poison, not seeing what they ought to see, nor understanding what they read, as if in vomit from the depth of their irreligious heart, have next proceeded to disparage our Lord's words, 'I in the Father and the Father in Me John 14:10;' saying, 'How can the One be contained in the Other and the Other in the One?' or 'How at all can the Father who is the greater be contained in the Son who is the less?' or 'What wonder, if the Son is in the Father,' considering it is written even of us, 'In Him we live and move and have our being ?' And this state of mind is consistent with their perverseness, who think God to be material, and understand not what is 'True Father?' and 'True Son,' nor 'Light Invisible' and 'Eternal,' and Its 'Radiance Invisible,' nor 'Invisible Subsistence,' and 'Immaterial Expression' and 'Immaterial Image.' For did they know, they would not dishonour and ridicule the Lord of glory, nor interpreting things immaterial after a material manner, pervert good words. It were sufficient indeed, on hearing only words which are the Lord's, at once to believe, since the faith of simplicity is better than an elaborate process of persuasion; but since they have endeavoured to profane even this passage to their own heresy, it becomes necessary to expose their perverseness and to show the mind of the truth, at least for the security of the faithful. For when it is said, 'I in the Father and the Father in Me,' They are not therefore, as these suppose, discharged into Each Other, filling the One the Other, as in the case of empty vessels, so that the Son fills the emptiness of the Father and the Father that of the Son, and Each of Them by Himself is not complete and perfect (for this is proper to bodies, and therefore the mere assertion of it is full of irreligion), for the Father is full and perfect, and the Son is the Fulness of Godhead. Nor again, as God, by coming into the Saints, strengthens them, thus is He also in the Son. For He is Himself the Father's Power and Wisdom, and by partaking of Him things originate are sanctified in the Spirit; but the Son Himself is not Son by participation, but is the Father's own Offspring. Nor again is the Son in the Father, in the sense of the passage, 'In Him we live and move and have our being;' for, He as being from the Fount of the Father is the Life, in which all things are both quickened and consist; for the Life does not live in life , else it would not be Life, but rather He gives life to all things.

2. But now let us see what Asterius the Sophist says, the retained pleader for the heresy. In imitation then of the Jews so far, he writes as follows; 'It is very plain that He has said, that He is in the Father and the Father again in Him, for this reason, that neither the word on which He was discoursing is, as He says, His own, but the Father's, nor the works belong to Him, but to the Father who gave Him the power.' Now this, if uttered at random by a little child, had been excused from his age; but when one who bears the title of Sophist, and professes universal knowledge , is the writer, what a serious condemnation does he deserve! And does he not show himself a stranger to the Apostle 1 Corinthians 2:4, as being puffed up with persuasive words of wisdom, and thinking thereby to succeed in deceiving, not understanding himself what he says nor whereof he affirms 1 Timothy 1:7? For what the Son has said as proper and suitable to a Son only, who is Word and Wisdom and Image of the Father's Essence, that he levels to all the creatures, and makes common to

the Son and to them; and he says, lawless man, that the Power of the Father receives power, that from this his irreligion it may follow to say that in a son the Son was made a son, and the Word received a word's authority; and, far from granting that He spoke this as a Son, He ranks Him with all things made as having learned it as they have. For if the Son said, 'I am in the Father and the Father in Me,' because His discourses were not His own words but the Father's, and so of His works, then — since David says, 'I will hear what the Lord God shall say in me ,' and again Solomon , 'My words are spoken by God,' and since Moses was minister of words which were from God, and each of the Prophets spoke not what was his own but what was from God, 'Thus says the Lord,' and since the works of the Saints, as they professed, were not their own but God's who gave the power, Elijah for instance and Elisha invoking God that He Himself would raise the dead, and Elisha saying to Naaman, on cleansing him from the leprosy, 'that you may know that there is a God in Israel 2 Kings 5:8, 15,' and Samuel too in the days of the harvest praying to God to grant rain, and the Apostles saying that not in their own power they did miracles but in the Lord's grace— it is plain that, according to Asterius such a statement must be common to all, so that each of them is able to say, 'I in the Father and the Father in me;' and as a consequence that He is no longer one Son of God and Word and Wisdom, but, as others, is only one out of many.

3. But if the Lord said this, His words would not rightly have been, 'I in the Father and the Father in Me,' but rather, 'I too am in the Father, and the Father is in Me too,' that He may have nothing of His own and by prerogative , relatively to the Father, as a Son, but the same grace in common with all. But it is not so, as they think; for not understanding that He is genuine Son from the Father, they belie Him who is such, whom alone it befits to say, 'I in the Father and the Father in Me.' For the Son is in the Father, as it is allowed us to know, because the whole Being of the Son is proper to the Father's essence , as radiance from light, and stream from fountain; so that whoever sees the Son, sees what is proper to the Father, and knows that the Son's Being, because from the Father, is therefore in the Father. For the Father is in the Son, since the Son is what is from the Father and proper to

Him, as in the radiance the sun, and in the word the thought, and in the stream the fountain: for whoever thus contemplates the Son, contemplates what is proper to the Father's Essence, and knows that the Father is in the Son. For whereas the Form and Godhead of the Father is the Being of the Son, it follows that the Son is in the Father and the Father in the Son.

4. On this account and reasonably, having said before, 'I and the Father are One,' He added, 'I in the Father and the Father in Me, John 10:30 ' by way of showing the identity of Godhead and the unity of Essence. For they are one, not as one thing divided into two parts, and these nothing but one, nor as one thing twice named, so that the Same becomes at one time Father, at another His own Son, for this Sabellius holding was judged an heretic. But They are two, because the Father is Father and is not also Son, and the Son is Son and not also Father ; but the nature is one; (for the offspring is not unlike its parent, for it is his image), and all that is the Father's, is the Son's. Wherefore neither is the Son another God, for He was not procured from without, else were there many, if a

godhead be procured foreign from the Father's ; for if the Son be other, as an Offspring, still He is the Same as God; and He and the Father are one in propriety and peculiarity of nature, and in the identity of the one Godhead, as has been said. For the radiance also is light, not second to the sun, nor a different light, nor from participation of it, but a whole and proper offspring of it. And such an offspring is necessarily one light; and no one would say that they are two lights, but sun and radiance two, yet one the light from the sun enlightening in its radiance all things. So also the Godhead of the Son is the Father's; whence also it is indivisible; and thus there is one God and none other but He. And so, since they are one, and the Godhead itself one, the same things are said of the Son, which are said of the Father, except His being said to be Father :— for instance, that He is God, 'And the Word was God John 1:1;' Almighty, 'Thus says He which was and is and is to come, the Almighty Revelation 1:8;' Lord, 'One Lord Jesus Christ 1 Corinthians 8:6;' that He is Light, 'I am the Light John 8:12;' that He wipes out sins, 'that you may know,' He says, 'that the Son of man has power upon earth to forgive sins Luke 5:24;' and so with other attributes. For 'all things,' says the Son Himself, 'whatsoever the Father has, are Mine;' and again, 'And Mine are Yours.'

5. And on hearing the attributes of the Father spoken of a Son, we shall thereby see the Father in the Son; and we shall contemplate the Son in the Father, when what is said of the Son is said of the Father also. And why are the attributes of the Father ascribed to the Son, except that the Son is an Offspring from Him? And why are the Son's attributes proper to the Father, except again because the Son is the proper Offspring of His Essence? And the Son, being the proper Offspring of the Father's Essence, reasonably says that the Father's attributes are His own also; whence suitably and consistently with saying, 'I and the Father are One,' He adds, 'that you may know that I am in the Father and the Father in Me.' Moreover, He has added this again, 'He that has seen Me, has seen the Father;' and there is one and the same sense in these three passages. For he who in this sense understands that the Son and the Father are one, knows that He is in the Father and the Father in the Son; for the Godhead of the Son is the Father's, and it is in the Son; and whoever

enters into this, is convinced that 'He that has seen the Son, has seen the Father.' for in the Son is contemplated the Father's Godhead. And we may perceive this at once from the illustration of the Emperor's image. For in the image is the shape and form of the Emperor, and in the Emperor is that shape which is in the image. For the likeness of the Emperor in the image is exact ; so that a person who looks at the image, sees in it the Emperor; and he again who sees the Emperor, recognises that it is he who is in the image. And from the likeness not differing, to one who after the image wished to view the Emperor, the image might say, 'I and the Emperor are one; for I am in him, and he in me; and what you see in me, that you behold in him, and what you have seen in him, that you hold in me.' Accordingly he who worships the image, in it worships the Emperor also; for the image is his form and appearance. Since then the Son too is the Father's Image, it must necessarily be understood that the Godhead and propriety of the Father is the Being of the Son.

6. And this is what is said, 'Who being in the form of God Philippians 2:6,' and 'the Father in Me.' Nor is this Form

of the Godhead partial merely, but the fullness of the Father's Godhead is the Being of the Son, and the Son is whole God. Therefore also, being equal to God, He 'thought it not a prize to be equal to God;' and again since the Godhead and the Form of the Son is none other's than the Father's, this is what He says, 'I in the Father.' Thus 'God was in Christ reconciling the world unto Himself 2 Corinthians 5:19;' for the propriety of the Father's Essence is that Son, in whom the creation was then reconciled with God. Thus what things the Son then wrought are the Father's works, for the Son is the Form of that Godhead of the Father, which wrought the works. And thus he who looks at the Son, sees the Father; for in the Father's Godhead is and is contemplated the Son; and the Father's Form which is in Him shows in Him the Father; and thus the Father is in the Son. And that propriety and Godhead which is from the Father in the Son, shows the Son in the Father, and His inseparability from Him; and whoever hears and beholds that what is said of the Father is also said of the Son, not as accruing to His Essence by grace or participation, but because the very Being of the Son is the proper Offspring of the Father's Essence, will fitly understand the words, as I said before, 'I in the Father, and the Father in Me;' and 'I and the Father are One.' For the Son is such as the Father is, because He has all that is the Father's. Wherefore also is He implied together with the Father. For, a son not being, one cannot say father; whereas when we call God a Maker, we do not of necessity intimate the things which have come to be; for a maker is before his works. But when we call God Father, at once with the Father we signify the Son's existence. Therefore also he who believes in the Son, believes also in the Father: for he believes in what is proper to the Father's Essence; and thus the faith is one in one God. And he who worships and honours the Son, in the Son worships and honours the Father; for one is the Godhead; and therefore one the honour and one the worship which is paid to the Father in and through the Son. And he who thus worships, worships one God; for there is one God and none other than He. Accordingly when the Father is called the only God, and we read that there is one God Mark 12:29, and 'I am,' and 'beside Me there is no God,' and 'I the first and I the last ,' this has a fit meaning. For God is One and Only and First; but this is not said to the denial of the Son , perish the thought; for He is in that One, and First and Only, as being of that

One and Only and First the Only Word and Wisdom and Radiance. And He too is the First, as the Fulness of the Godhead of the First and Only, being whole and full God. This then is not said on His account, but to deny that there is other such as the Father and His Word.

Chapter XXIV. Texts Explained; Eighthly, John XVII. 3. And the Like.

Our Lord's divinity cannot interfere with His Father's prerogatives, as the One God, which were so earnestly upheld by the Son. 'One' is used in contrast to false gods and idols, not to the Son, through whom the Father spoke. Our Lord adds His Name to the Father's, as included in Him. The Father the First, not as if the Son were not First too, but as Origin.

7. Now that this is the sense of the Prophet is clear and manifest to all; but since the irreligious men, alleging such passages also, dishonour the Lord and reproach us, saying, 'Behold God is said to be One and Only and First; how say ye that the Son is God? For if He were God, He had

not said, I Alone, nor God is One ;' it is necessary to declare the sense of these phrases in addition, as far as we can, that all may know from this also that the Arians are really contending with God. If there then is rivalry of the Son towards the Father, then be such words uttered against Him; and if according to what is said to David concerning Adonijah and Absalom , so also the Father looks upon the Son, then let Him utter and urge such words against Himself, lest He the Son, calling Himself God, make any to revolt from the Father. But if he who knows the Son, on the contrary, knows the Father, the Son Himself revealing Him to him, and in the Word he shall rather see the Father, as has been said, and if the Son on coming, glorified not Himself but the Father, saying to one who came to Him, 'Why do you call Me good? None is good save One, that is, God ;' and to one who asked, what was the great commandment in the Law, answering, 'Hear, O Israel, the Lord our God is One Lord Mark 12:29;' and saying to the multitudes, 'I came down from heaven, not to do My own will, but the will of Him that sent Me ;' and teaching the disciples, 'My Father is greater than I,' and 'He that honours Me, honours Him that sent Me ;' if the Son is such towards His own Father, what is the difficulty, that one must need take such a view of such passages? And on the other hand, if the Son is the Father's Word, who is so wild, besides these Christ-opposers, as to think that God has thus spoken, as traducing and denying His own Word? This is not the mind of Christians; perish the thought; for not with reference to the Son is it thus written, but for the denial of those falsely called gods, invented by men.

8. And this account of the meaning of such passages is satisfactory; for since those who are devoted to gods falsely so called, revolt from the True God, therefore God, being good and careful for mankind, recalling the wanderers, says, 'I am Only God,' and 'I Am,' and 'Besides Me there is no God,' and the like; that He may condemn things which are not, and may convert all men to Himself. And as, supposing in the daytime when the sun was shining, a man were rudely to paint a piece of wood, which had not even the appearance of light, and call that image the cause of light, and if the sun with regard to it were to say, 'I alone am the light of the day, and there is no other light of the day but I,' he would say this, with regard, not to his

own radiance, but to the error arising from the wooden image and the dissimilitude of that vain representation; so it is with 'I am,' and 'I am Only God,' and 'There is none other besides Me,' viz. that He may make men renounce falsely called gods, and that they may recognise Him the true God instead. Indeed when God said this, He said it through His own Word, unless forsooth the modern Jews add this too, that He has not said this through His Word; but so has He spoken, though they rave, these followers of the devil. For the Word of the Lord came to the Prophet, and this was what was heard; nor is there a thing which God says or does, but He says and does it in the Word. Not then with reference to Him is this said, O Christ's enemies, but to things foreign to Him and not from Him. For according to the aforesaid illustration, if the sun had spoken those words, he would have been setting right the error and have so spoken, not as having his radiance without him, but in the radiance showing his own light. Therefore not for the denial of the Son, nor with reference to Him, are such passages, but to the overthrow of falsehood. Accordingly God spoke not such words to Adam at the beginning, though His Word was with Him, by whom all things came to be; for there was no need, before idols came in; but when men made insurrection against the truth and named for themselves gods such as they would , then it was that need arose of such words, for the denial of gods that were not. Nay I would add, that they were said even in anticipation of the folly of these Christ-opposers , that they might know, that whatsoever god they devise external to the Father's Essence, he is not True God, nor Image and Son of the Only and First.

9. If then the Father be called the only true God, this is said not to the denial of Him who said, 'I am the Truth John 14:6,' but of those on the other hand who by nature are not true, as the Father and His Word are. And hence the Lord Himself added at once, 'And Jesus Christ whom You sent.' Now had He been a creature, He would not have added this, and ranked Himself with His Creator (for what fellowship is there between the True and the not true?); but as it is, by adding Himself to the Father, He has shown that He is of the Father's nature; and He has given us to know that of the True Father He is True Offspring. And John too, as he had learned , so he teaches this, writing in his Epistle, 'And we are in the True, even in His

Son Jesus Christ; This is the True God and eternal life 1 John 5:20.' And when the Prophet says concerning the creation, 'That stretches forth the heavens alone Isaiah 44:24,' and when God says, 'I only stretch out the heavens,' it is made plain to every one, that in the Only is signified also the Word of the Only, in whom 'all things were made,' and without whom 'was made not one thing.' Therefore, if they were made through the Word, and yet He says, 'I Only,' and together with that Only is understood the Son, through whom the heavens were made, so also then, if it be said, 'One God,' and 'I Only,' and 'I the First,' in that One and Only and First is understood the Word coexisting, as in the Light the Radiance. And this can be understood of no other than the Word alone. For all other things subsisted out of nothing through the Son, and are greatly different in nature; but the Son Himself is natural and true Offspring from the Father; and thus the very passage which these insensates have thought fit to adduce, 'I the First,' in defense of their heresy, does rather expose their perverse spirit. For God says, 'I the First and I the Last;' if then, as though ranked with the things after Him, He is said to be first of them, so that they come next to Him, then certainly you will have shown that He Himself precedes the works in time only ; which, to go no further, is extreme irreligion; but if it is in order to prove that He is not from any, nor any before Him, but that He is Origin and Cause of all things, and to destroy the Gentile fables, that He has said 'I the First,' it is plain also, that when the Son is called First-born, this is done not for the sake of ranking Him with the creation, but to prove the framing and adoption of all things through the Son. For as the Father is First, so also is He both First , as Image of the First, and because the First is in Him, and also Offspring from the Father, in whom the whole creation is created and adopted into sonship.

Chapter XXV. Texts Explained; Ninthly, John X. 30; XVII. 11, Etc.

Arian explanation, that the Son is one with the Father in will and judgment; but so are all good men, nay things inanimate; contrast of the Son. Oneness between Them is in nature, because oneness in operation. Angels not objects of prayer, because they do not work together with God, but the Son; texts quoted. Seeing an Angel, is not seeing God. Ariansin fact hold two Gods, and tend to Gentile polytheism. Arianexplanation that the Father and Son are one as we are one with Christ, is put aside by the Regula Fidei, and shown invalid by the usage of Scripture in illustrations; the true force of the comparison; force of the terms used. Force of 'in us;' force of 'as;' confirmed by St. John. In what sense we are 'in God' and His 'sons.'

10. However here too they introduce their private fictions, and contend that the Son and the Father are not in such wise 'one,' or 'like,' as the Church preaches, but, as they themselves would have it. For they say, since what the Father wills, the Son wills also, and is not contrary either in what He thinks or in what He judges, but is in all respects concordant with Him, declaring doctrines which are the same, and a word consistent and united with the Father's teaching, therefore it is that He and the Father are One; and some of them have dared to write as well as say this. Now what can be more unseemly or irrational than this? For if therefore the Son and the Father are One and if in this way the Word is like the Father, it follows

immediately that the Angels too, and the other beings above us, Powers and Authorities, and Thrones and Dominions, and what we see, Sun and Moon, and the Stars, should be sons also, as the Son; and that it should be said of them too, that they and the Father are one, and that each is God's Image and Word. For what God wills, that will they; and neither in judging nor in doctrine are they discordant, but in all things are obedient to their Maker. For they would not have remained in their own glory, unless, what the Father willed, that they had willed also. He, for instance, who did not remain, but went astray, heard the words, 'How are you fallen from heaven, O Lucifer, son of the morning Isaiah 14:12?' But if this be so, how is only He Only-begotten Son and Word and Wisdom? Or how, whereas so many are like the Father, is He only an Image? For among men too will be found many like the Father, numbers, for instance, of martyrs, and before them the Apostles and Prophets, and again before them the Patriarchs. And many now too keep the Saviour's command, being merciful 'as their Father which is in heaven ,' and observing the exhortation, 'Be therefore followers of God as dear children, and walk in love, as Christ also has loved us Ephesians 5:1-2;' many too have become followers of Paul as he also of Christ. 1 Corinthians 11:1 And yet no one of these is Word or Wisdom or Only-begotten Son or Image; nor did any one of them make bold to say, 'I and the Father are One,' or, 'I in the Father, and the Father in Me ;' but it is said of all of them, 'Who is like You among the gods, O Lord? And who shall be likened to the Lord among the sons of Gods ?' and of Him on the contrary that He only is Image true and natural of the Father. For though we have been made after the Image, and called both image and glory of God, yet not on our own account still, but for that Image and true Glory of God inhabiting us, which is His Word, who was for us afterwards made flesh, have we this grace of our designation.

11. This their notion then being evidently unseemly and irrational as well as the rest, the likeness and the oneness must be referred to the very Essence of the Son; for unless it be so taken, He will not be shown to have anything beyond things originate, as has been said, nor will He be like the Father, but He will be like the Father's doctrines; and He differs from the Father, in that the Father is

Father, but the doctrines and teaching are the Father's. If then in respect to the doctrines and the teaching the Son is like the Father, then the Father according to them will be Father in name only, and the Son will not be an exact Image, or rather will be seen to have no propriety at all or likeness of the Father; for what likeness or propriety has he who is so utterly different from the Father? For Paul taught like the Saviour, yet was not like 'Him in essence.' Having then such notions, they speak falsely; whereas the Son and the Father are one in such wise as has been said, and in such wise is the Son like the Father Himself and from Him, as we may see and understand son to be towards father, and as we may see the radiance towards the sun. Such then being the Son, therefore when the Son works, the Father is the Worker, and the Son coming to the Saints, the Father is He who comes in the Son, as He promised when He said, 'I and My Father will come, and will make Our abode with him John 14:23;' for in the Image is contemplated the Father, and in the Radiance is the Light. Therefore also, as we said just now, when the Father gives grace and peace, the Son also gives it, as Paul signifies in every Epistle, writing, 'Grace to you and peace from God our Father and the Lord Jesus Christ.' For one and the same grace is from the Father in the Son, as the light of the sun and of the radiance is one, and as the sun's illumination is effected through the radiance; and so too when he prays for the Thessalonians, in saying, 'Now God Himself even our Father, and the Lord Jesus Christ, may He direct our way unto you 1 Thessalonians 3:11,' he has guarded the unity of the Father and of the Son. For he has not said, 'May they direct,' as if a double grace were given from two Sources, This and That, but 'May He direct,' to show that the Father gives it through the Son;— at which these irreligious ones will not blush, though they well might.

12. For if there were no unity, nor the Word the own Offspring of the Father's Essence, as the radiance of the light, but the Son were divided in nature from the Father, it were sufficient that the Father alone should give, since none of originate things is a partner with his Maker in His givings; but, as it is, such a mode of giving shows the oneness of the Father and the Son. No one, for instance, would pray to receive from God and the Angels , or from any other creature, nor would any one say, 'May God and

the Angel give you;' but from Father and the Son, because of Their oneness and the oneness of Their giving. For through the Son is given what is given; and there is nothing but the Father operates it through the Son; for thus is grace secure to him who receives it. And if the Patriarch Jacob, blessing his grandchildren Ephraim and Manasses, said, 'God which fed me all my life long unto this day, the Angel which delivered me from all evil, bless the lads ,' yet none of created and natural Angels did he join to God their Creator, nor rejecting God that fed him, did he from Angel ask the blessing on his grandsons; but in saying, 'Who delivered me from all evil,' he showed that it was no created Angel, but the Word of God, whom he joined to the Father in his prayer, through whom, whomsoever He will, God does deliver. For knowing that He is also called the Father's 'Angel of great Counsel ,' he said that none other than He was the Giver of blessing, and Deliverer from evil. Nor was it that he desired a blessing for himself from God but for his grandchildren from the Angel, but whom He Himself had besought saying, 'I will not let You go except Thou bless me ' (for that was God, as he says himself, 'I have seen God face to face'), Him he prayed to bless also the sons of Joseph. It is proper then to an Angel to minister at the command of God, and often does he go forth to cast out the Amorite, and is sent to guard the people in the way; but these are not his doings, but of God who commanded and sent him, whose also it is to deliver, whom He will deliver. Therefore it was no other than the Lord God Himself whom he had seen, who said to him, 'And behold I am with you, to guard you in all the way wherever you go;' and it was no other than God whom he had seen, who kept Laban from his treachery, ordering him not to speak evil words to Jacob; and none other than God did he himself beseech, saying, 'Rescue me from the hand of my brother Esau, for I fear him;' for in conversation too with his wives he said, 'God has not suffered Laban to injure me.'

13. Therefore it was none other than God Himself that David too besought concerning his deliverance, 'When I was in trouble, I called upon the Lord, and He heard me; deliver my soul, O Lord, from lying lips and from a deceitful tongue.' To Him also giving thanks he spoke the words of the Song in the seventeenth Psalm, in the day in which the Lord delivered him from the hand of all his

enemies and from the hand of Saul, saying, 'I will love You, O Lord my strength; the Lord is my strong rock and my defense and deliverer.' And Paul, after enduring many persecutions, to none other than God gave thanks, saying, 'Out of them all the Lord delivered me; and He will deliver in Whom we trust.' And none other than God blessed Abraham and Isaac; and Isaac praying for Jacob, said, 'May God bless you and increase you and multiply you, and you shall be for many companies of nations, and may He give you the blessing of Abraham my father.' But if it belong to none other than God to bless and to deliver, and none other was the deliverer of Jacob than the Lord Himself and Him that delivered him the Patriarch besought for his grandsons, evidently none other did he join to God in his prayer, than God's Word, whom therefore he called Angel, because it is He alone who reveals the Father. Which the Apostle also did when he said, 'Grace unto you and peace from God our Father and the Lord Jesus Christ.' For thus the blessing was secure, because of the Son's indivisibility from the Father, and for that the grace given by Them is one and the same. For though the Father gives it, through the Son is the gift; and though the Son be said to vouchsafe it, it is the Father who supplies it through and in the Son; for 'I thank my God,' says the Apostle writing to the Corinthians, 'always on your behalf, for the grace of God which is given you in Christ Jesus 1 Corinthians 1:4.' And this one may see in the instance of light and radiance; for what the light enlightens, that the radiance irradiates; and what the radiance irradiates, from the light is its enlightenment. So also when the Son is beheld, so is the Father, for He is the Father's radiance; and thus the Father and the Son are one.

14. But this is not so with things originate and creatures; for when the Father works, it is not that any Angel works, or any other creature; for none of these is an efficient cause , but they are of things which come to be; and moreover being separate and divided from the only God, and other in nature, and being works, they can neither work what God works, nor, as I said before, when God gives grace, can they give grace with Him. Nor, on seeing an Angel would a man say that he had seen the Father; for Angels, as it is written, are 'ministering spirits sent forth to minister Hebrews 1:14,' and are heralds of gifts given by

Him through the Word to those who receive them. And the Angel on his appearance, himself confesses that he has been sent by his Lord; as Gabriel confessed in the case of Zacharias, and also in the case of Mary, bearer of God. And he who beholds a vision of Angels, knows that he has seen the Angel and not God. For Zacharias saw an Angel; and Isaiah saw the Lord. Manoah, the father of Samson, saw an Angel; but Moses beheld God. Gideon saw an Angel, but to Abraham appeared God. And neither he who saw God, beheld an Angel, nor he who saw an Angel, considered that he saw God; for greatly, or rather wholly, do things by nature originate differ from God the Creator. But if at any time, when the Angel was seen, he who saw it heard God's voice, as took place at the bush; for 'the Angel of the Lord was seen in a flame of fire out of the bush, and the Lord called Moses out of the bush, saying, I am the God of your father, the God of Abraham and the God of Isaac and the God of Jacob ,' yet was not the Angel the God of Abraham, but in the Angel God spoke. And what was seen was an Angel; but God spoke in him. For as He spoke to Moses in the pillar of a cloud in the tabernacle, so also God appears and speaks in Angels. So again to the son of Nun He spoke by an Angel. But what God speaks, it is very plain He speaks through the Word, and not through another. And the Word, as being not separate from the Father, nor unlike and foreign to the Father's Essence, what He works, those are the Father's works, and His framing of all things is one with His; and what the Son gives, that is the Father's gift. And he who has seen the Son, knows that, in seeing Him, he has seen, not Angel, nor one merely greater than Angels, nor in short any creature, but the Father Himself. And he who hears the Word, knows that he hears the Father; as he who is irradiated by the radiance, knows that he is enlightened by the sun.

15. For divine Scripture wishing us thus to understand the matter, has given such illustrations, as we have said above, from which we are able both to press the traitorous Jews, and to refute the allegation of Gentiles who maintain and think, on account of the Trinity, that we profess many gods. For, as the illustration shows, we do not introduce three Origins or three Fathers, as the followers of Marcion and Manichæus; since we have not suggested the image of three suns, but sun and radiance. And one is the light from

the sun in the radiance; and so we know of but one origin; and the All-framing Word we profess to have no other manner of godhead, than that of the Only God, because He is born from Him. Rather then will the Ario-maniacs with reason incur the charge of polytheism or else of atheism , because they idly talk of the Son as external and a creature, and again the Spirit as from nothing. For either they will say that the Word is not God; or saying that He is God , because it is so written, but not proper to the Father's Essence, they will introduce many because of their difference of kind (unless forsooth they shall dare to say that by participation only, He, as all things else, is called God; though, if this be their sentiment, their irreligion is the same, since they consider the Word as one among all things). But let this never even come into our mind. For there is but one form of Godhead, which is also in the Word; and one God, the Father, existing by Himself according as He is above all, and appearing in the Son according as He pervades all things, and in the Spirit according as in Him He acts in all things through the Word. For thus we confess God to be one through the Triad, and we say that it is much more religious than the godhead of the heretics with its many kinds , and many parts, to entertain a belief of the One Godhead in a Triad.

16. For if it be not so, but the Word is a creature and a work out of nothing, either He is not True God because He is Himself one of the creatures, or if they name Him God from regard for the Scriptures, they must of necessity say that there are two Gods , one Creator, the other creature, and must serve two Lords, one Unoriginate, and the other originate and a creature; and must have two faiths, one in the True God, and the other in one who is made and fashioned by themselves and called God. And it follows of necessity in so great blindness, that, when they worship the Unoriginate, they renounce the originate, and when they come to the creature, they turn from the Creator. For they cannot see the One in the Other, because their natures and operations are foreign and distinct. And with such sentiments, they will certainly be going on to more gods, for this will be the essay of those who revolt from the One God. Wherefore then, when the Arians have these speculations and views, do they not rank themselves with the Gentiles? For they too, as these, worship the creature rather than God the Creator of all ,

and though they shrink from the Gentile name, in order to deceive the unskilful, yet they secretly hold a like sentiment with them. For their subtle saying which they are accustomed to urge, We say not two 'Unoriginates ,' they plainly say to deceive the simple; for in their very professing 'We say not two Unoriginates,' they imply two Gods, and these with different natures, one originate and one Unoriginate. And though the Greeks worship one Unoriginate and many originate, but these one Unoriginate and one originate, this is no difference from them; for the God whom they call originate is one out of many, and again the many gods of the Greeks have the same nature with this one, for both he and they are creatures. Unhappy are they, and the more for that their hurt is from thinking against Christ; for they have fallen from the truth, and are greater traitors than the Jews in denying the Christ, and they wallow with the Gentiles, hateful as they are to God, worshipping the creature and many deities. For there is One God, and not many, and One is His Word, and not many; for the Word is God, and He alone has the Form of the Father. Being then such, the Saviour Himself troubled the Jews with these words, 'The Father Himself which has sent Me, has borne witness of Me; you have neither heard His voice at any time nor seen His Form; and you have not His Word abiding in you; for whom He has sent, Him ye believe not John 5:37.' Suitably has He joined the 'Word' to the 'Form,' to show that the Word of God is Himself Image and Expression and Form of His Father; and that the Jews who did not receive Him who spoke to them, thereby did not receive the Word, which is the Form of God. This too it was that the Patriarch Jacob having seen, received a blessing from Him and the name of Israel instead of Jacob, as divine Scripture witnesses, saying, 'And as he passed by the Form of God, the Sun rose upon him.' And This it was who said, 'He that has seen Me has seen the Father,' and, 'I in the Father and the Father in Me,' and, 'I and the Father are one ;' for thus God is One, and one the faith in the Father and Son; for, though the Word be God, the Lord our God is one Lord; for the Son is proper to that One, and inseparable according to the propriety and peculiarity of His Essence.

17. The Arians, however, not even thus abashed, reply, 'Not as you say, but as we will ;' for, whereas you have

overthrown our former expedients, we have invented a new one, and it is this:— So are the Son and the Father One, and so is the Father in the Son and the Son in the Father, as we too may become one in Him. For this is written in the Gospel according to John, and Christ desired it for us in these words, 'Holy Father, keep through Your own Name, those whom You have given Me, that they may be one, as We are John 17:11.' And shortly after; 'Neither pray I for these alone, but for them also which shall believe in Me through their Word; that they all may be one, as You, Father, are in Me, and I in You, that they also may be one in Us, that the world may believe that You have sent Me. And the glory which You gave Me I have given them, that they may be one, even as We are one; I in them, and You in Me, that they may be made perfect in one, and that the world may know that You sent Me.' Then, as having found an evasion, these men of craft add, 'If, as we become one in the Father, so also He and the Father are one, and thus He too is in the Father, how pretend you from His saying, I and the Father are One, and I in the Father and the Father in Me, that He is proper and like the Father's Essence? For it follows either that we too are proper to the Father's Essence, or He foreign to it, as we are foreign.' Thus they idly babble; but in this their perverseness I see nothing but unreasoning audacity and recklessness from the devil, since it is saying after his pattern, 'We will ascend to heaven, we will be like the Most High.' For what is given to man by grace, this they would make equal to the Godhead of the Giver. Thus hearing that men are called sons, they thought themselves equal to the True Son by nature such. And now again hearing from the Saviour, 'that they may be one as We are John 8:44,' they deceive themselves, and are arrogant enough to think that they may be such as the Son is in the Father and the Father in the Son; not considering the fall of their 'father the devil,' which happened upon such an imagination.

18. If then, as we have many times said, the Word of God is the same with us, and nothing differs from us except in time, let Him be like us, and have the same place with the Father as we have; nor let Him be called Only-begotten, nor Only Word or Wisdom of the Father; but let the same name be of common application to all us who are like Him. For it is right, that they who have one nature, should

have their name in common, though they differ from each other in point of time. For Adam was a man, and Paul a man, and he who is now born is a man, and time is not that which alters the nature of the race. If then the Word also differs from us only in time, then we must be as He. But in truth neither we are Word or Wisdom, nor is He creature or work; else why are we all sprung from one, and He the Only Word? But though it be suitable in them thus to speak, in us at least it is unsuitable to entertain their blasphemies. And yet, needless though it be to refine upon these passages, considering their so clear and religious sense, and our own orthodox belief, yet that their irreligion may be shown here also, come let us shortly, as we have received from the fathers, expose their heterodoxy from the passage. It is a custom with divine Scripture to take the things of nature as images and illustrations for mankind; and this it does, that from these physical objects the moral impulses of man may be explained; and thus their conduct shown to be either bad or righteous. For instance, in the case of the bad, as when it charges, 'Be not like to horse and mule which have no understanding.' Or as when it says, complaining of those who have become such, 'Man, being in honour, has no understanding, but is compared unto the beasts that perish.' And again, 'They were as wanton horses Jeremiah 5:8.' And the Saviour to expose Herod said, 'Tell that fox Luke 13:32;' but, on the other hand, charged His disciples, 'Behold I send you forth as sheep in the midst of wolves; be ye therefore wise as serpents and harmless as doves Matthew 10:16.' And He said this, not that we may become in nature beasts of burden, or become serpents and doves; for He has not so made us Himself, and therefore nature does not allow of it; but that we might eschew the irrational motions of the one, and being aware of the wisdom of that other animal, might not be deceived by it, and might take on us the meekness of the dove.

19. Again, taking patterns for man from divine subjects, the Saviour says; 'Be merciful, as your Father which is in heaven is merciful Luke 6:36;' and, 'Be perfect, as your heavenly Father is perfect Matthew 5:48.' And He said this too, not that we might become such as the Father; for to become as the Father, is impossible for us creatures, who have been brought to be out of nothing; but as He charged us, 'Be not like to horse,' not lest we should

become as draught animals, but that we should not imitate their want of reason, so, not that we might become as God, did He say, 'Be merciful as your Father,' but that looking at His beneficent acts, what we do well, we might do, not for men's sake, but for His sake, so that from Him and not from men we may have the reward. For as, although there be one Son by nature, True and Only-begotten, we too become sons, not as He in nature and truth, but according to the grace of Him that calls, and though we are men from the earth, are yet called gods, not as the True God or His Word, but as has pleased God who has given us that grace; so also, as God do we become merciful, not by being made equal to God, nor becoming in nature and truth benefactors (for it is not our gift to benefit but belongs to God), but in order that what has accrued to us from God Himself by grace, these things we may impart to others, without making distinctions, but largely towards all extending our kind service. For only in this way can we anyhow become imitators, and in no other, when we minister to others what comes from Him. And as we put a fair and right sense upon these texts, such again is the sense of the lection in John. For he does not say, that, as the Son is in the Father, such we must become:

— whence could it be? When He is God's Word and Wisdom, and we were fashioned out of the earth, and He is by nature and essence Word and true God (for thus speaks John, 'We know that the Son of God has come, and He has given us an understanding to know Him that is true, and we are in Him that is true, even in His Son Jesus Christ; this is the true God and eternal life 1 John 5:20 ') and we are made sons through Him by adoption and grace, as partaking of His Spirit (for 'as many as received Him,' he says, 'to them gave He power to become children of God, even to them that believe in His Name John 1:12 '), and therefore also He is the Truth (saying, 'I am the Truth,' and in His address to His Father, He said, 'Sanctify them through Your Truth, Your Word is Truth '); but we by imitation become virtuous and sons:— therefore not that we might become such as He, did He say 'that they may be one as We are;' but that as He, being the Word, is in His own Father, so that we too, taking an examplar and looking at Him, might become one towards each other in concord and oneness of spirit, nor be at variance as the Corinthians, but mind the same thing, as those five thousand in the Acts Acts 4:4, 32, who were as one.

20. For it is as 'sons,' not as the Son; as 'gods,' not as He Himself; and not as the Father, but 'merciful as the Father.' And, as has been said, by so becoming one, as the Father and the Son, we shall be such, not as the Father is by nature in the Son and the Son in the Father, but according to our own nature, and as it is possible for us thence to be moulded and to learn how we ought to be one, just as we learned also to be merciful. For like things are naturally one with like; thus all flesh is ranked together in kind ; but the Word is unlike us and like the Father. And therefore, while He is in nature and truth one with His own Father, we, as being of one kind with each other (for from one were all made, and one is the nature of all men), become one with each other in good disposition , having as our copy the Son's natural unity with the Father. For as He taught us meekness from Himself, saying, 'Learn of Me for I am meek and lowly in heart Matthew 11:29,' not that we may become equal to Him, which is impossible, but that looking towards Him, we may remain meek continually, so also here wishing that our good disposition towards each other should be true and firm and indissoluble, from Himself taking the pattern, He says, 'that they may be one as We are,' whose oneness is

indivisible; that is, that they learning from us of that indivisible Nature, may preserve in like manner agreement one with another. And this imitation of natural conditions is especially safe for man, as has been said; for, since they remain and never change, whereas the conduct of men is very changeable, one may look to what is unchangeable by nature, and avoid what is bad and remodel himself on what is best.

21. And for this reason also the words, 'that they may be one in Us,' have a right sense. If, for instance, it were possible for us to become as the Son in the Father, the words ought to run, 'that they may be one in You,' as the Son is in the Father; but, as it is, He has not said this; but by saying 'in Us' He has pointed out the distance and difference; that He indeed is alone in the Father alone, as Only Word and Wisdom; but we in the Son, and through Him in the Father. And thus speaking, He meant this only, 'By Our unity may they also be so one with each other, as We are one in nature and truth; for otherwise they could not be one, except by learning unity in Us.' And that 'in Us' has this signification, we may learn from

Paul, who says, 'These things I have in a figure transferred to myself and to Apollos, that you may learn in us not to be puffed up above that is written 1 Corinthians 4:6.' The words 'in Us' then, are not 'in the Father,' as the Son is in Him; but imply an example and image, instead of saying, 'Let them learn of Us.' For as Paul to the Corinthians, so is the oneness of the Son and the Father a pattern and lesson to all, by which they may learn, looking to that natural unity of the Father and the Son, how they themselves ought to be one in spirit towards each other. Or if it needs to account for the phrase otherwise, the words 'in Us' may mean the same as saying, that in the power of the Father and the Son they may be one, speaking the same things ; for without God this is impossible. And this mode of speech also we may find in the divine writings, as 'In God will we do great acts;' and 'In God I shall leap over the wall ;' and 'In You will we tread down our enemies.' Therefore it is plain, that in the Name of Father and Son we shall be able, becoming one, to hold firm the bond of charity. For, dwelling still on the same thought, the Lord says, 'And the glory which You gave Me, I have given to them, that they may be one as We are one.' Suitably has He here too said, not, 'that they may be in You as I am,' but 'as We are;' now he who says 'as', signifies not identity, but an image and example of the matter in hand.

22. The Word then has the real and true identity of nature with the Father; but to us it is given to imitate it, as has been said; for He immediately adds, 'I in them and You in Me; that they may be made perfect in one.' Here at length the Lord asks something greater and more perfect for us; for it is plain that the Word has come to be in us, for He has put on our body. 'And Thou Father in Me;' 'for I am Your Word, and since You are in Me, because I am Your Word, and I in them because of the body, and because of You the salvation of men is perfected in Me, therefore I ask that they also may become one, according to the body that is in Me and according to its perfection; that they too may become perfect, having oneness with It, and having become one in It; that, as if all were carried by Me, all may be one body and one spirit, and may grow up unto a perfect man.' For we all, partaking of the Same, become one body, having the one Lord in ourselves. The passage then having this meaning, still more plainly is refuted the

heterodoxy of Christ's enemies. I repeat it; if He had said simply and absolutely 'that they may be one in You,' or 'that they and I may be one in You,' God's enemies had had some plea, though a shameless one; but in fact He has not spoken simply, but, 'As Thou, Father, in Me, and I in You, that they may be all one.' Moreover, using the word 'as,' He signifies those who become distantly as He is in the Father; distantly not in place but in nature; for in place nothing is far from God , but in nature only all things are far from Him. And, as I said before, whoever uses the particle 'as' implies, not identity, nor equality, but a pattern of the matter in question, viewed in a certain respect.

23. Indeed we may learn also from the Saviour Himself, when He says, 'For as Jonah was three days and three nights in the whale's belly, so shall the Son of man be three days and three nights in the heart of the earth Matthew 12:40.' For Jonah was not as the Saviour, nor did Jonah go down to hades; nor was the whale hades; nor did Jonah, when swallowed up, bring up those who had before been swallowed by the whale, but he alone came forth, when the whale was bidden. Therefore there is no identity

nor equality signified in the term 'as,' but one thing and another; and it shows a certain kind of parallel in the case of Jonah, on account of the three days. In like manner then we too, when the Lord says 'as,' neither become as the Son in the Father, nor as the Father is in the Son. For we become one as the Father and the Son in mind and agreement of spirit, and the Saviour will be as Jonah in the earth; but as the Saviour is not Jonah, nor, as he was swallowed up, so did the Saviour descend into hades, but it is but a parallel, in like manner, if we too become one, as the Son in the Father, we shall not be as the Son, nor equal to Him; for He and we are but parallel. For on this account is the word 'as' applied to us; since things differing from others in nature, become as they, when viewed in a certain relation. Wherefore the Son Himself, simply and without any condition is in the Father; for this attribute He has by nature; but for us, to whom it is not natural, there is needed an image and example, that He may say of us, 'As Thou in Me, and I in You.' 'And when they shall be so perfected,' He says, 'then the world knows that You have sent Me, for unless I had come and borne this their body, no one of them had been perfected, but one and all had remained corruptible. Work Thou then in them, O Father, and as You have given to Me to bear this, grant to them Your Spirit, that they too in It may become one, and may be perfected in Me. For their perfecting shows that Your Word has sojourned among them; and the world seeing them perfect and full of God , will believe altogether that You have sent Me, and I have sojourned here. For whence is this their perfecting, but that I, Your Word, having borne their body, and become man, have perfected the work, which You gave Me, O Father? And the work is perfected, because men, redeemed from sin, no longer remain dead; but being deified , have in each other, by looking at Me, the bond of charity. '

24. We then, by way of giving a rude view of the expressions in this passage, have been led into many words, but blessed John will show from his Epistle the sense of the words, concisely and much more perfectly than we can. And he will both disprove the interpretation of these irreligious men, and will teach how we become in God and God in us; and how again we become One in Him, and how far the Son differs in nature from us, and will stop the Arians from any longer thinking that they shall

be as the Son, lest they hear it said to them, 'You are a man and not God,' and 'Stretch not yourself, being poor, beside a rich man.' John then thus writes; 'Hereby know we that we dwell in Him and He in us, because He has given us of His Spirit 1 John 4:13.' Therefore because of the grace of the Spirit which has been given to us, in Him we come to be, and He in us ; and since it is the Spirit of God, therefore through His becoming in us, reasonably are we, as having the Spirit, considered to be in God, and thus is God in us. Not then as the Son in the Father, so also we become in the Father; for the Son does not merely partake the Spirit, that therefore He too may be in the Father; nor does He receive the Spirit, but rather He supplies It Himself to all; and the Spirit does not unite the Word to the Father , but rather the Spirit receives from the Word. And the Son is in the Father, as His own Word and Radiance; but we, apart from the Spirit, are strange and distant from God, and by the participation of the Spirit we are knit into the Godhead; so that our being in the Father is not ours, but is the Spirit's which is in us and abides in us, while by the true confession we preserve it in us, John again saying, 'Whosoever shall confess that Jesus is the Son of God, God dwells in him and he in God 1

John 4:15.' What then is our likeness and equality to the Son? Rather, are not the Arians confuted on every side? And especially by John, that the Son is in the Father in one way, and we become in Him in another, and that neither we shall ever be as He, nor is the Word as we; except they shall dare, as commonly, so now to say, that the Son also by participation of the Spirit and by improvement of conduct came to be Himself also in the Father. But here again is an excess of irreligion, even in admitting the thought. For He, as has been said, gives to the Spirit, and whatever the Spirit has, He has from the Word.

25. The Saviour, then, saying of us, 'As Thou, Father, art in Me, and I in You, that they too may be one in Us,' does not signify that we were to have identity with Him; for this was shown from the instance of Jonah; but it is a request to the Father, as John has written, that the Spirit should be vouchsafed through Him to those who believe, through whom we are found to be in God, and in this respect to be conjoined in Him. For since the Word is in the Father, and the Spirit is given from the Word, He wills

that we should receive the Spirit, that, when we receive It, thus having the Spirit of the Word which is in the Father, we too may be found on account of the Spirit to become One in the Word, and through Him in the Father. And if He say, 'as we,' this again is only a request that such grace of the Spirit as is given to the disciples may be without failure or revocation. For what the Word has by nature , as I said, in the Father, that He wishes to be given to us through the Spirit irrevocably; which the Apostle knowing, said, 'Who shall separate us from the love of Christ.' for 'the gifts of God?' and 'grace of His calling are without repentance.' It is the Spirit then which is in God, and not we viewed in our own selves; and as we are sons and gods because of the Word in us , so we shall be in the Son and in the Father, and we shall be accounted to have become one in Son and in Father, because that that Spirit is in us, which is in the Word which is in the Father. When then a man falls from the Spirit for any wickedness, if he repent upon his fall, the grace remains irrevocably to such as are willing ; otherwise he who has fallen is no longer in God (because that Holy Spirit and Paraclete which is in God has deserted him), but the sinner shall be in him to whom he has subjected himself, as took place in

Saul's instance; for the Spirit of God departed from him and an evil spirit was afflicting him. 1 Samuel 16:14 God's enemies hearing this ought to be henceforth abashed, and no longer to feign themselves equal to God. But they neither understand (for 'the irreligious,' he says, 'does not understand knowledge') nor endure religious words, but find them heavy even to hear.

Chapter XXVI. Introductory to Texts from the Gospels on the Incarnation.

Enumeration of texts still to be explained. Arians compared to the Jews. We must recur to the Regula Fidei. Our Lord did not come into, but became, man, and therefore had the acts and affections of the flesh. The same works divine and human. Thus the flesh was purified, and men were made immortal. Reference to I Peter 4:1.

26. For behold, as if not wearied in their words of irreligion, but hardened with Pharaoh, while they hear and see the Saviour's human attributes in the Gospels , they

have utterly forgotten, like the Samosatene, the Son's paternal Godhead , and with arrogant and audacious tongue they say, 'How can the Son be from the Father by nature, and be like Him in essence,' who says, 'All power is given unto Me;' and 'The Father judges no man, but has committed all judgment unto the Son.' and 'The Father loves the Son, and has given all things into His hand; he that believes in the Son has everlasting life;' and again, 'All things were delivered unto Me of My Father, and no one knows the Father save the Son, and he to whomsoever the Son will reveal Him;' and again, 'All that the Father has given unto Me, shall come to Me.' On this they observe, 'If He was, as you say, Son by nature, He had no need to receive, but He had by nature as a Son.' Or how can He be the natural and true Power of the Father, who near upon the season of the passion says, 'Now is My soul troubled, and what shall I say? Father, save Me from this hour; but for this came I unto this hour. Father, glorify Your Name. Then came there a voice from heaven, saying, I have both glorified it, and will glorify it again John 12:27-28.' And He said the same another time; 'Father, if it be possible, let this cup pass from Me;' and 'When Jesus had thus said, He was troubled in spirit and testified and said, Verily,

verily, I say unto you, that one of you shall betray Me.' Then these perverse men argue; 'If He were Power, He had not feared, but rather He had supplied power to others.' Further they say; 'If He were by nature the true and own Wisdom of the Father,' how is it written, 'And Jesus increased in wisdom and stature, and in favour with God and man?' In like manner, when He had come into the parts of Cæsarea Philippi, He asked the disciples whom men said that He was; and when He was at Bethany He asked where Lazarus lay; and He said besides to His disciples, 'How many loaves have ye? How then,' say they, 'is He Wisdom, who increased in wisdom and was ignorant of what He asked of others?' This too they urge; How can He be the own Word of the Father, without whom the Father never was, through whom He makes all things, as you think, who said upon the Cross 'My God, My God, why have You forsaken Me?' and before that had prayed, 'Glorify Your Name,' and, 'O Father, glorify Thou Me with the glory which I had with You before the world was.' And He used to pray in the deserts and charge His disciples to pray lest they should enter into temptation; and, 'The spirit indeed is willing,' He said, 'but the flesh is weak.' And, 'Of that day and that hour knows no man, no, nor the Angels, neither the Son.' Upon this again say the miserable men, If the Son were, according to your interpretation, eternally existent with God, He had not been ignorant of the Day, but had known as Word; nor had been forsaken as being coexistent; nor had asked to receive glory, as having it in the Father; nor would have prayed at all; for, being the Word, He had needed nothing; but since He is a creature and one of things originate, therefore He thus spoke, and needed what He had not; for it is proper to creatures to require and to need what they have not.

27. This then is what the irreligious men allege in their discourses; and if they thus argue, they might consistently speak yet more daringly; 'Why did the Word become flesh at all?' and they might add; 'For how could He, being God, become man?' or, 'How could the Immaterial bear a body?' or they might speak with Caiaphas still more Judaically, 'Wherefore at all did Christ, being a man, make Himself God?' for this and the like the Jews then muttered when they saw, and now the Ario-maniacs disbelieve when they read, and have fallen away into

blasphemies. If then a man should carefully parallel the words of these and those, he will of a certainty find them both arriving at the same unbelief, and the daring of their irreligion equal, and their dispute with us a common one. For the Jews said; 'How, being a man, can He be God.' And the Arians, 'If He were very God from God, how could He become man?' And the Jews were offended then and mocked, saying, 'Had He been Son of God, He had not endured the Cross;' and the Arians standing over against them, urge upon us, 'How dare ye say that He is the Word proper to the Father's Essence, who had a body, so as to endure all this?' Next, while the Jews sought to kill the Lord, because He said that God was His own Father and made Himself equal to Him, as working what the Father works, the Arians also, not only have learned to deny, both that He is equal to God and that God is the own and natural Father of the Word, but those who hold this they seek to kill. Again, whereas the Jews said, 'Is not this the Son of Joseph, whose father and mother we know? How then is it that He says, Before Abraham was, I am, and I came down from heaven?' the Arians on the other hand make response and say conformably, 'How can He be Word or God who slept as man, and wept, and inquired?' Thus both parties deny the Eternity and Godhead of the Word in consequence of those human attributes which the Saviour took on Him by reason of that flesh which He bore.

28. Such error then being Judaic, and Judaic after the mind of Judas the traitor, let them openly confess themselves scholars of Caiaphas and Herod, instead of cloking Judaism with the name of Christianity, and let them deny outright, as we have said before, the Saviour's appearance in the flesh, for this doctrine is akin to their heresy; or if they fear openly to Judaize and be circumcised , from servility towards Constantius and for their sake whom they have beguiled, then let them not say what the Jews say; for if they disown the name, let them in fairness renounce the doctrine. For we are Christians, O Arians, Christians we; our privilege is it well to know the Gospels concerning the Saviour, and neither, with Jews to stone Him, if we hear of His Godhead and Eternity, nor with you to stumble at such lowly sayings as He may speak for our sakes as man. If then you would become Christians , put off Arius's madness, and cleanse with the words of

religion those ears of yours which blaspheming has defiled; knowing that, by ceasing to be Arians, you will cease also from the malevolence of the present Jews. Then at once will truth shine on you out of darkness, and you will no longer reproach us with holding two Eternals, but you will yourselves acknowledge that the Lord is God's true Son by nature, and not as merely eternal, but revealed as co-existing in the Father's eternity. For there are things called eternal of which He is Framer; for in the twenty-third Psalm it is written, 'Lift up your gates, O you rulers, and be lifted up, you everlasting gates;' and it is plain that through Him these things were made; but if even of things everlasting He is the Framer, who of us shall be able henceforth to dispute that He is anterior to those things eternal, and in consequence is proved to be Lord not so much from His eternity, as in that He is God's Son; for being the Son, He is inseparable from the Father, and never was there when He was not, but He was always; and being the Father's Image and Radiance, He has the Father's eternity. Now what has been briefly said above may suffice to show their misunderstanding of the passages they then alleged; and that of what they now allege from the Gospels they certainly give an unsound interpretation , we may easily see, if we now consider the scope of that faith which we Christians hold, and using it as a rule, apply ourselves, as the Apostle teaches, to the reading of inspired Scripture. For Christ's enemies, being ignorant of this scope, have wandered from the way of truth, and have stumbled Romans 9:32 on a stone of stumbling, thinking otherwise than they should think.

29. Now the scope and character of Holy Scripture, as we have often said, is this — it contains a double account of the Saviour; that He was ever God, and is the Son, being the Father's Word and Radiance and Wisdom ; and that afterwards for us He took flesh of a Virgin, Mary Bearer of God , and was made man. And this scope is to be found throughout inspired Scripture, as the Lord Himself has said, 'Search the Scriptures, for they are they which testify of Me John 5:39.' But lest I should exceed in writing, by bringing together all the passages on the subject, let it suffice to mention as a specimen, first John saying, 'In the beginning was the Word, and the Word was with God, and the Word was God. The same was in the beginning with God. All things were made by Him, and without

Him was made not one thing ;' next, 'And the Word was made flesh and dwelt among us, and we beheld His glory, the glory as of one Only-begotten from the Father ;' and next Paul writing, 'Who being in the form of God, thought it not a prize to be equal with God, but emptied Himself, taking the form of a servant, being made in the likeness of men, and being found in fashion like a man, He humbled Himself, becoming obedient unto death, even the death of the Cross Philippians 2:6-8.' Any one, beginning with these passages and going through the whole of the Scripture upon the interpretation which they suggest, will perceive how in the beginning the Father said to Him, 'Let there be light,' and 'Let there be a firmament,' and 'Let us make man ;' but in fullness of the ages, He sent Him into the world, not that He might judge the world, but that the world by Him might be saved, and how it is written 'Behold, the Virgin shall be with child, and shall bring forth a Son, and they shall call his Name Emmanuel, which, being interpreted, is God with us Matthew 1:23.'

30. The reader then of divine Scripture may acquaint himself with these passages from the ancient books; and from the Gospels on the other hand he will perceive that the Lord became man; for 'the Word,' he says, 'became flesh, and dwelt among us John 1:14.' And He became man, and did not come into man; for this it is necessary to know, lest perchance these irreligious men fall into this notion also, and beguile any into thinking, that, as in former times the Word was used to come into each of the Saints, so now He sojourned in a man, hallowing him also, and manifesting Himself as in the others. For if it were so, and He only appeared in a man, it were nothing strange, nor had those who saw Him been startled, saying, Whence is He? And wherefore do You, being a man, make Yourself God? For they were familiar with the idea, from the words, 'And the Word of the Lord came' to this or that of the Prophets. But now, since the Word of God, by whom all things came to be, endured to become also Son of man, and humbled Himself, taking a servant's form, therefore to the Jews the Cross of Christ is a scandal, but to us Christ is 'God's power' and 'God's wisdom 1 Corinthians 1:24;' for 'the Word,' as John says, 'became flesh' (it being the custom of Scripture to call man by the name of 'flesh,' as it

says by Joel the Prophet, 'I will pour out My Spirit upon all flesh;' and as Daniel said to Astyages, 'I do not worship idols made with hands, but the Living God, who has created the heaven and the earth, and has sovereignty over all flesh ;' for both he and Joel call mankind flesh).

31. Of old time He was wont to come to the Saints individually, and to hallow those who rightly received Him; but neither, when they were begotten was it said that He had become man, nor, when they suffered, was it said that He Himself suffered. But when He came among us from Mary once at the end of the ages for the abolition of sin (for so it was pleasing to the Father, to send His own Son 'made of a woman, made under the Law'), then it is said, that He took flesh and became man, and in that flesh He suffered for us (as Peter says, 'Christ therefore having suffered for us in the flesh Galatians 4:4; 1 Peter 4:1,' that it might be shown, and that all might believe, that whereas He was ever God, and hallowed those to whom He came, and ordered all things according to the Father's will , afterwards for our sakes He became man, and 'bodily Colossians 2:9,' as the Apostle says, the Godhead dwelt in

the flesh; as much as to say, 'Being God, He had His own body, and using this as an instrument, He became man for our sakes.' And on account of this, the properties of the flesh are said to be His, since He was in it, such as to hunger, to thirst, to suffer, to weary, and the like, of which the flesh is capable; while on the other hand the works proper to the Word Himself, such as to raise the dead, to restore sight to the blind, and to cure the woman with an issue of blood, He did through His own body. And the Word bore the infirmities of the flesh, as His own, for His was the flesh; and the flesh ministered to the works of the Godhead, because the Godhead was in it, for the body was God's. And well has the Prophet said 'carried Isaiah 53:4;' and has not said, 'He remedied our infirmities,' lest, as being external to the body, and only healing it, as He has always done, He should leave men subject still to death; but He carries our infirmities, and He Himself bears our sins, that it might be shown that He has become man for us, and that the body which in Him bore them, was His own body; and, while He received no hurt Himself by 'bearing our sins in His body on the tree,' as Peter speaks, we men were redeemed from our own affections, and were filled with the righteousness of the Word.

32. Whence it was that, when the flesh suffered, the Word was not external to it; and therefore is the passion said to be His: and when He did divinely His Father's works, the flesh was not external to Him, but in the body itself did the Lord do them. Hence, when made man, He said , 'If I do not the works of the Father, believe Me not; but if I do, though ye believe not Me, believe the works, that you may know that the Father is in Me and I in Him.' And thus when there was need to raise Peter's wife's mother, who was sick of a fever, He stretched forth His hand humanly, but He stopped the illness divinely. And in the case of the man blind from the birth, human was the spittle which He gave forth from the flesh, but divinely did He open the eyes through the clay. And in the case of Lazarus, He gave forth a human voice as man; but divinely, as God, did He raise Lazarus from the dead. These things were so done, were so manifested, because He had a body, not in appearance, but in truth ; and it became the Lord, in putting on human flesh, to put it on whole with the affections proper to it; that, as we say that the body was His own, so also we may say that the affections of the body were proper to Him alone, though they did not touch Him according to His Godhead. If then the body

had been another's, to him too had been the affections attributed; but if the flesh is the Word's (for 'the Word became flesh'), of necessity then the affections also of the flesh are ascribed to Him, whose the flesh is. And to whom the affections are ascribed, such namely as to be condemned, to be scourged, to thirst, and the cross, and death, and the other infirmities of the body, of Him too is the triumph and the grace. For this cause then, consistently and fittingly such affections are ascribed not to another, but to the Lord; that the grace also may be from Him, and that we may become, not worshippers of any other, but truly devout towards God, because we invoke no originate thing, no ordinary man, but the natural and true Son from God, who has become man, yet is not the less Lord and God and Saviour.

33. Who will not admire this? Or who will not agree that such a thing is truly divine? For if the works of the Word's Godhead had not taken place through the body, man had not been deified; and again, had not the properties of the flesh been ascribed to the Word, man had not been thoroughly delivered from them; but though they had

ceased for a little while, as I said before, still sin had remained in him and corruption, as was the case with mankind before Him; and for this reason:— Many for instance have been made holy and clean from all sin; nay, Jeremiah was hallowed even from the womb, and John, while yet in the womb, leapt for joy at the voice of Mary Bearer of God ; nevertheless 'death reigned from Adam to Moses, even over those that had not sinned after the similitude of Adam's transgression Romans 5:14;' and thus man remained mortal and corruptible as before, liable to the affections proper to their nature. But now the Word having become man and having appropriated what pertains to the flesh, no longer do these things touch the body, because of the Word who has come in it, but they are destroyed by Him, and henceforth men no longer remain sinners and dead according to their proper affections, but having risen according to the Word's power, they abide ever immortal and incorruptible. Whence also, whereas the flesh is born of Mary Bearer of God , He Himself is said to have been born, who furnishes to others an origin of being; in order that He may transfer our origin into Himself, and we may no longer, as mere earth, return to earth, but as being knit into the Word from heaven, may be carried to heaven by Him. Therefore in like manner not without reason has He transferred to Himself the other affections of the body also; that we, no longer as being men, but as proper to the Word, may have share in eternal life. For no longer according to our former origin in Adam do we die; but henceforward our origin and all infirmity of flesh being transferred to the Word, we rise from the earth, the curse from sin being removed, because of Him who is in us , and who has become a curse for us. And with reason; for as we are all from earth and die in Adam, so being regenerated from above of water and Spirit, in the Christ we are all quickened; the flesh being no longer earthly, but being henceforth made Word , by reason of God's Word who for our sake 'became flesh.'

34. And that one may attain to a more exact knowledge of the impassibility of the Word's nature and of the infirmities ascribed to Him because of the flesh, it will be well to listen to the blessed Peter; for he will be a trustworthy witness concerning the Saviour. He writes then in his Epistle thus; 'Christ then having suffered for us in the flesh 1 Peter 4:1.' Therefore also when He is said

to hunger and thirst and to toil and not to know, and to sleep, and to weep, and to ask, and to flee, and to be born, and to deprecate the cup, and in a word to undergo all that belongs to the flesh , let it be said, as is congruous, in each case 'Christ then hungering and thirsting for us in the flesh;' and saying 'He did not know, and being buffeted, and toiling for us in the flesh;' and 'being exalted too, and born, and growing in the flesh;' and 'fearing and hiding in the flesh;' and 'saying, If it be possible let this cup pass from Me Matthew 26:39, and being beaten, and receiving, for us in the flesh;' and in a word all such things 'for us in the flesh.' For on this account has the Apostle himself said, 'Christ then having suffered,' not in His Godhead, but 'for us in the flesh,' that these affections may be acknowledged as, not proper to the very Word by nature, but proper by nature to the very flesh.

Let no one then stumble at what belongs to man, but rather let a man know that in nature the Word Himself is impassible, and yet because of that flesh which He put on, these things are ascribed to Him, since they are proper to the flesh, and the body itself is proper to the Saviour. And while He Himself, being impassible in nature, remains as He is, not harmed by these affections, but rather obliterating and destroying them, men, their passions as if changed and abolished in the Impassible, henceforth become themselves also impassible and free from them for ever, as John taught, saying, 'And ye know that He was manifested to take away our sins, and in Him is no sin 1 John 3:5.' And this being so, no heretic shall object, 'Wherefore rises the flesh, being by nature mortal? And if it rises, why not hunger too and thirst, and suffer, and remain mortal? For it came from the earth, and how can its natural condition pass from it?' since the flesh is able now to make answer to this so contentious heretic, 'I am from earth, being by nature mortal, but afterwards I have become the Word's flesh,' and He 'carried' my affections, though He is without them; and so I became free from them, being no more abandoned to their service because of the Lord who has made me free from them. For if you object to my being rid of that corruption which is by nature, see that you object not to God's Word having taken my form of servitude; for as the Lord, putting on the body, became man, so we men are deified by the Word as being taken to Him through His flesh, and henceforward inherit life 'everlasting.'

35. These points we have found it necessary first to examine, that, when we see Him doing or saying anything divinely through the instrument of His own body, we may know that He so works, being God, and also, if we see Him speaking or suffering humanly, we may not be ignorant that He bore flesh and became man, and hence He so acts and so speaks. For if we recognise what is proper to each, and see and understand that both these things and those are done by One , we are right in our faith, and shall never stray. But if a man looking at what is done divinely by the Word, deny the body, or looking at what is proper to the body, deny the Word's presence in the flesh, or from what is human entertain low thoughts concerning the Word, such a one, as a Jewish vintner , mixing water with the wine, shall account the Cross an offense, or as a Gentile, will deem the preaching folly. This then is what happens to God's enemies the Arians; for looking at what is human in the Saviour, they have judged Him a creature. Therefore they ought, looking also at the divine works of the Word, to deny the origination of His

body, and henceforth to rank themselves with Manichees. But for them, learn they, however tardily, that 'the Word became flesh;' and let us, retaining the general scope of the faith, acknowledge that what they interpret ill, has a right interpretation.

Chapter XXVII. Texts Explained; Tenthly, Matthew XI. 27: John III. 35, Etc.

These texts intended to preclude the Sabellian notion of the Son; they fall in with the Catholic doctrine concerning the Son; they are explained by 'so' in John 5:26. (Anticipation of the next chapter.) Again they are used with reference to our Lord's human nature; for our sake, that we might receive and not lose, as receiving in Him. And consistently with other parts of Scripture, which show that He had the power, etc., before He received it. He was God and man, and His actions are often at once divine and human.

35 (continued). For, 'The Father loves the Son, and has given all things into His hand;' and, 'All things were given

unto Me of My Father.' and, 'I can do nothing of Myself, but as I hear, I judge;' and the like passages do not show that the Son once had not these prerogatives — (for had not He eternally what the Father has, who is the Only Word and Wisdom of the Father in essence, who also says, 'All that the Father has are Mine,' and what are Mine, are the Father's? For if the things of the Father are the Son's and the Father has them ever, it is plain that what the Son has, being the Father's, were ever in the Son) — not then because once He had them not, did He say this, but because, whereas the Son has eternally what He has, yet He has them from the Father.

36. For lest a man, perceiving that the Son has all that the Father has, from the exact likeness and identity of that He has, should wander into the irreligion of Sabellius, considering Him to be the Father, therefore He has said 'Was given unto Me,' and 'I received,' and 'Were delivered to Me John 10:18; Matthew 28:18,' only to show that He is not the Father, but the Father's Word, and the Eternal Son, who because of His likeness to the Father, has eternally what He has from Him, and because He is the

Son, has from the Father what He has eternally. Moreover that 'Was given' and 'Were delivered,' and the like, do not impair the Godhead of the Son, but rather show Him to be truly Son, we may learn from the passages themselves. For if all things are delivered unto Him, first, He is other than that all which He has received; next, being Heir of all things, He alone is the Son and proper according to the Essence of the Father. For if He were one of all, then He were not 'heir of all Hebrews 1:2,' but every one had received according as the Father willed and gave. But now, as receiving all things, He is other than them all, and alone proper to the Father. Moreover that 'Was given' and 'Were delivered' do not show that once He had them not, we may conclude from a similar passage, and in like manner concerning them all; for the Saviour Himself says, 'As the Father has life in Himself, so has He given also to the Son to have life in Himself John 5:26.' Now from the words 'Hath given,' He signifies that He is not the Father; but in saying 'so,' He shows the Son's natural likeness and propriety towards the Father. If then once the Father had not, plainly the Son once had not; for as the Father, 'so' also the Son has. But if this is irreligious to say, and religious on the contrary to say that the Father had ever, is it not unseemly in them when the Son says that, 'as' the Father has, 'so' also the Son has, to say that He has not 'so ,' but otherwise? Rather then is the Word faithful, and all things which He says that He has received, He has always, yet has from the Father; and the Father indeed not from any, but the Son from the Father. For as in the instance of the radiance, if the radiance itself should say, 'All places the light has given me to enlighten, and I do not enlighten from myself, but as the light wills,' yet, in saying this, it does not imply that it once had not, but it means, 'I am proper to the light, and all things of the light are mine;' so, and much more, must we understand in the instance of the Son. For the Father, having given all things to the Son, in the Son still has all things; and the Son having, still the Father has them; for the Son's Godhead is the Father's Godhead, and thus the Father in the Son exercises His Providence over all things.

37. And while such is the sense of expressions like these, those which speak humanly concerning the Saviour admit of a religious meaning also. For with this end have we examined them beforehand, that, if we should hear Him

asking where Lazarus is laid , or when He asks on coming into the parts of Cæsarea, 'Whom do men say that I am?' or, 'How many loaves do you have?' and, 'What will you that I shall do unto you ?' we may know, from what has been already said, the right sense of the passages, and may not stumble as Christ's enemies the Arians. First then we must put this question to the irreligious, why they consider Him ignorant? For one who asks, does not for certain ask from ignorance; but it is possible for one who knows, still to ask concerning what He knows. Thus John was aware that Christ, when asking, 'How many loaves do you have?' was not ignorant, for he says, 'And this He said to prove him, for He Himself knew what He would do John 6:6.' But if He knew what He was doing, therefore not in ignorance, but with knowledge did He ask. From this instance we may understand similar ones; that, when the Lord asks, He does not ask in ignorance, where Lazarus lies, nor again, whom men do say that He is; but knowing the thing which He was asking, aware what He was about to do. And thus with ease is their clever point exploded; but if they still persist on account of His asking, then they must be told that in the Godhead indeed ignorance is not, but to the flesh ignorance is proper, as has been said. And that this is really so, observe how the Lord who inquired where Lazarus lay, Himself said, when He was not on the spot but a great way off, 'Lazarus is dead John 11:14,' and where he was dead; and how that He who is considered by them as ignorant, is He Himself who foreknew the reasonings of the disciples, and was aware of what was in the heart of each, and of 'what was in man,' and, what is greater, alone knows the Father and says, 'I in the Father and the Father in Me.'

38. Therefore this is plain to every one, that the flesh indeed is ignorant, but the Word Himself, considered as the Word, knows all things even before they come to be. For He did not, when He became man, cease to be God ; nor, whereas He is God does He shrink from what is man's; perish the thought; but rather, being God, He has taken to Him the flesh, and being in the flesh deifies the flesh. For as He asked questions in it, so also in it did He raise the dead; and He showed to all that He who quickens the dead and recalls the soul, much more discerns the secret of all. And He knew where Lazarus lay, and yet He asked; for the All-holy Word of God, who endured all

things for our sakes, did this, that so carrying our ignorance, He might vouchsafe to us the knowledge of His own only and true Father, and of Himself, sent because of us for the salvation of all, than which no grace could be greater. When then the Saviour uses the words which they allege in their defense, 'Power is given to Me,' and, 'Glorify Your Son,' and Peter says, 'Power is given unto Him,' we understand all these passages in the same sense, that humanly because of the body He says all this. For though He had no need, nevertheless He is said to have received what He received humanly, that on the other hand, inasmuch as the Lord has received, and the grant is lodged with Him, the grace may remain sure. For while mere man receives, he is liable to lose again (as was shown in the case of Adam, for he received and he lost), but that the grace may be irrevocable, and may be kept sure by men, therefore He Himself appropriates the gift; and He says that He has received power, as man, which He ever had as God, and He says, 'Glorify Me,' who glorifies others, to show that He has a flesh which has need of these things. Wherefore, when the flesh receives, since that which receives is in Him, and by taking it He has become man, therefore He is said Himself to have received.

39. If then (as has many times been said) the Word has not become man, then ascribe to the Word, as you would have it, to receive, and to need glory, and to be ignorant; but if He has become man (and He has become), and it is man's to receive, and to need, and to be ignorant, wherefore do we consider the Giver as receiver, and the Dispenser to others do we suspect to be in need, and divide the Word from the Father as imperfect and needy, while we strip human nature of grace? For if the Word Himself, considered as Word, has received and been glorified for His own sake, and if He according to His Godhead is He who is hallowed and has risen again, what hope is there for men? For they remain as they were, naked, and wretched, and dead, having no interest in the things given to the Son. Why too did the Word come among us, and become flesh? If that He might receive these things, which He says that He has received, He was without them before that, and of necessity will rather owe thanks Himself to the body, because, when He came into it, then He receives these things from the Father, which He had not before His descent into the flesh. For on this showing He seems rather to be Himself promoted because of the body, than the body promoted because of Him. But

this notion is Judaic. But if that He might redeem mankind , the Word did come among us; and that He might hallow and deify them, the Word became flesh (and for this He did become), who does not see that it follows, that what He says that He received, when He became flesh, that He mentions, not for His own sake, but for the flesh? For to it, in which He was speaking, pertained the gifts given through Him from the Father. But let us see what He asked, and what the things altogether were which He said that He had received, that in this way also they may be brought to feeling. He asked then glory, yet He had said, 'All things were delivered unto Me Luke 10:22.' And after the resurrection, He says that He has received all power; but even before that He had said, 'All things were delivered unto Me,' He was Lord of all, for 'all things were made by Him;' and 'there is One Lord by whom are all things 1 Corinthians 8:6.' And when He asked glory, He was as He is, the Lord of glory; as Paul says, 'If they had known it, they would not have crucified the Lord of glory 1 Corinthians 2:8;' for He had that glory which He asked when He said, 'the glory which I had with You before the world was John 17:5.'

40. Also the power which He said He received after the resurrection, that He had before He received it, and before the resurrection. For He of Himself rebuked Satan, saying, 'Get behind Me, Satan Luke 4:8;' and to the disciples He gave the power against him, when on their return He said, 'I beheld Satan, as lightning, fall from heaven Luke 10:18-19.' And again, that what He said that He had received, that He possessed before receiving it, appears from His driving away the demons, and from His unbinding what Satan had bound, as He did in the case of the daughter of Abraham; and from His remitting sins, saying to the paralytic, and to the woman who washed His feet, 'Your sins be forgiven you ;' and from His both raising the dead, and repairing the first nature of the blind, granting to him to see. And all this He did, not waiting till He should receive, but being 'possessed of power.' From all this it is plain that what He had as Word, that when He had become man and was risen again, He says that He received humanly ; that for His sake men might henceforward upon earth have power against demons, as having become partakers of a divine nature; and in heaven, as being delivered from corruption, might reign everlastingly. Thus we must acknowledge this once for all,

that nothing which He says that He received, did He receive as not possessing before; for the Word, as being God, had them always; but in these passages He is said humanly to have received, that, whereas the flesh received in Him, henceforth from it the gift might abide surely for us. For what is said by Peter, 'receiving from God honour and glory, Angels being made subject unto Him ,' has this meaning. As He inquired humanly, and raised Lazarus divinely, so 'He received' is spoken of Him humanly, but the subjection of the Angels marks the Word's Godhead.

41. Cease then, O abhorred of God , and degrade not the Word; nor detract from His Godhead, which is the Father's , as though He needed or were ignorant; lest ye be casting your own arguments against the Christ, as the Jews who once stoned Him. For these belong not to the Word, as the Word; but are proper to men and, as when He spat, and stretched forth the hand, and called Lazarus, we did not say that the triumphs were human, though they were done through the body, but were God's, so, on the other hand, though human things are ascribed to the Saviour in the Gospel, let us, considering the nature of what is said

and that they are foreign to God, not impute them to the Word's Godhead, but to His manhood. For though 'the Word became flesh,' yet to the flesh are the affections proper; and though the flesh is possessed by God in the Word, yet to the Word belong the grace and the power. He did then the Father's works through the flesh; and as truly contrariwise were the affections of the flesh displayed in Him; for instance, He inquired and He raised Lazarus, He chid His Mother, saying, 'My hour is not yet come,' and then at once He made the water wine. For He was Very God in the flesh, and He was true flesh in the Word. Therefore from His works He revealed both Himself as Son of God, and His own Father, and from the affections of the flesh He showed that He bore a true body, and that it was His own.

Chapter XXVIII. Texts Explained; Eleventhly, Mark XIII. 32 And Luke II. 52.

Arianexplanation of the former text is against the Regula Fidei; and against the context. Our Lord said He was ignorant of the Day, by reason of His human nature. If the

Holy Spirit knows the Day, therefore the Son knows; if the Son knows the Father, therefore He knows the Day; if He has all that is the Father's, therefore knowledge of the Day; if in the Father, He knows the Day in the Father; if He created and upholds all things, He knows when they will cease to be. He knows not as Man, argued from Matthew 24:42. As He asked about Lazarus's grave, etc., yet knew, so He knows; as St. Paul says, 'whether in the body I know not,' etc., yet knew, so He knows. He said He knew not for our profit, that we be not curious as in Acts 1:7, where on the contrary He did not say He knew not. As the Almighty asks of Adam and of Cain, yet knew, so the Son knows [as God]. Again, He advanced in wisdom also as man, else He made Angels perfect before Himself. He advanced, in that the Godhead was manifested in Him more fully as time went on.

42. These things being so, come let us now examine into 'But of that day and that hour knows no man, neither the Angels of God, nor the Son;' for being in great ignorance as regards these words, and being stupefied about them, they think they have in them an important argument for

their heresy. But I, when the heretics allege it and prepare themselves with it, see in them the giants again fighting against God. For the Lord of heaven and earth, by whom all things were made, has to litigate before them about day and hour; and the Word who knows all things is accused by them of ignorance about a day; and the Son who knows the Father is said to be ignorant of an hour of a day; now what can be spoken more contrary to sense, or what madness can be likened to this? Through the Word all things have been made, times and seasons and night and day and the whole creation; and is the Framer of all said to be ignorant of His work? And the very context of the lection shows that the Son of God knows that hour and that day, though the Arians fall headlong in their ignorance. For after saying, 'nor the Son,' He relates to the disciples what precedes the day, saying, 'This and that shall be, and then the end.' But He who speaks of what precedes the day, knows certainly the day also, which shall be manifested subsequently to the things foretold. But if He had not known the hour, He had not signified the events before it, as not knowing when it should be. And as any one, who, by way of pointing out a house or city to those who were ignorant of it, gave an account of what comes before the house or city, and having described all, said, 'Then immediately comes the city or the house,' would know of course where the house or the city was (for had he not known, he had not described what comes before lest from ignorance he should throw his hearers far out of the way, or in speaking he should unawares go beyond the object), so the Lord saying what precedes that day and that hour, knows exactly, nor is ignorant, when the hour and the day are at hand.

43. Now why it was that, though He knew, He did not tell His disciples plainly at that time, no one may be curious where He has been silent; for 'Who has known the mind of the Lord, or who has been His counsellor Romans 11:34?' but why, though He knew, He said, 'no, not the Son knows,' this I think none of the faithful is ignorant, viz. that He made this as those other declarations as man by reason of the flesh. For this as before is not the Word's deficiency , but of that human nature whose property it is to be ignorant. And this again will be well seen by honestly examining into the occasion, when and to whom the Saviour spoke thus. Not then when the heaven was

made by Him, nor when He was with the Father Himself, the Word 'disposing all things ,' nor before He became man did He say it, but when 'the Word became flesh John 1:14.' On this account it is reasonable to ascribe to His manhood everything which, after He became man, He speaks humanly. For it is proper to the Word to know what was made, nor be ignorant either of the beginning or of the end of these (for the works are His), and He knows how many things He wrought, and the limit of their consistence. And knowing of each the beginning and the end, He knows surely the general and common end of all. Certainly when He says in the Gospel concerning Himself in His human character, 'Father, the hour has come, glorify Your Son ,' it is plain that He knows also the hour of the end of all things, as the Word, though as man He is ignorant of it, for ignorance is proper to man , and especially ignorance of these things. Moreover this is proper to the Saviour's love of man; for since He was made man, He is not ashamed, because of the flesh which is ignorant , to say 'I know not,' that He may show that knowing as God, He is but ignorant according to the flesh. And therefore He said not, 'no, not the Son of God knows,' lest the Godhead should seem ignorant, but simply, 'no, not the Son,' that the ignorance might be the Son's as born from among men.

44. On this account, He alludes to the Angels, but He did not go further and say, 'not the Holy Ghost;' but He was silent, with a double intimation; first that if the Spirit knew, much more must the Word know, considered as the Word, from whom the Spirit receives ; and next by His silence about the Spirit, He made it clear, that He said of His human ministry, 'no, not the Son.' And a proof of it is this; that, when He had spoken humanly 'No, not the Son knows,' He yet shows that divinely He knew all things. For that Son whom He declares not to know the day, Him He declares to know the Father; for 'No one,' He says, 'knows the Father save the Son Matthew 11:27.' And all men but the Arians would join in confessing, that He who knows the Father, much more knows the whole of the creation; and in that whole, its end. And if already the day and the hour be determined by the Father, it is plain that through the Son are they determined, and He knows Himself what through Him has been determined , for there is nothing but has come to be and has been

determined through the Son. Therefore He, being the Framer of the universe, knows of what nature, and of what magnitude, and with what limits, the Father has willed it to be made; and in the how much and how far is included its period. And again, if all that is the Father's, is the Son's (and this He Himself has John 16:15 said), and it is the Father's attribute to know the day, it is plain that the Son too knows it, having this proper to Him from the Father. And again, if the Son be in the Father and the Father in the Son, and the Father knows the day and the hour, it is clear that the Son, being in the Father and knowing the things of the Father, knows Himself also the day and the hour. And if the Son is also the Father's Very Image, and the Father knows the day and the hour, it is plain that the Son has this likeness also to the Father of knowing them. And it is not wonderful if He, through whom all things were made, and in whom the universe consists, Himself knows what has been brought to be, and when the end will be of each and of all together; rather is it wonderful that this audacity, suitable as it is to the madness of the Ariomaniacs, should have forced us to have recourse to so long a defense. For ranking the Son of God, the Eternal Word, among things originate, they are not far from venturing to maintain that the Father Himself is second to the creation; for if He who knows the Father knows not the day nor the hour, I fear lest the knowledge of the creation, or rather of the lower portion of it, be greater, as they in their madness would say, than knowledge concerning the Father.

45. But for them, when they thus blaspheme the Spirit, they must expect no remission ever of such irreligion, as the Lord has said ; but let us, who love Christ and bear Christ within us, know that the Word, not as ignorant, considered as Word, has said 'I know not,' for He knows, but as showing His manhood , in that to be ignorant is proper to man, and that He had put on flesh that was ignorant , being in which, He said according to the flesh, 'I know not.' And for this reason, after saying, 'No not the Son knows,' and mentioning the ignorance of the men in Noah's day, immediately He added, 'Watch therefore, for you know not in what hour your Lord does come,' and again, 'In such an hour as you think not, the Son of man comes Matthew 24:42, 44.' For I too, having become as you for you, said 'no, not the Son.' For, had He been ignorant divinely, He must have said, 'Watch therefore, for

I know not,' and, 'In an hour when I think not;' but in fact this has He not said; but by saying 'You know not' and 'When ye think not,' He has signified that it belongs to man to be ignorant; for whose sake He too having a flesh like theirs and having become man, said 'No, not the Son knows,' for He knew not in flesh, though knowing as Word. And again the example from Noah exposes the shamelessness of Christ's enemies; for there too He said not, 'I knew not,' but 'They knew not until the flood came Matthew 24:39.' For men did not know, but He who brought the flood (and it was the Saviour Himself) knew the day and the hour in which He opened the cataracts of heaven and broke up the great deep, and said to Noah, 'Come thou and all your house into the ark Genesis 7:1.' For were He ignorant, He had not foretold to Noah, 'Yet seven days and I will bring a flood upon the earth.' But if in describing the day He makes use of the parallel of Noah's time, and He did know the day of the flood, therefore He knows also the day of His own coming.

46. Moreover, after narrating the parable of the Virgins, again He shows more clearly who they are who are

ignorant of the day and the hour, saying, 'Watch therefore, for you know neither the day nor the hour Matthew 25:13.' He who said shortly before, 'No one knows, no not the Son,' now says not 'I know not,' but 'ye know not.' In like manner then, when His disciples asked about the end, suitably said He then, 'no, nor the Son,' according to the flesh because of the body; that He might show that, as man, He knows not; for ignorance is proper to man. If however He is the Word, if it is He who is to come, He to be Judge, He to be the Bridegroom, He knows when and in what hour He comes, and when He is to say, 'Awake, you that sleep, and arise from the dead, and Christ shall give you light Ephesians 5:14.' For as, on becoming man, He hungers and thirsts and suffers with men, so with men as man He knows not; though divinely, being in the Father Word and Wisdom, He knows, and there is nothing which He knows not. In like manner also about Lazarus He asks humanly, who was on His way to raise him, and knew whence He should recall Lazarus's soul; and it was a greater thing to know where the soul was, than to know where the body lay; but He asked humanly, that He might raise divinely. So too He asks of the disciples, on coming into the parts of Cæsarea, though knowing even before Peter made answer. For if the Father revealed to Peter the answer to the Lord's question, it is plain that through the Son was the revelation, for 'No one knows the Son,' says He, 'save the Father, neither the Father save the Son, and he to whomsoever the Son will reveal Him Luke 10:22.' But if through the Son is revealed the knowledge both of the Father and the Son, there is no room for doubting that the Lord who asked, having first revealed it to Peter from the Father, next asked humanly; in order to show, that asking after the flesh, He knew divinely what Peter was about to say. The Son then knew, as knowing all things, and knowing His own Father, than which knowledge nothing can be greater or more perfect.

47. This is sufficient to confute them; but to show still further that they are hostile to the truth and Christ's enemies, I could wish to ask them a question. The Apostle in the Second Epistle to the Corinthians writes, 'I knew a man in Christ, above fourteen years ago, whether in the body I do not know, or whether out of the body I do not know; God knows.' What now say ye? Knew the Apostle

what had happened to him in the vision, though he says 'I know not,' or knew he not? If he knew not, see to it, lest, being familiar with error, you err in the trespass of the Phrygians , who say that the Prophets and the other ministers of the Word know neither what they do nor concerning what they announce. But if he knew when he said 'I know not,' for he had Christ within him revealing to him all things, is not the heart of God's enemies indeed perverted and 'self-condemned?' for when the Apostle says, 'I know not,' they say that he knows; but when the Lord says, 'I know not,' they say that He does not know. For if since Christ was within him, Paul knew that of which he says, 'I know not,' does not much more Christ Himself know, though He say, 'I know not?' The Apostle then, the Lord revealing it to him, knew what happened to him; for on this account he says, 'I knew a man in Christ.' and knowing the man, he knew also how the man was caught away. Thus Elisha, who beheld Elijah, knew also how he was taken up; but though knowing, yet when the sons of the Prophets thought that Elijah was cast upon one of the mountains by the Spirit, he knowing from the first what he had seen, tried to persuade them; but when they urged it, he was silent, and suffered them to go after him. Did he then not know, because he was silent? He knew indeed, but as if not knowing, he suffered them, that they being convinced, might no more doubt about the taking up of Elijah. Therefore much more Paul, himself being the person caught away, knew also how he was caught; for Elijah knew; and had any one asked, he would have said how. And yet Paul says 'I know not,' for these two reasons, as I think at least; one, as he has said himself, lest because of the abundance of the revelations any one should think of him beyond what he saw; the other, because, our Saviour having said 'I know not,' it became him also to say 'I know not,' lest the servant should appear above his Lord, and the disciple above his Master.

48. Therefore He who gave to Paul to know, much rather knew Himself; for since He spoke of the antecedents of the day, He also knew, as I said before, when the Day and when the Hour, and yet though knowing, He says, 'No, not the Son knows.' Why then said He at that time 'I know not,' what He as Lord , knew? As we may by searching conjecture, for our profit , as I think at least, did He this; and may He grant to what we are now proposing

a true meaning! On both sides did the Saviour secure our advantage; for He has made known what comes before the end, that, as He said Himself, we might not be startled nor scared, when they happen, but from them may expect the end after them. And concerning the day and the hour He was not willing to say according to His divine nature, 'I know,' but after the flesh, 'I know not,' for the sake of the flesh which was ignorant, as I have said before; lest they should ask Him further, and then either He should have to pain the disciples by not speaking, or by speaking might act to the prejudice of them and us all. For whatever He does, that altogether He does for our sakes, since also for us 'the Word became flesh.' For us therefore He said 'No, not the Son knows;' and neither was He untrue in thus saying (for He said humanly, as man, 'I know not'), nor did He suffer the disciples to force Him to speak, for by saying 'I know not' He stopped their inquiries. And so in the Acts of the Apostles it is written, when He went upon the Angels, ascending as man, and carrying up to heaven the flesh which He bore, on the disciples seeing this, and again asking, 'When shall the end be, and when will You be present?' He said to them more clearly, 'It is not for you to know the times or the seasons which the Father has put in

His own power Acts 1:7.' And He did not then say, 'No, not the Son,' as He said before humanly, but, 'It is not for you to know.' For now the flesh had risen and put off its mortality and been deified; and no longer did it become Him to answer after the flesh when He was going into the heavens; but henceforth to teach after a divine manner, 'It is not for you to know times or seasons which the Father has put in His own power; but you shall receive Power.' And what is that Power of the Father but the Son? For Christ is 'God's Power and God's Wisdom.'

49. The Son then did know, as being the Word; for He implied this in what He said —'I know but it is not for you to know;' for it was for your sakes that sitting also on the mount I said according to the flesh, 'No, not the Son knows,' for the profit of you and all. For it is profitable to you to hear so much both of the Angels and of the Son, because of the deceivers which shall be afterwards; that though demons should be transfigured as Angels, and should attempt to speak concerning the end, you should not believe, since they are ignorant; and that, if Antichrist too, disguising himself, should say, 'I am Christ,' and

should try in his turn to speak of that day and end, to deceive the hearers, ye, having these words from Me, 'No, not the Son,' may disbelieve him also. And further, not to know when the end is, or when the day of the end, is expedient for man, lest knowing, they might become negligent of the time between, awaiting the days near the end; for they will argue that then only must they attend to themselves. Therefore also has He been silent of the time when each shall die, lest men, being elated on the ground of knowledge, should immediately neglect themselves for the greater part of their time. Both then, the end of all things and the limit of each of us has the Word concealed from us (for in the end of all is the end of each, and in the end of each the end of all is comprehended), that, whereas it is uncertain and always in prospect, we may advance day by day as if summoned, reaching forward to the things before us and forgetting the things behind. For who, knowing the day of the end, would not be dilatory with the interval? But, if ignorant, would not be ready day by day? It was on this account that the Saviour added, 'Watch therefore, for you know not what hour your Lord does come;' and, 'In such an hour as you think not, the Son of man comes Matthew 24:42; Luke 12:40.' For the advantage then which comes of ignorance has He said this; for in saying it, He wishes that we should always be prepared; 'for you,' He says, 'know not; but I, the Lord, know when I come, though the Arians do not wait for Me, who am the Word of the Father.'

50. The Lord then, knowing what is good for us beyond ourselves, thus secured the disciples; and they, being thus taught, set right those of Thessalonica when likely on this point to run into error. However, since Christ's enemies do not yield even to these considerations, I wish, though knowing that they have a heart harder than Pharaoh, to ask them again concerning this. In Paradise God asks, 'Adam, where are You ' and He inquires of Cain also, 'Where is Abel your brother ?' What then say you to this? For if you think Him ignorant and therefore to have asked, you are already of the party of the Manichees, for this is their bold thought; but if, fearing the open name, you force yourselves to say, that He asks knowing, what is there extravagant or strange in the doctrine, that you should thus fall, on finding that the Son, in whom God then inquired, that same Son who now is clad in flesh,

inquires of the disciples as man? Unless forsooth, having become Manichees, you are willing to blame the question then put to Adam and all that you may give full play to your perverseness. For being exposed on all sides, you still make a whispering from the words of Luke, which are rightly said, but ill understood by you. And what this is, we must state, that so also their corrupt meaning may be shown.

51. Now Luke says, 'And Jesus advanced in wisdom and stature, and in grace with God and man Luke 2:52.' This then is the passage, and since they stumble in it, we are compelled to ask them, like the Pharisees and the Sadducees, of the person concerning whom Luke speaks. And the case stands thus. Is Jesus Christ man, as all other men, or is He God bearing flesh? If then He is an ordinary man as the rest, then let Him, as a man, advance; this however is the sentiment of the Samosatene, which virtually indeed you entertain also, though in name you deny it because of men. But if He be God bearing flesh, as He truly is, and 'the Word became flesh,' and being God descended upon earth, what advance had He who existed

equal to God? Or how had the Son increase, being ever in the Father? For if He who was ever in the Father, advanced, what, I ask, is there beyond the Father from which His advance might be made? Next it is suitable here to repeat what was said upon the point of His receiving and being glorified. If He advanced when He became man, it is plain that, before He became man, He was imperfect; and rather the flesh became to Him a cause of perfection, than He to the flesh. And again, if, as being the Word, He advances, what has He more to become than Word and Wisdom and Son and God's Power? For the Word is all these, of which if one can anyhow partake as it were one ray, such a man becomes all perfect among men, and equal to Angels. For Angels, and Archangels, and Dominions, and all the Powers, and Thrones, as partaking the Word, behold always the face of His Father. How then does He who to others supplies perfection, Himself advance later than they? For Angels even ministered to His human birth, and the passage from Luke comes later than the ministration of the Angels. How then at all can it even come into thought of man? Or how did Wisdom advance in wisdom? Or how did He who to others gives grace (as Paul says in every Epistle, knowing that through

Him grace is given, 'The grace of our Lord Jesus Christ be with you all'), how did He advance in grace? For either let them say that the Apostle is untrue, and presume to say that the Son is not Wisdom, or else if He is Wisdom as Solomon said, and if Paul wrote, 'Christ God's Power and God's Wisdom,' of what advance did Wisdom admit further?

52. For men, creatures as they are, are capable in a certain way of reaching forward and advancing in virtue. Enoch, for instance, was thus translated, and Moses increased and was perfected; and Isaac 'by advancing became great;' and the Apostle said that he 'reached forth Philippians 3:13 ' day by day to what was before him. For each had room for advancing, looking to the step before him. But the Son of God, who is One and Only, what room had He for reaching forward? For all things advance by looking at Him; and He, being One and Only, is in the Only Father, from whom again He does not reach forward, but in Him abides ever. To men then belongs advance; but the Son of God, since He could not advance, being perfect in the Father, humbled Himself for us, that in His humbling we

on the other hand might be able to increase. And our increase is no other than the renouncing things sensible, and coming to the Word Himself; since His humbling is nothing else than His taking our flesh. It was not then the Word, considered as the Word, who advanced; who is perfect from the perfect Father , who needs nothing, nay brings forward others to an advance; but humanly is He here also said to advance, since advance belongs to man. Hence the Evangelist, speaking with cautious exactness , has mentioned stature in the advance; but being Word and God He is not measured by stature, which belongs to bodies. Of the body then is the advance; for, it advancing, in it advanced also the manifestation of the Godhead to those who saw it. And, as the Godhead was more and more revealed, by so much more did His grace as man increase before all men. For as a child He was carried to the Temple; and when He became a boy, He remained there, and questioned the priests about the Law. And by degrees His body increasing, and the Word manifesting Himself in it, He is confessed henceforth by Peter first, then also by all, 'Truly this is the Son of God ;' however wilfully the Jews, both the ancient and these modern , shut fast their eyes, lest they see that to advance in wisdom is not the advance of Wisdom Itself, but rather the manhood's advance in It. For 'Jesus advanced in wisdom and grace;' and, if we may speak what is explanatory as well as true, He advanced in Himself; for 'Wisdom built herself a house,' and in herself she gave the house advancement.

53. (What moreover is this advance that is spoken of, but, as I said before, the deifying and grace imparted from Wisdom to men, sin being obliterated in them and their inward corruption, according to their likeness and relationship to the flesh of the Word?) For thus, the body increasing in stature, there developed in it the manifestation of the Godhead also, and to all was it displayed that the body was God's Temple , and that God was in the body. And if they urge, that 'The Word become flesh' is called Jesus, and refer to Him the term 'advanced,' they must be told that neither does this impair the Father's Light , which is the Son, but that it still shows that the Word has become man, and bore true flesh. And as we said that He suffered in the flesh, and hungered in the flesh, and was fatigued in the flesh, so also reasonably

may He be said to have advanced in the flesh; for neither did the advance, such as we have described it, take place with the Word external to the flesh, for in Him was the flesh which advanced and His is it called, and that as before, that man's advance might abide and fail not, because of the Word which is with it. Neither then was the advance the Word's, nor was the flesh Wisdom, but the flesh became the body of Wisdom. Therefore, as we have already said, not Wisdom, as Wisdom, advanced in respect of Itself; but the manhood advanced in Wisdom, transcending by degrees human nature, and being deified, and becoming and appearing to all as the organ of Wisdom for the operation and the shining forth of the Godhead. Wherefore neither said he, 'The Word advanced,' but Jesus, by which Name the Lord was called when He became man; so that the advance is of the human nature in such wise as we explained above.

Chapter XXIX. Texts Explained; Twelfthly, Matthew XXVI. 39; John XII. 27, Etc.

Arianinferences are against the Regula Fidei, as before. He wept and the like, as man. Other texts prove Him God. God could not fear. He feared because His flesh feared.

54. Therefore as, when the flesh advanced, He is said to have advanced, because the body was His own, so also what is said at the season of His death, that He was troubled, that He wept, must be taken in the same sense. For they, going up and down , as if thereby recommending their heresy anew, allege; Behold, 'He wept,' and said, 'Now is My soul troubled,' and He besought that the cup might pass away; how then, if He so spoke, is He God, and Word of the Father? Yea, it is written that He wept, O God's enemies, and that He said, 'I am troubled,' and on the Cross He said, 'Eloi, Eloi, lama sabachthani,' that is, 'My God, My God, why have You forsaken Me?' and He besought that the cup might pass away. Thus certainly it is written; but again I would ask you (for the same rejoinder must of necessity be made to each of your objections), If

the speaker is mere man, let him weep and fear death, as being man; but if He is the Word in flesh (for one must not be reluctant to repeat), whom had He to fear being God? Or wherefore should He fear death, who was Himself Life, and was rescuing others from death? Or how, whereas He said, 'Fear not him that kills the body Luke 12:4,' should He Himself fear? And how should He who said to Abraham, 'Fear not, for I am with you,' and encouraged Moses against Pharaoh, and said to the son of Nun, 'Be strong, and of a good courage ,' Himself feel terror before Herod and Pilate? Further, He who succours others against fear (for 'the Lord,' says Scripture, 'is on my side, I will not fear what man shall do unto me '), did He fear governors, mortal men? Did He who Himself had come against death, feel terror of death? Is it not both unseemly and irreligious to say that He was terrified at death or hades, whom the keepers of the gates of hades saw and shuddered? But if, as you would hold, the Word was in terror wherefore, when He spoke long before of the conspiracy of the Jews, did He not flee, nay said when actually sought, 'I am He?' for He could have avoided death, as He said, 'I have power to lay down My life, and I have power to take it again;' and 'No one takes it from Me.'

55. But these affections were not proper to the nature of the Word, as far as He was Word; but in the flesh which was thus affected was the Word, O Christ's enemies and unthankful Jews! For He said not all this prior to the flesh; but when the 'Word became flesh,' and has become man, then is it written that He said this, that is, humanly. Surely He of whom this is written was He who raised Lazarus from the dead, and made the water wine, and vouchsafed sight to the man born blind, and said, 'I and My Father are one.' If then they make His human attributes a ground for low thoughts concerning the Son of God, nay consider Him altogether man from the earth, and not from heaven, wherefore not from His divine works recognise the Word who is in the Father, and henceforward renounce their self-willed irreligion? For they are given to see, how He who did the works is the same as He who showed that His body was passible by His permitting it to weep and hunger, and to show other properties of a body. For while by means of such He made it known that, though God

impassible, He had taken a passible flesh; yet from the works He showed Himself the Word of God, who had afterwards become man, saying, Though you believe not Me, beholding Me clad in a human body, yet believe the works, that you may know that I am in the Father, and the Father in Me. 'And Christ's enemies seem to me to show plain shamelessness and blasphemy;' for, when they hear 'I and the Father are one ,' they violently distort the sense, and separate the unity of the Father and the Son; but reading of His tears or sweat or sufferings, they do not advert to His body, but on account of these rank in the creation Him by whom the creation was made. What then is left for them to differ from the Jews in? For as the Jews blasphemously ascribed God's works to Beelzebub, so also will these, ranking with the creatures the Lord who wrought those works, undergo the same condemnation as theirs without mercy.

56. But they ought, when they hear 'I and the Father are one,' to see in Him the oneness of the Godhead and the propriety of the Father's Essence; and again when they hear, 'He wept' and the like, to say that these are proper to

the body; especially since on each side they have an intelligible ground, viz. that this is written as of God and that with reference to His manhood. For in the incorporeal, the properties of body had not been, unless He had taken a body corruptible and mortal ; for mortal was Holy Mary, from whom was His body. Wherefore of necessity when He was in a body suffering, and weeping, and toiling, these things which are proper to the flesh, are ascribed to Him together with the body. If then He wept and was troubled, it was not the Word, considered as the Word, who wept and was troubled, but it was proper to the flesh; and if too He besought that the cup might pass away, it was not the Godhead that was in terror, but this affection too was proper to the manhood. And that the words 'Why have You forsaken Me?' are His, according to the foregoing explanations (though He suffered nothing, for the Word was impassible), is notwithstanding declared by the Evangelists; since the Lord became man, and these things are done and said as from a man, that He might Himself lighten these very sufferings of the flesh, and free it from them. Whence neither can the Lord be forsaken by the Father, who is ever in the Father, both before He spoke, and when He uttered this cry. Nor is it lawful to say that the Lord was in terror, at whom the keepers of hell's gates shuddered and set open hell, and the graves did gape, and many bodies of the saints arose and appeared to their own people. Therefore be every heretic dumb, nor dare to ascribe terror to the Lord whom death, as a serpent, flees, at whom demons tremble, and the sea is in alarm; for whom the heavens are rent and all the powers are shaken. For behold when He says, 'Why have You forsaken Me?' the Father showed that He was ever and even then in Him; for the earth knowing its Lord who spoke, straightway trembled, and the veil was rent, and the sun was hidden, and the rocks were torn asunder, and the graves, as I have said, did gape, and the dead in them arose; and, what is wonderful, they who were then present and had before denied Him, then seeing these signs, confessed that 'truly He was the Son of God.'

57. And as to His saying, 'If it be possible, let the cup pass,' observe how, though He thus spoke, He rebuked Peter, saying, 'You savour not the things that be of God, but those that be of men.' For He willed what He deprecated, for therefore had He come; but His was the

willing (for for it He came), but the terror belonged to the flesh. Wherefore as man He utters this speech also, and yet both were said by the Same, to show that He was God, willing in Himself, but when He had become man, having a flesh that was in terror. For the sake of this flesh He combined His own will with human weakness , that destroying this affection He might in turn make man undaunted in face of death. Behold then a thing strange indeed! He to whom Christ's enemies impute words of terror, He by that so-called tenor renders men undaunted and fearless. And so the Blessed Apostles after Him from such words of His conceived so great a contempt of death, as not even to care for those who questioned them, but to answer, 'We ought to obey God rather than men Acts 5:29.' And the other Holy Martyrs were so bold, as to think that they were rather passing to life than undergoing death. Is it not extravagant then, to admire the courage of the servants of the Word, yet to say that the Word Himself was in terror, through whom they despised death? But from that most enduring purpose and courage of the Holy Martyrs is shown, that the Godhead was not in terror, but the Saviour took away our terror. For as He abolished death by death, and by human means all human evils, so by this so-called terror did He remove our terror, and brought about that never more should men fear death. His word and deed go together. For human were the sayings, 'Let the cup pass,' and 'Why have You forsaken Me?' and divine the act whereby the Same did cause the sun to fail and the dead to rise. Again He said humanly, 'Now is My soul troubled;' and He said divinely, 'I have power to lay down My life, and power to take it again.' For to be troubled was proper to the flesh, and to have power to lay down His life and take it again, when He will, was no property of men but of the Word's power. For man dies, not by his own power, but by necessity of nature and against his will; but the Lord, being Himself immortal, but having a mortal flesh, had power, as God, to become separate from the body and to take it again, when He would. Concerning this too speaks David in the Psalm, 'You shall not leave My soul in hades, neither shall Thou suffer Your Holy One to see corruption.' For it beseemed that the flesh, corruptible as it was, should no longer after its own nature remain mortal, but because of the Word who had put it on, should abide incorruptible. For as He, having come in our body, was conformed to our condition, so we, receiving Him, partake of the immortality that is from Him.

58. Idle then is the excuse for stumbling, and petty the notions concerning the Word, of these Ario-maniacs, because it is written, 'He was troubled,' and 'He wept.' For they seem not even to have human feeling, if they are thus ignorant of man's nature and properties; which do but make it the greater wonder, that the Word should be in such a suffering flesh, and neither prevented those who were conspiring against Him, nor took vengeance of those who were putting Him to death, though He was able, He who hindered some from dying, and raised others from the dead. And He let His own body suffer, for therefore did He come, as I said before, that in the flesh He might suffer, and thenceforth the flesh might be made impassible and immortal , and that, as we have many times said, contumely and other troubles might determine upon Him and come short of others after Him, being by Him annulled utterly; and that henceforth men might for ever abide incorruptible, as a temple of the Word. Had Christ's enemies thus dwelt on these thoughts, and recognised the ecclesiastical scope as an anchor for the faith, they would

not have made shipwreck of the faith, nor been so shameless as to resist those who would fain recover them from their fall, and to deem those as enemies who are admonishing them to be religious.

Chapter XXX. Objections Continued, as in Chapters VII.-X.

Whether the Son is begotten of the Father's will? This virtually the same as whether once He was not? And used by the Arians to introduce the latter question. The Regula Fidei answers it at once in the negative by contrary texts. The Arians follow the Valentinians in maintaining a precedent will; which really is only exercised by God towards creatures. Instances from Scripture. Inconsistency of Asterius. If the Son by will, there must be another Word before Him. If God is good, or exist, by His will, then is the Son by His will. If He willed to have reason or wisdom, then is His Word and Wisdom at His will. The Son is the Living Will, and has all titles which denote connaturality. That will which the Father has to the Son, the Son has to the Father.

The Father wills the Son and the Son wills the Father

58. (continued). But, as it seems, a heretic is a wicked thing in truth, and in every respect his heart is depraved and irreligious. For behold, though convicted on all points, and shown to be utterly bereft of understanding, they feel no shame; but as the hydra of Gentile fable, when its former serpents were destroyed, gave birth to fresh ones, contending against the slayer of the old by the production of new, so also they, hostile and hateful to God, as hydras, losing their life in the objections which they advance, invent for themselves other questions Judaic and foolish, and new expedients, as if Truth were their enemy, thereby to show the rather that they are Christ's opponents in all things.

59. After so many proofs against them, at which even the devil who is their father had himself been abashed and gone back, again as from their perverse heart they mutter forth other expedients, sometimes in whispers, sometimes with the drone of gnats; 'Be it so,' say they; 'interpret these

places thus, and gain the victory in reasonings and proofs; still you must say that the Son has received being from the Father at His will and pleasure;' for thus they deceive many, putting forward the will and the pleasure of God. Now if any of those who believe aright were to say this in simplicity, there would be no cause to be suspicious of the expression, the right intention prevailing over that somewhat simple use of words. But since the phrase is from the heretics and the words of heretics are suspicious, and, as it is written, 'The wicked are deceitful,' and 'The words of the wicked are deceit ,' even though they but make signs , for their heart is depraved, come let us examine this phrase also, lest, though convicted on all sides, still, as hydras, they invent a fresh word, and by such clever language and specious evasion, they sow again that irreligion of theirs in another way. For he who says, 'The Son came to be at the Divine will,' has the same meaning as another who says, 'Once He was not,' and 'The Son came to be out of nothing,' and 'He is a creature.' But since they are now ashamed of these phrases, these crafty ones have endeavoured to convey their meaning in another way, putting forth the word 'will,' as cuttlefish their blackness, thereby to blind the simple , and to keep in mind their peculiar heresy. For whence bring they 'by will and pleasure?' or from what Scripture? Let them say, who are so suspicious in their words and so inventive of irreligion. For the Father who revealed from heaven His own Word, declared, 'This is My beloved Son.' and by David He said, 'My heart uttered a good Word.' and John He bade say, 'In the beginning was the Word.' and David says in the Psalm, 'With You is the well of life, and in Your light shall we see light;' and the Apostle writes, 'Who being the Radiance of Glory,' and again, 'Who being in the form of God,' and, 'Who is the Image of the invisible God.'

60. All everywhere tell us of the being of the Word, but none of His being 'by will,' nor at all of His making; but they, where, I ask, did they find will or pleasure 'precedent ' to the Word of God, unless forsooth, leaving the Scriptures, they simulate the perverseness of Valentinus? For Ptolemy the Valentinian said that the Unoriginate had a pair of attributes, Thought and Will, and first He thought and then He willed; and what He thought, He could not put forth , unless when the power of the Will

was added. Thence the Arians taking a lesson, wish will and pleasure to precede the Word. For them then, let them rival the doctrine of Valentinus; but we, when we read the divine discourses, found 'He was' applied to the Son, but of Him only did we hear as being in the Father and the Father's Image; while in the case of things originate only, since also by nature these things once were not, but afterwards came to be , did we recognise a precedent will and pleasure, David saying in the hundred and thirteenth Psalm, 'As for our God He is in heaven, He has done whatsoever pleased Him,' and in the hundred and tenth, 'The works of the Lord are great, sought out unto all His good pleasure;' and again, in the hundred and thirty-fourth, 'Whatsoever the Lord pleased, that did He in heaven, and in earth, and in the sea, and in all deep places.' If then He be work and thing made, and one among others, let Him, as others, be said 'by will?' to have come to be, and Scripture shows that these are thus brought into being. And Asterius, the advocate for the heresy, acquiesces, when he thus writes, 'For if it be unworthy of the Framer of all, to make at pleasure, let His being pleased be removed equally in the case of all, that His Majesty be preserved unimpaired. Or if it be befitting God to will, then let this better way obtain in the case of the first Offspring. For it is not possible that it should be fitting for one and the same God to make things at His pleasure, and not at His will also.' In spite of the Sophist having introduced abundant irreligion in his words, namely, that the Offspring and the thing made are the same, and that the Son is one offspring out of all offsprings that are, He ends with the conclusion that it is fitting to say that the works are by will and pleasure.

61. Therefore if He be other than all things, as has been above shown , and through Him the works rather came to be, let not 'by will?' be applied to Him, or He has similarly come to be as the things consist which through Him come to be. For Paul, whereas he was not before, became afterwards an Apostle 'by the will of God ;' and our own calling, as itself once not being, but now taking place afterwards, is preceded by will, and, as Paul himself says again, has been made 'according to the good pleasure of His will Ephesians 1:5.' And what Moses relates, 'Let there be light,' and 'Let the earth appear,' and 'Let Us make man,' is, I think, according to what has gone before ,

significant of the will of the Agent. For things which once were not but happened afterwards from external causes, these the Framer counsels to make; but His own Word begotten from Him by nature, concerning Him He did not counsel beforehand; for in Him the Father makes, in Him frames, other things whatever He counsels; as also James the Apostle teaches, saying, 'Of His own will begot He us with the Word of truth James 1:18.' Therefore the Will of God concerning all things, whether they be begotten again or are brought into being at the first, is in His Word, in whom He both makes and begets again what seems right to Him; as the Apostle 1 Thessalonians 5:18 again signifies, writing to Thessalonica; 'for this is the will of God in Christ Jesus concerning you.' But if, in whom He makes, in Him also is the will, and in Christ is the pleasure of the Father, how can He, as others, come into being by will and pleasure? For if He too came to be as you maintain, by will, it follows that the will concerning Him consists in some other Word, through whom He in turn comes to be; for it has been shown that God's will is not in the things which He brings into being, but in Him through whom and in whom all things made are brought to be. Next, since it is all one to say 'By will?' and Once

He was not,' let them make up their minds to say, 'Once He was not,' that, perceiving with shame that times are signified by the latter, they may understand that to say 'by will?' is to place times before the Son; for counselling goes before things which once were not, as in the case of all creatures. But if the Word is the Framer of the creatures, and He coexists with the Father, how can to counsel precede the Everlasting as if He were not? For if counsel precedes, how through Him are all things? For rather He too, as one among others is by will begotten to be a Son, as we too were made sons by the Word of Truth; and it rests, as was said, to seek another Word, through whom He too has come to be, and was begotten together with all things, which were according to God's pleasure.

62. If then there is another Word of God, then be the Son originated by a word; but if there be not, as is the case, but all things by Him have come to be, which the Father has willed, does not this expose the many-headed craftiness of these men? That feeling shame at saying 'work,' and 'creature,' and 'God's Word was not before His generation,' yet in another way they assert that He is a

creature, putting forward 'will,' and saying, 'Unless He has by will come to be, therefore God had a Son by necessity and against His good pleasure.' And who is it then who imposes necessity on Him, O men most wicked, who draw everything to the purpose of your heresy? For what is contrary to will they see; but what is greater and transcends it has escaped their perception. For as what is beside purpose is contrary to will, so what is according to nature transcends and precedes counselling. A man by counsel builds a house, but by nature he begets a son; and what is in building began to come into being at will, and is external to the maker; but the son is proper offspring of the father's essence, and is not external to him; wherefore neither does he counsel concerning him, lest he appear to counsel about himself. As far then as the Son transcends the creature, by so much does what is by nature transcend the will. And they, on hearing of Him, ought not to measure by will what is by nature; forgetting however that they are hearing about God's Son, they dare to apply human contrarieties in the instance of God, 'necessity' and 'beside purpose,' to be able thereby to deny that there is a true Son of God. For let them tell us themselves — that God is good and merciful, does this attach to Him by will or not? If by will, we must consider that He began to be good, and that His not being good is possible; for to counsel and choose implies an inclination two ways, and is incidental to a rational nature. But if it be too unseemly that He should be called good and merciful upon will, then what they have said themselves must be retorted on them —'therefore by necessity and not at His pleasure He is good;' and, 'who is it that imposes this necessity on Him?' But if it be unseemly to speak of necessity in the case of God, and therefore it is by nature that He is good, much more is He, and more truly, Father of the Son by nature and not by will.

63. Moreover let them answer us this:— (for against their shamelessness I wish to urge a further question, bold indeed, but with a religious intent; be propitious, O Lord!)— the Father Himself, does He exist, first having counselled, then being pleased, or before counselling? For since they are so bold in the instance of the Word, they must receive the like answer, that they may know that this their presumption reaches even to the Father Himself. If then they shall themselves take counsel about will, and say

that even He is from will, what then was He before He counselled, or what gained He, as you consider, after counselling? But if such a question be unseemly and self-destructive, and shocking even to ask (for it is enough only to hear God's Name for us to know and understand that He is He that Is), will it not also be against reason to have parallel thoughts concerning the Word of God, and to make pretences of will and pleasure? For it is enough in like manner only to hear the Name of the Word, to know and understand that He who is God not by will, has not by will but by nature His own Word. And does it not surpass all conceivable madness, to entertain the thought only, that God Himself counsels and considers and chooses and proceeds to have a good pleasure, that He be not without Word and without Wisdom, but have both? For He seems to be considering about Himself, who counsels about what is proper to His Essence. There being then much blasphemy in such a thought, it will be religious to say that things originate have come to be 'by favour and will,' but the Son is not a work of will, nor has come after , as the creation, but is by nature the own Offspring of God's Essence. For being the own Word of the Father, He allows us not to account of will as before

Himself, since He is Himself the Father's Living Counsel, and Power, and Framer of the things which seemed good to the Father. And this is what He says of Himself in the Proverbs; 'Counsel is mine and security, mine is understanding, and mine strength Proverbs 8:14.' For as, although Himself the 'Understanding,' in which He prepared the heavens, and Himself 'Strength and Power' (for Christ is 'God's Power and God's Wisdom' 1 Corinthians 1:24), He here has altered the terms and said, 'Mine is understanding' and 'Mine strength,' so while He says, 'Mine is counsel,' He must Himself be the Living Counsel of the Father; as we have learned from the Prophet also, that He becomes 'the Angel of great Counsel Isaiah 9:6,' and was called the good pleasure of the Father; for thus we must refute them, using human illustrations concerning God.

64. Therefore if the works subsist 'by will and favour,' and the whole creature is made 'at God's good pleasure,' and Paul was called to be an Apostle 'by the will of God,' and our calling has come about 'by His good pleasure and will,' and all things have come into being through the Word, He

is external to the things which have come to be by will, but rather is Himself the Living Counsel of the Father, by which all these things have come to be; by which David also gives thanks in the seventy-second Psalm. 'You have holden me by my right hand; You shall guide me with Your Counsel.' How then can the Word, being the Counsel and Good Pleasure of the Father, come into being Himself 'by good pleasure and will,' like every one else? Unless, as I said before, in their madness they repeat that He has come into being through Himself, or through some other. Who then is it through whom He has come to be? Let them fashion another Word; and let them name another Christ, rivalling the doctrine of Valentinus ; for Scripture it is not. And though they fashion another, yet assuredly he too comes into being through some one; and so, while we are thus reckoning up and investigating the succession of them, the many-headed heresy of the Atheists is discovered to issue in polytheism and madness unlimited; in the which, wishing the Son to be a creature and from nothing, they imply the same thing in other words by pretending the words will and pleasure, which rightly belong to things originate and creatures. Is it not irreligious then to impute the characteristics of things originate to the Framer of all? And is it not blasphemous to say that will was in the Father before the Word? For if will precedes in the Father, the Son's words are not true, 'I in the Father.' or even if He is in the Father, yet He will hold but a second place, and it became Him not to say 'I in the Father,' since will was before Him, in which all things were brought into being and He Himself subsisted, as you hold. For though He excel in glory, He is not the less one of the things which by will come into being. And, as we have said before, if it be so, how is He Lord and they servants ? But He is Lord of all, because He is one with the Father's Lordship; and the creation is all in bondage, since it is external to the Oneness of the Father, and, whereas it once was not, was brought to be.

65. Moreover, if they say that the Son is by will, they should say also that He came to be by understanding; for I consider understanding and will to be the same. For what a man counsels, about that also he has understanding; and what he has in understanding, that also he counsels. Certainly the Saviour Himself has made them correspond, as being cognate, when He says, 'Counsel is mine and

security; mine is understanding, and mine strength Proverbs 8:14.' For as strength and security are the same (for they mean one attribute), so we may say that Understanding and Counsel are the same, which is the Lord. But these irreligious men are unwilling that the Son should be Word and Living Counsel; but they fable that there is with God , as if a habit , coming and going , after the manner of men, understanding, counsel, wisdom; and they leave nothing undone, and they put forward the 'Thought' and 'Will' of Valentinus, so that they may but separate the Son from the Father, and may call Him a creature instead of the proper Word of the Father. To them then must be said what was said to Simon Magus; 'the irreligion of Valentinus perish with you Acts 8:20;' and let every one rather trust to Solomon, who says, that the Word is Wisdom and Understanding. For he says, 'The Lord by Wisdom founded the earth, by Understanding He established the heavens.' And as here by Understanding, so in the Psalms, 'By the Word of the Lord were the heavens made.' And as by the Word the heavens, so 'He has done whatsoever pleased Him.' And as the Apostle writes to Thessalonians, 'the will of God is in Christ Jesus.' The Son of God then, He is the 'Word' and the 'Wisdom;' He the 'Understanding' and the Living 'Counsel;' and in Him is the 'Good Pleasure of the Father.' He is 'Truth' and 'Light' and 'Power' of the Father. But if the Will of God is Wisdom and Understanding, and the Son is Wisdom, he who says that the Son is 'by will,' says virtually that Wisdom has come into being in wisdom, and the Son is made in a son, and the Word created through the Word ; which is incompatible with God and is opposed to His Scriptures. For the Apostle proclaims the Son to be the own Radiance and Expression, not of the Father's will , but of His Essence Itself, saying, 'Who being the Radiance of His glory and the Expression of His Subsistence Hebrews 1:3.' But if, as we have said before, the Father's Essence and Subsistence be not from will, neither, as is very plain, is what is proper to the Father's Subsistence from will; for such as, and so as, that Blessed Subsistence, must also be the proper Offspring from It. And accordingly the Father Himself said not, 'This is the Son originated at My will,' nor 'the Son whom I have by My favour,' but simply 'My Son,' and more than that, 'in whom I am well pleased;' meaning by this, This is the Son by nature; and 'in Him is lodged My will about what pleases Me.'

66. Since then the Son is by nature and not by will, is He without the pleasure of the Father and not with the Father's will? No, verily; but the Son is with the pleasure of the Father, and, as He says Himself, 'The Father loves the Son, and shows Him all things.' For as not 'from will?' did He begin to be good, nor yet is good without will and pleasure (for what He is, that also is His pleasure), so also that the Son should be, though it came not 'from will,' yet it is not without His pleasure or against His purpose. For as His own Subsistence is by His pleasure, so also the Son, being proper to His Essence, is not without His pleasure. Be then the Son the object of the Father's pleasure and love; and thus let every one religiously account of the pleasure and the not-unwillingness of God. For by that good pleasure wherewith the Son is the object of the Father's pleasure, is the Father the object of the Son's love, pleasure, and honour; and one is the good pleasure which is from Father in Son, so that here too we may contemplate the Son in the Father and the Father in the Son. Let no one then, with Valentinus, introduce a precedent will; nor let any one, by this pretence of 'counsel,' intrude between the Only Father and the Only Word; for it were madness to place will and consideration

between them. For it is one thing to say, 'Of will He came to be,' and another, that the Father has love and good pleasure towards His Son who is His own by nature. For to say, 'Of will He came to be,' in the first place implies that once He was not; and next it implies an inclination two ways, as has been said, so that one might suppose that the Father could even not will the Son. But to say of the Son, 'He might not have been,' is an irreligious presumption reaching even to the Essence of the Father, as if what is His own might not have been. For it is the same as saying, 'The Father might not have been good.' And as the Father is always good by nature, so He is always generative by nature; and to say, 'The Father's good pleasure is the Son,' and 'The Word's good pleasure is the Father,' implies, not a precedent will, but genuineness of nature, and propriety and likeness of Essence. For as in the case of the radiance and light one might say, that there is no will preceding radiance in the light, but it is its natural offspring, at the pleasure of the light which begot it, not by will and consideration, but in nature and truth, so also in the instance of the Father and the Son, one might rightly say, that the Father has love and good pleasure towards the Son, and the Son has love and good pleasure towards the Father.

67. Therefore call not the Son a work of good pleasure; nor bring in the doctrine of Valentinus into the Church; but be He the Living Counsel, and Offspring in truth and nature, as the Radiance from the Light. For thus has the Father spoken, 'My heart uttered a good Word.' and the Son conformably, 'I in the Father and the Father in Me.' But if the Word be in the heart, where is will? And if the Son in the Father, where is good pleasure? And if He be Will Himself, how is counsel in Will? It is unseemly; lest the Word come into being in a word, and the Son in a son, and Wisdom in a wisdom, as has been repeatedly said. For the Son is the Father's All; and nothing was in the Father before the Word; but in the Word is will also, and through Him the objects of will are carried into effect, as holy Scriptures have shown. And I could wish that the irreligious men, having fallen into such want of reason as to be considering about will, would now ask their childbearing women no more, whom they used to ask, 'Had you a son before conceiving him?' but the father,

'Do ye become fathers by counsel, or by the natural law of your will.' or 'Are your children like your nature and essence?' that, even from fathers they may learn shame, from whom they assumed this proposition about birth, and from whom they hoped to gain knowledge in point. For they will reply to them, 'What we beget, is like, not our good pleasure, but like ourselves; nor become we parents by previous counsel, but to beget is proper to our nature; since we too are images of our fathers.' Either then let them condemn themselves, and cease asking women about the Son of God, or let them learn from them, that the Son is begotten not by will, but in nature and truth. Becoming and suitable to them is a refutation from human instances, since the perverse-minded men dispute in a human way concerning the Godhead. Why then are Christ's enemies still mad? For this, as well as their other pretences, is shown and proved to be mere fantasy and fable; and on this account, they ought, however late, contemplating the precipice of folly down which they have fallen, to rise again from the depth and to flee the snare of the devil, as we admonish them. For Truth is loving unto men and cries continually, 'If because of My clothing of the body ye believe Me not, yet believe the works, that you may know that I am in the Father and the Father in Me, and I and the Father are one, and He that has seen Me has seen the Father.' But the Lord according to His wont is loving to man, and would fain 'help them that are fallen,' as the praise of David says; but the irreligious men, not desirous to hear the Lord's voice, nor bearing to see Him acknowledged by all as God and God's Son, go about, miserable men, as beetles, seeking with their father the devil pretexts for irreligion. What pretexts then, and whence will they be able next to find? Unless they borrow blasphemies of Jews and Caiaphas, and take atheism from Gentiles? For the divine Scriptures are closed to them, and from every part of them they are refuted as insensate and Christ's enemies.

Discourse IV

1-5. The substantiality of the Word proved from Scripture. If the One Origin be substantial, Its Word is substantial. Unless the Word and Son be a second Origin, or a work, or an attribute (and so God be compounded), or at the same time Father, or involve a second nature in God, He is from the Father's Essence and distinct from Him. Illustration of John 10:30, drawn from Deuteronomy 4:4.

1. The Word is God from God; for 'the Word was God John 1:1,' and again, 'Of whom are the Fathers, and of whom Christ, who is God over all, blessed forever. Amen Romans 9:5.' And since Christ is God from God, and God's Word, Wisdom, Son, and Power, therefore but One God is declared in the divine Scriptures. For the Word, being Son of the One God, is referred to Him of whom also He is; so that Father and Son are two, yet the Monad of the Godhead is indivisible and inseparable. And thus too we preserve One Beginning of Godhead and not two Beginnings, whence there is strictly a Monarchy. And of this very Beginning the Word is by nature Son, not as if another beginning, subsisting by Himself, nor having

come into being externally to that Beginning, lest from that diversity a Dyarchy and Polyarchy should ensue; but of the one Beginning He is own Son, own Wisdom, own Word, existing from It. For, according to John, 'in' that 'Beginning was the Word, and the Word was with God,' for the Beginning was God; and since He is from It, therefore also 'the Word was God.' And as there is one Beginning and therefore one God, so one is that Essence and Subsistence which indeed and truly and really is, and which said 'I am that I am Exodus 3:14,' and not two, that there be not two Beginnings; and from the One, a Son in nature and truth, is Its own Word, Its Wisdom, Its Power, and inseparable from It. And as there is not another essence, lest there be two Beginnings, so the Word which is from that One Essence has no dissolution, nor is a sound significative, but is an essential Word and essential Wisdom, which is the true Son. For were He not essential, God will be speaking into the air 1 Corinthians 14:9, and having a body, in nothing differently from men; but since He is not man, neither is His Word according to the infirmity of man. For as the Beginning is one Essence, so Its Word is one, essential, and subsisting, and Its Wisdom. For as He is God from God, and Wisdom from the Wise, and Word from the Rational, and Son from Father, so is He from Subsistence Subsistent, and from Essence Essential and Substantive, and Being from Being.

2. Since were He not essential Wisdom and substantive Word, and Son existing, but simply Wisdom and Word and Son in the Father, then the Father Himself would have a nature compounded of Wisdom and Word. But if so, the forementioned absurdities would follow; and He will be His own Father, and the Son begetting and begotten by Himself; or Word, Wisdom, Son, is a name only, and He does not subsist who owns, or rather who is, these titles. If then He does not subsist, the names are idle and empty, unless we say that God is Very Wisdom and Very Word. But if so, He is His own Father and Son; Father, when Wise, Son, when Wisdom; but these things are not in God as a certain quality; away with the dishonourable thought; for it will issue in this, that God is compounded of essence and quality. For whereas all quality is in essence, it will clearly follow that the Divine Monad, indivisible as it is, must be compound, being severed into essence and accident. We must ask then these

headstrong men; The Son was proclaimed as God's Wisdom and Word; how then is He such? If as a quality, the absurdity has been shown; but if God is that Very Wisdom, then it is the absurdity of Sabellius; therefore He is so, as an Offspring in a proper sense from the Father Himself, according to the illustration of light. For as there is light from fire, so from God is there a Word, and Wisdom from the Wise, and from the Father a Son. For in this way the Monad remains undivided and entire, and Its Son, Word not unessential, nor not subsisting, but essential truly. For were it not so, all that is said would be said notionally and verbally. But if we must avoid that absurdity, then is a true Word essential. For as there is a Father truly, so Wisdom truly. In this respect then they are two; not because, as Sabellius said, Father and Son are the same, but because the Father is Father and the Son Son, and they are one, because He is Son of the Essence of the Father by nature, existing as His own Word. This the Lord said, viz. 'I and the Father are One John 10:30;' for neither is the Word separated from the Father, nor was or is the Father ever Wordless; on this account He says, 'I in the Father and the Father in Me.'

3. And again, Christ is the Word of God. Did He then subsist by Himself, and subsisting, has He become joined to the Father, or did God make Him or call Him His Word? If the former, I mean if He subsisted by Himself and is God, then there are two Beginnings; and moreover, as is plain, He is not the Father's own, as being not of the Father, but of Himself. But if on the contrary He be made externally, then is He a creature. It remains then to say that He is from God Himself; but if so, that which is from another is one thing, and that from which it is, is a second; according to this then there are two. But if they be not two, but the names belong to the same, cause and effect will be the same, and begotten and begetting, which has been shown absurd in the instance of Sabellius. But if He be from Him, yet not another, He will be both begetting and not begetting; begetting because He produces from Himself, and not begetting, because it is nothing other than Himself. But if so, the same is called Father and Son notionally. But if it be unseemly so to say, Father and Son must be two; and they are one, because the Son is not from without, but begotten of God. But if any one shrinks from saying 'Offspring,' and only says that the Word exists with God, let such a one fear lest, shrinking from what is

said in Scripture, he fall into absurdity, making God a being of double nature. For not granting that the Word is from the Monad, but simply as if He were joined to the Father, he introduces a twofold essence, and neither of them Father of the other. And the same of Power. And we may see this more clearly, if we consider it with reference to the Father; for there is One Father, and not two, but from that One the Son. As then there are not two Fathers, but One, so not two Beginnings, but One, and from that One the Son essential.

4. But the Arians we must ask contrariwise: (for the Sabellianisers must be confuted from the notion of a Son, and the Arians from that of a Father:) let us say then — Is God wise and not word-less: or on the contrary, is He wisdom-less and word-less? If the latter, there is an absurdity at once; if the former, we must ask, how is He wise and not word-less? Does He possess the Word and the Wisdom from without, or from Himself? If from without, there must be one who first gave to Him, and before He received He was wisdom-less and word-less. But if from Himself, it is plain that the Word is not from

nothing, nor once was not; for He was ever; since He of whom He is the Image, exists ever. But if they say that He is indeed wise and not word-less, but that He has in Himself His own wisdom and own word, and that, not Christ, but that by which He made Christ, we must answer that, if Christ in that word was brought to be, plainly so were all things; and it must be He of whom John says, 'All things were made by Him,' and the Psalmist, 'In Wisdom have You made them all.' And Christ will be found to speak untruly, 'I in the Father,' there being another in the Father. And 'the Word became flesh John 1:14 ' is not true according to them. For if He in whom 'all things came to be,' Himself became flesh, but Christ is not in the Father, as Word 'by whom all things came to be,' then Christ has not become flesh, but perhaps Christ was named Word. But if so, first, there will be another besides the name, next, all things were not by Him brought to be, but in that other, in whom Christ also was made. But if they say that Wisdom is in the Father as a quality or that He is Very Wisdom , the absurdities will follow already mentioned. For He will be compound , and will prove His own Son and Father. Moreover, we must confute and silence them on the ground, that the Word which is in God cannot be a creature nor out of nothing; but if once a Word be in God, then He must be Christ who says, 'I am in the Father and the Father in Me John 14:20,' who also is therefore the Only-begotten, since no other was begotten from Him. This is One Son, who is Word, Wisdom, Power; for God is not compounded of these, but is generative of them. For as He frames the creatures by the Word, so according to the nature of His own Essence has He the Word as an Offspring, through whom He frames and creates and dispenses all things. For by the Word and the Wisdom all things have come to be, and all things together remain according to His ordinance. And the same concerning the word 'Son;' if God be without Son , then is He without Work; for the Son is His Offspring through whom He works ; but if not, the same questions and the same absurdities will follow their audacity.

5. From Deuteronomy; 'But ye that did attach yourselves unto the Lord your God are alive every one of you this day Deuteronomy 4:4.' From this we may see the difference, and know that the Son of God is not a creature. For the

Son says, 'I and the Father are One,' and, 'I in the Father, and the Father in Me;' but things originate, when they make advance, are attached unto the Lord. The Word then is in the Father as being His own; but things originate, being external, are attached, as being by nature foreign, and attached by free choice. For a son which is by nature, is one with him who begot him; but he who is from without, and is made a son, will be attached to the family. Therefore he immediately adds, 'What nation is there so great who has God drawing near unto them ?' and elsewhere, 'I a God drawing near ;' for to things originate He draws near, as being strange to Him, but to the Son, as being His own, He does not draw near, but He is in Him. And the Son is not attached to the Father, but co-exists with Him; whence also Moses says again in the same Deuteronomy, 'You shall obey His voice, and apply yourselves unto Him Deuteronomy 13:4;' but what is applied, is applied from without.

6, 7. When the Word and Son hungered, wept, and was wearied, He acted as our Mediator, taking on Him what was ours, that He might impart to us what was His.

6. But in answer to the weak and human notion of the Arians, their supposing that the Lord is in want, when He says, 'Is given unto Me,' and 'I received,' and if Paul says, 'Wherefore He highly exalted Him,' and 'He set Him at the right hand ,' and the like, we must say that our Lord, being Word and Son of God, bore a body, and became Son of Man, that, having become Mediator between God, and men, He might minister the things of God to us, and ours to God. When then He is said to hunger and weep and weary, and to cry Eloi, Eloi, which are our human affections, He receives them from us and offers to the Father , interceding for us, that in Him they may be annulled. And when it is said, 'All power is given unto Me,' and 'I received,' and 'Wherefore God highly exalted Him,' these are gifts given from God to us through Him. For the Word was never in want , nor has come into being ; nor again were men sufficient to minister these things for themselves, but through the Word they are given to us; therefore, as if given to Him, they are imparted to us. For this was the reason of His becoming man, that, as being given to Him, they might pass on to us. For of such gifts mere man had not become worthy; and again the mere Word had not needed them ; the Word

then was united to us, and then imparted to us power, and highly exalted us. For the Word being in man, highly exalted man himself; and, when the Word was in man, man himself received. Since then, the Word being in flesh, man himself was exalted, and received power, therefore these things are referred to the Word, since they were given on His account; for on account of the Word in man were these gifts given. And as 'the Word became flesh John 1:14,' so also man himself received the gifts which came through the Word. For all that man himself has received, the Word is said to have received ; that it might be shown, that man himself, being unworthy to receive, as far as his own nature is concerned, yet has received because of the Word become flesh. Wherefore if anything be said to be given to the Lord, or the like, we must consider that it is given, not to Him as needing it, but to man himself through the Word. For every one interceding for another, receives the gift in his own person, not as needing, but on his account for whom he intercedes.

7. For as He takes our infirmities, not being infirm , and hungers not hungering, but sends up what is ours that it

may be abolished, so the gifts which come from God instead of our infirmities, does He too Himself receive, that man, being united to Him, may be able to partake them. Hence it is that the Lord says, 'All things whatsoever You have given Me, I have given them,' and again, 'I pray for them John 17:7-9.' For He prayed for us, taking on Him what is ours, and He was giving what He received. Since then, the Word being united to man himself, the Father, regarding Him, vouchsafed to man to be exalted, to have all power and the like; therefore are referred to the Word Himself, and are as if given to Him, all things which through Him we receive. For as He for our sake became man, so we for His sake are exalted. It is no absurdity then, if, as for our sake He humbled Himself, so also for our sake He is said to be highly exalted. So 'He gave to Him,' that is, 'to us for His sake;' 'and He highly exalted Him Philippians 2:9,' that is, 'us in Him.' And the Word Himself, when we are exalted, and receive, and are succoured, as if He Himself were exalted and received and were succoured, gives thanks to the Father, referring what is ours to Himself, and saying, 'All things, whatsoever You have given Me, I have given unto them John 17:7-8.'

8. Ariansdate the Son's beginning earlier than Marcellus, etc.

8. Eusebius and his fellows, that is, the Ario-maniacs, ascribing a beginning of being to the Son, yet pretend not to wish Him to have a beginning of kingship. But this is ridiculous; for he who ascribes to the Son a beginning of being, very plainly ascribes to Him also a beginning of reigning; so blind are they, confessing what they deny. Again, those who say that the Son is only a name, and that the Son of God, that is, the Word of the Father, is unessential and non-subsistent, pretend to be angry with those who say, 'Once He was not.' This is ridiculous also; for they who give Him no being at all, are angry with those who at least grant Him to be in time. Thus these also confess what they deny, in the act of censuring the others. And again Eusebius and his fellows, confessing a Son, deny that He is the Word by nature, and would have the Son called Word notionally; and the others confessing Him to be Word, deny Him to be Son, and would have the Word called Son notionally, equally void of footing.

9, 10. Unless Father and Son are two in name only, or as parts and so each imperfect, or two gods, they are coessential, one in Godhead, and the Son from the Father.

9. 'I and the Father are One John 10:30.' You say that the two things are one, or that the one has two names, or again that the one is divided into two. Now if the one is divided into two, that which is divided must need be a body, and neither part perfect, for each is a part and not a whole. But if again the one have two names, this is the expedient of Sabellius, who said that Son and Father were the same, and did away with either, the Father when there is a Son, and the Son when there is a Father. But if the two are one, then of necessity they are two, but one according to the Godhead, and according to the Son's coessentiality with the Father, and the Word's being from the Father Himself; so that there are two, because there is Father, and Son, namely the Word; and one because one God. For if not, He would have said, 'I am the Father,' or 'I and the Father am;' but, in fact, in the 'I' He signifies the Son, and in the 'And the Father,' Him who begot Him; and in the 'One' the one Godhead and His coessentiality. For the Same is not, as the Gentiles hold,

Wise and Wisdom, or the Same Father and Word; for it were unfit for Him to be His own Father, but the divine teaching knows Father and Son, and Wise and Wisdom, and God and Word; while it ever guards Him indivisible and inseparable and indissoluble in all respects.

10. But if any one, on hearing that the Father and the Son are two, misrepresent us as preaching two Gods (for this is what some feign to themselves, and immediately mock, saying, 'You hold two God.'), we must answer to such, If to acknowledge Father and Son, is to hold two Gods, it instantly follows that to confess but one we must deny the Son and Sabellianise. For if to speak of two is to fall into Gentilism, therefore if we speak of one, we must fall into Sabellianism. But this is not so; perish the thought! But, as when we say that Father and Son are two, we still confess one God, so when we say that there is one God, let us consider Father and Son two, while they are one in the Godhead, and in the Father's Word being indissoluble and indivisible and inseparable from Him. And let the fire and the radiance from it be a similitude of man, which are two in being and in appearance,

but one in that its radiance is from it indivisibly.

11, 12. Marcellus and his disciples, like Arians, say that the Word was, not indeed created, but issued, to create us, as if the Divine silence were a state of inaction, and when God spoke by the Word, He acted; or that there was a going forth and return of the Word; a doctrine which implies change and imperfection in Father and Son.

11. They fall into the same folly with the Arians; for Arians also say that He was created for us, that He might create us, as if God waited till our creation for His issue, as the one party say, or His creation, as the other. Arians then are more bountiful to us than to the Son; for they say, not we for His sake, but He for ours, came to be; that is, if He was therefore created, and subsisted, that God through Him might create us. And these, as irreligious or more so, give to God less than to us. For we oftentimes, even when silent, yet are active in thinking, so as to form the results of our thoughts into images; but God they would have inactive when silent, and when He speaks then to exert strength; if, that is, when silent He could not make, and when speaking He began to create. For it is just to ask

them, whether the Word, when He was in God, was perfect, so as to be able to make. If on the one hand He was imperfect, when in God, but by being begotten became perfect , we are the cause of His perfection, that is, if He has been begotten for us; for on our behalf He has received the power of making. But if He was perfect in God, so as to be able to make, His generation is superfluous; for He, even when in the Father, could frame the world; so that either He has not been begotten, or He was begotten, not for us, but because He is ever from the Father. For His generation evidences, not that we were created, but that He is from God; for He was even before our creation.

12. And the same presumption will be proved against them concerning the Father; for if, when silent, He could not make, of necessity He has gained power by begetting, that is, by speaking. And whence has He gained it? And wherefore? If, when He had the Word within Him, He could make, He begets needlessly, being able to make even in silence. Next, if the Word was in God before He was begotten, then being begotten He is without and external

to Him. But if so, how says He now, 'I in the Father and the Father in Me John 14:10?' but if He is now in the Father, then always was He in the Father, as He is now, and needless is it to say, 'For us was He begotten, and He reverts after we are formed, that He may be as He was.' For He was not anything which He is not now, nor is He what He was not; but He is as He ever was, and in the same state and in the same respects; otherwise He will seem to be imperfect and alterable. For if, what He was, that He shall be afterwards, as if now He were not so, it is plain, He is not now what He was and shall be. I mean, if He was before in God, and afterwards shall be again, it follows that now the Word is not in God. But the Lord refutes such persons when He says, 'I in the Father and the Father in Me;' for so is He now as He ever was. But if so He now is, as He was ever, it follows, not that at one time He was begotten and not at another, nor that once there was silence with God, and then He spoke, but there is ever a Father, and a Son who is His Word, not in name alone a Word, nor the Word in notion only a Son, but existing coessential with the Father, not begotten for us, for we are brought into being for Him. For, if He were begotten for us, and in His begetting we were created, and in His generation the creature consists, and then He returns that He may be what He was before, first, He that was begotten will be again not begotten. For if His progression be generation, His return will be the close of that generation, for when He has come to be in God, God will be silent again. But if He shall be silent, there will be what there was when He was silent, stillness and not creation, for the creation will cease to be. For, as on the Word's outgoing, the creation came to be, and existed, so on the Word's retiring, the creation will not exist. What use then for it to come into being, if it is to cease? Or why did God speak, that then He should be silent? And why did He issue One whom He recalls? And why did He beget One whose generation He willed to cease? Again it is uncertain what He shall be. For either He will ever be silent, or He will again beget, and will devise a different creation (for He will not make the same, else that which was made would have remained, but another); and in due course He will bring that also to a close, and will devise another, and so on without end.

13, 14. Such a doctrine precludes all real distinctions of personality in the Divine Nature. Illustration of the Scripture doctrine from 2 Corinthians 6:11, etc.

13. This perhaps he borrowed from the Stoics, who maintain that their God contracts and again expands with the creation, and then rests without end. For what is dilated is first straitened; and what is expanded is at first contracted; and it is what it was, and does but undergo an affection. If then the Monad being dilated became a Triad, and the Monad was the Father, and the Triad is Father, Son, and Holy Ghost, first the Monad being dilated, underwent an affection and became what it was not; for it was dilated, whereas it had not been dilate. Next, if the Monad itself was dilated into a Triad, and that, Father and Son and Holy Ghost, then Father and Son and Spirit prove the same, as Sabellius held, unless the Monad which he speaks of is something besides the Father, and then he ought not to speak of dilatation, since the Monad was to make Three, so that there was a Monad, and then Father, Son, and Spirit. For if the Monad were dilated, and expanded itself, it must itself be that which was expanded. And a Triad when dilated is no longer a Monad, and when

a Monad it is not yet a Triad. And so, He that was Father was not yet Son and Spirit; but, when become These, is no longer only Father. And a man who thus should lie, must ascribe a body to God, and represent Him as passible; for what is dilatation, but an affection of that which is dilated? Or what the dilated, but what before was not so, but was strait indeed; for it is the same, in time only differing from itself.

14. And this the divine Apostle knows, when he writes to the Corinthians, 'Be not straitened in us, but be yourselves dilated, O Corinthians 2 Corinthians 6:12-13;' for he advises identical persons to change from straitness to dilatation. And as, supposing the Corinthians being straitened were in turn dilated, they had not been others, but still Corinthians, so if the Father was dilated into a Triad, the Triad again is the Father alone. And he says again the same thing, 'Our heart is dilated ;' and Noah says, 'May God dilate for Japheth ,' for the same heart and the same Japheth is in the dilatation. If then the Monad dilated, it would dilate for others; but if it dilated for itself, then it would be that which was dilated; and what is that

but the Son and Holy Spirit? And it is well to ask him, when thus speaking, what was the action of this dilatation? Or, in very truth, wherefore at all it took place? For what does not remain the same, but is in course of time dilated, must necessarily have a cause of dilatation. If then it was in order that Word and Spirit should be with Him, it is beside the purpose to say, 'First Monad, and then dilated;' for Word and Spirit were not afterwards, but ever, or God would be wordless, as the Arians hold. So that if Word and Spirit were ever, ever was it dilated, and not at first a Monad; but if it were dilated afterwards, then afterwards is there a Word. But if for the Incarnation it was dilated, and then became a Triad, then before the Incarnation there was not yet a Triad. And it will seem even that the Father became flesh, if, that is, He be the Monad, and was dilated in the Man; and thus perhaps there will only be a Monad, and flesh, and thirdly Spirit; if, that is, He was Himself dilated; and there will be in name only a Triad. It is absurd too to say that it was dilated for creating; for it were possible for it, remaining a Monad, to make all; for the Monad did not need dilatation, nor was wanting in power before being dilated; it is absurd surely and impious, to think or speak thus in the case of God. Another absurdity too will follow. For if it was dilated for the sake of the creation, and while it was a Monad the creation was not, but upon the Consummation it will be again a Monad after dilatation, then the creation too will come to nought. For as for the sake of creating it was dilated, so, the dilatation ceasing, the creation will cease also.

15-24. Since the Word is from God, He must be Son. Since the Son is from everlasting, He must be the Word; else either He is superior to the Word, or the Word is the Father. Texts of the New Testament which state the unity of the Son with the Father; therefore the Son is the Word. Three hypotheses refuted — 1. That the Man is the Son; 2. That the Word and Man together are the Son; 3. That the Word became Son on His incarnation. Texts of the Old Testament which speak of the Son. If they are merely prophetical, then those concerning the Word may be such also.

15. Such absurdities will be the consequence of saying that the Monad is dilated into a Triad. But since those who say

so venture to separate Word and Son, and to say that the Word is one and the Son another, and that first was the Word and then the Son, come let us consider this doctrine also. Now their presumption takes various forms; for some say that the man whom the Saviour assumed is the Son; and others both that the man and the Word then became Son, when they were united. And others say that the Word Himself then became Son when He became man; for from being Word, they say, He has become Son, not being Son before, but only Word. Now both are Stoic doctrines, whether to say that God was dilated or to deny the Son, but especially is it absurd to name the Word, yet deny Him to be Son. For if the Word be not from God, reasonably might they deny Him to be Son; but if He is from God, how see they not that what exists from anything is son of him from whom it is? Next, if God is Father of the Word, why is not the Word Son of His own Father? For one is and is called father, whose is the son; and one is and is called son of another, whose is the father. If then God is not Father of Christ, neither is the Word Son; but if God be Father, then reasonably also the Word is Son. But if afterwards there is Father, and first God, this is an Arian thought. Next, it is absurd that God should change; for that belongs to bodies; but if they argue that in the instance of creation He became afterwards a Maker, let them know that the change is in the things which afterwards came to be, and not in God.

16. If then the Son too were a work, well might God begin to be a Father towards Him as others; but if the Son is not a work, then ever was the Father and ever the Son. But if the Son was ever, He must be the Word; for if the Word be not Son, and this is what a man waxes bold to say, either he holds that Word to be Father or the Son superior to the Word. For the Son being 'in the bosom of the Father John 1:18,' of necessity either the Word is not before the Son (for nothing is before Him who is in the Father), or if the Word be other than the Son, the Word must be the Father in whom is the Son. But if the Word is not Father but Word, the Word must be external to the Father, since it is the Son who is 'in the bosom of the Father.' For not both the Word and the Son are in the bosom, but one must be, and He the Son, who is Only-begotten. And it follows for another reason, if the Word is one, and the Son another, that the Son is superior to the

Word; for 'no one knows the Father save the Son Matthew 11:27,' not the Word. Either then the Word does not know, or if He knows, it is not true that 'no one knows.' And the same of 'He that has seen Me, has seen the Father,' and 'I and the Father are One,' for this is uttered by the Son, not the Word, as they would have it, as is plain from the Gospel; for according to John when the Lord said, 'I and the Father are One,' the Jews took up stones to stone Him. 'Jesus answered them, Many good works have I showed you from My Father, for which of those works do ye stone Me? The Jews answered Him, saying, For a good work we stone You not, but for blasphemy, and because that You, being a man, make Yourself God. Jesus answered them, Is it not written in your law, I said, You are gods? If he called them gods unto whom the Word of God came, and the Scripture cannot be broken, say ye of Him, whom the Father has sanctified and sent into the world, Thou blaspheme, because I said, I am the Son of God? If I do not the works of My Father, believe Me not. But if I do, though ye believe not Me, believe the works, that you may know and believe that the Father is in Me, and I in the Father.' And yet, as far as the surface of the words intimated, He said neither 'I am

God,' nor 'I am Son of God,' but 'I and the Father are One.'

17. The Jews then, when they heard 'One,' thought like Sabellius that He said that He was the Father, but our Saviour shows their sin by this argument: 'Though I had said God, you should have remembered what is written, I said, You are gods;' then to clear up 'I and the Father are One,' He has explained the Son's oneness with the Father in the words, 'Because I said, I am the Son of God.' For if He did not say it in words, still He has referred the sense of 'are One' to the Son. For nothing is one with the Father, but what is from Him. What is that which is from Him but the Son? And therefore He adds, 'that you may know that I am in the Father, and the Father in Me.' For, when expounding the 'One,' He said that the union and the inseparability lay, not in This being That, with which It was One, but in His being in the Father and the Father in the Son. For thus He overthrows both Sabellius, in saying, 'I am' not, the Father, but, 'the Son of God;' and Arius, in saying, 'are One.' If then the Son and the Word are not the same, it is not that the Word is one with the

Father, but the Son; nor he that has seen the Word 'has seen the Father,' but 'he that has seen' the Son. And from this it follows, either that the Son is greater than the Word, or the Word has nothing beyond the Son. For what can be greater or more perfect than 'One,' and 'I in the Father and the Father in Me,' and 'He that has seen Me, has seen the Father.' for these utterances also belong to the Son. And hence the same John says, 'He that has seen Me, has seen Him that sent Me,' and, 'He that receives Me, receives Him that sent Me;' and, 'I have come a light into the world, that whosoever believes in Me, should not abide in darkness. And, if any one hear My words and observe them not, I judge him not; for I came not to judge the world, but to save the world. The word which he shall hear, the same shall judge him in the last day, because I go unto the Father.' The preaching, He says, judges him who has not observed the commandment; 'for if,' He says, 'I had not come and spoken unto them, they had not had sin; but now they shall have no cloke John 15:22,' He says, having heard My words, through which those who observe them shall reap salvation.

18. Perhaps they will have so little shame as to say, that this utterance belongs not to the Son but to the Word; but from what preceded it appeared plainly that the speaker was the Son. For He who here says, 'I came not to judge the world but to save John 12:47,' is shown to be no other than the Only-begotten Son of God, by the same John's saying before , 'For God so loved the world that He gave His Only-begotten Son, that whosoever believes in Him should not perish, but have everlasting life. For God sent not His Son into the world to condemn the world, but that the world through Him might be saved. He that believes in Him is not condemned, but he that believes not is condemned already, because he has not believed in the Name of the Only-begotten Son of God. And this is the condemnation, that light has come into the world, and men loved darkness rather than light, because their deeds are evil.' If He who says, 'For I came not to judge the world, but that I might save it,' is the Same as says, 'He that sees Me, sees Him that sent Me ,' and if He who came to save the world and not judge it is the Only-begotten Son of God, it is plain that it is the same Son who says, 'He that sees Me, sees Him that sent Me.' For He who said, 'He that believes in Me,' and, 'If any one

hear My words, I judge him not,' is the Son Himself, of whom Scripture says, 'He that believes in Him is not condemned, but He that believes not is condemned already, because He has not believed in the Name of the Only-begotten Son of God.' And again: 'And this is the condemnation' of him who believes not on the Son, 'that light has come into the world,' and they believed not in Him, that is, in the Son; for He must be 'the Light which lights every man that comes into the world.' And as long as He was upon earth according to the Incarnation, He was Light in the world, as He said Himself, 'While you have light, believe in the light, that you may be the children of light;' for 'I,' says He, 'have come a light into the world.'

19. This then being shown, it follows that the Word is the Son. But if the Son is the Light, which has come into the world, beyond all dispute the world was made by the Son. For in the beginning of the Gospel, the Evangelist, speaking of John the Baptist, says, 'He was not that Light, but that he might bear witness concerning that Light.' For Christ Himself was, as we have said before, the True Light

that lights every man that comes into the world. For if 'He was in the world, and the world was made by Him ,' of necessity He is the Word of God, concerning whom also the Evangelist witnesses that all things were made by Him. For either they will be compelled to speak of two worlds, that the one may have come into being by the Son and the other by the Word, or, if the world is one and the creation one, it follows that Son and Word are one and the same before all creation, for by Him it came into being. Therefore if as by the Word, so by the Son also all things came to be, it will not be contradictory, but even identical to say, for instance, 'In the beginning was the Word,' or, 'In the beginning was the Son.' But if because John did not say, 'In the beginning was the Son,' they shall maintain that the attributes of the Word do not suit with the Son, it at once follows that the attributes of the Son do not suit with the Word. But it was shown that to the Son belongs, 'I and the Father are One,' and that it is He 'Who is in the bosom of the Father,' and, 'He that sees Me, sees Him that sent Me ;' and that 'the world was brought into being by Him,' is common to the Word and the Son; so that from this the Son is shown to be before the world; for of necessity the Framer is before the things brought into being. And what is said to Philip must belong, according to them, not to the Word, but to the Son. For, 'Jesus said,' says Scripture, 'Have I been so long time with you, and yet you have not known Me, Philip? He that has seen Me, has seen the Father. And how do you say then, Show us the Father? Do you not believe, that I am in the Father and the Father in Me? The words that I speak unto you, I speak not of Myself, but the Father that dwells in Me, He does the works. Believe Me that I am in the Father and the Father in Me, or else, believe Me for the very works' sake. Verily, verily, I say unto you, he that believes in Me, the works that I do shall he do also, and greater works than these shall he do, because I go unto the Father. And whatsoever you shall ask in My Name, that will I do, that the Father may be glorified in the Son.' Therefore if the Father be glorified in the Son, the Son must be He who said, 'I in the Father and the Father in Me;' and He who said, 'He that has seen Me, has seen the Father.' for He, the same who thus spoke, shows Himself to be the Son, by adding, 'that the Father may be glorified in the Son.'

20. If then they say that the Man whom the Word wore, and not the Word, is the Son of God the Only-begotten, the Man must be by consequence He who is in the Father, in whom also the Father is; and the Man must be He who is One with the Father, and who is in the bosom of the Father, and the True Light. And they will be compelled to say that through the Man Himself the world came into being, and that the Man was He who came not to judge the world but to save it; and that He it was who was in being before Abraham came to be. For, says Scripture, Jesus said to them, 'Verily, verily, I say unto you, before Abraham was, I am John 8:58.' And is it not absurd to say, as they do, that one who came of the seed of Abraham after two and forty generations , should exist before Abraham came to be? Is it not absurd, if the flesh, which the Word bore, itself is the Son, to say that the flesh from Mary is that by which the world was made? And how will they retain 'He was in the world?' for the Evangelist, by way of signifying the Son's antecedence to the birth according to the flesh, goes on to say, 'He was in the world.' And how, if not the Word but the Man is the Son, can He save the world, being Himself one of the world? And if this does not shame them, where shall be the

Word, the Man being in the Father? And where will the Word stand to the Father, the Man and the Father being One? But if the Man be Only-begotten, what will be the place of the Word? Either one must say that He comes second, or, if He be above the Only-begotten, He must be the Father Himself. For as the Father is One, so also the Only-begotten from Him is One; and what has the Word above the Man, if the Word is not the Son? For, while Scripture says that through the Son and the Word the world was brought to be, and it is common to the Word and to the Son to frame the world, yet Scripture proceeds to place the sight of the Father, not in the Word but in the Son, and to attribute the saving of the world, not to the Word, but to the Only-begotten Son. For, says it, Jesus said, 'Have I been so long while with you, and yet have you not known Me, Philip? He that has seen Me, has seen the Father.' Nor does Scripture say that the Word knows the Father, but the Son; and that not the Word sees the Father, but the Only-begotten Son who is in the bosom of the Father.

21. And what more does the Word contribute to our salvation than the Son, if, as they hold, the Son is one, and the Word another? For the command is that we should believe, not in the Word, but in the Son. For John says, 'He that believes in the Son, has everlasting life; but he that believes not the Son, shall not see life John 3:36.' And Holy Baptism, in which the substance of the whole faith is lodged, is administered not in the Word, but in Father, Son, and Holy Ghost. If then, as they hold, the Word is one and the Son another, and the Word is not the Son, Baptism has no connection with the Word. How then are they able to hold that the Word is with the Father, when He is not with Him in the giving of Baptism? But perhaps they will say, that in the Father's Name the Word is included? Wherefore then not the Spirit also? Or is the Spirit external to the Father? And the Man indeed (if the Word is not Son) is named after the Father, but the Spirit after the Man? And then the Monad, instead of dilating into a Triad, dilates according to them into a Tetrad, Father, Word, Son, and Holy Ghost. Being brought to shame on this ground, they have recourse to another, and say that not the Man by Himself whom the Lord bore, but both together, the Word and the Man, are the Son; for

both joined together are named Son, as they say. Which then is cause of which? And which has made which a Son? Or, to speak more clearly, is the Word a Son because of the flesh? Or is the flesh called Son because of the Word? Or is neither the cause, but the concurrence of the two? If then the Word be a Son because of the flesh, of necessity the flesh is Son, and all those absurdities follow which have been already drawn from saying that the Man is Son. But if the flesh is called Son because of the Word, then even before the flesh the Word certainly, being such, was Son. For how could a being make other sons, not being himself a son, especially when there was a father? If then He makes sons for Himself, then is He Himself Father; but if for the Father, then must He be Son, or rather that Son, by reason of Whom the rest are made sons.

22. For if, while He is not Son, we are sons, God is our Father and not His. How then does He appropriate the name instead, saying, 'My Father,' and 'I from the Father?' for if He be common Father of all, He is not His Father only, nor did He alone come out from the Father.

But he says, that He is sometimes called our Father also, because He has Himself become partaker in our flesh. For on this account the Word has become flesh, that, since the Word is Son, therefore, because of the Son dwelling in us, He may be called our Father also; for 'He sent forth,' says Scripture, 'the Spirit of His Son into our hearts, crying, Abba, Father Galatians 4:6.' Therefore the Son in us, calling upon His own Father, causes Him to be named our Father also. Surely in whose hearts the Son is not, of them neither can God be called Father. But if because of the Word the Man is called Son, it follows necessarily, since the ancients are called sons even before the Incarnation, that the Word is Son even before His sojourn among us; for 'I begot sons,' says Scripture; and in the time of Noah, 'When the sons of God saw,' and in the Song, 'Is not He your Father?' Therefore there was also that True Son, for whose sake they too were sons. But if, as they say again, neither of the two is Son, but it depends on the concurrence of the two, it follows that neither is Son; I say, neither the Word nor the Man, but some cause, on account of which they were united; and accordingly that cause which makes the Son will precede the uniting. Therefore in this way also the Son was before the flesh.

both joined together are named Son, as they say. Which then is cause of which? And which has made which a Son? Or, to speak more clearly, is the Word a Son because of the flesh? Or is the flesh called Son because of the Word? Or is neither the cause, but the concurrence of the two? If then the Word be a Son because of the flesh, of necessity the flesh is Son, and all those absurdities follow which have been already drawn from saying that the Man is Son. But if the flesh is called Son because of the Word, then even before the flesh the Word certainly, being such, was Son. For how could a being make other sons, not being himself a son, especially when there was a father? If then He makes sons for Himself, then is He Himself Father; but if for the Father, then must He be Son, or rather that Son, by reason of Whom the rest are made sons.

22. For if, while He is not Son, we are sons, God is our Father and not His. How then does He appropriate the name instead, saying, 'My Father,' and 'I from the Father?' for if He be common Father of all, He is not His Father only, nor did He alone come out from the Father.

But he says, that He is sometimes called our Father also, because He has Himself become partaker in our flesh. For on this account the Word has become flesh, that, since the Word is Son, therefore, because of the Son dwelling in us, He may be called our Father also; for 'He sent forth,' says Scripture, 'the Spirit of His Son into our hearts, crying, Abba, Father Galatians 4:6.' Therefore the Son in us, calling upon His own Father, causes Him to be named our Father also. Surely in whose hearts the Son is not, of them neither can God be called Father. But if because of the Word the Man is called Son, it follows necessarily, since the ancients are called sons even before the Incarnation, that the Word is Son even before His sojourn among us; for 'I begot sons,' says Scripture; and in the time of Noah, 'When the sons of God saw,' and in the Song, 'Is not He your Father?' Therefore there was also that True Son, for whose sake they too were sons. But if, as they say again, neither of the two is Son, but it depends on the concurrence of the two, it follows that neither is Son; I say, neither the Word nor the Man, but some cause, on account of which they were united; and accordingly that cause which makes the Son will precede the uniting. Therefore in this way also the Son was before the flesh.

Word, the Man being in the Father? And where will the Word stand to the Father, the Man and the Father being One? But if the Man be Only-begotten, what will be the place of the Word? Either one must say that He comes second, or, if He be above the Only-begotten, He must be the Father Himself. For as the Father is One, so also the Only-begotten from Him is One; and what has the Word above the Man, if the Word is not the Son? For, while Scripture says that through the Son and the Word the world was brought to be, and it is common to the Word and to the Son to frame the world, yet Scripture proceeds to place the sight of the Father, not in the Word but in the Son, and to attribute the saving of the world, not to the Word, but to the Only-begotten Son. For, says it, Jesus said, 'Have I been so long while with you, and yet have you not known Me, Philip? He that has seen Me, has seen the Father.' Nor does Scripture say that the Word knows the Father, but the Son; and that not the Word sees the Father, but the Only-begotten Son who is in the bosom of the Father.

21. And what more does the Word contribute to our salvation than the Son, if, as they hold, the Son is one, and the Word another? For the command is that we should believe, not in the Word, but in the Son. For John says, 'He that believes in the Son, has everlasting life; but he that believes not the Son, shall not see life John 3:36.' And Holy Baptism, in which the substance of the whole faith is lodged, is administered not in the Word, but in Father, Son, and Holy Ghost. If then, as they hold, the Word is one and the Son another, and the Word is not the Son, Baptism has no connection with the Word. How then are they able to hold that the Word is with the Father, when He is not with Him in the giving of Baptism? But perhaps they will say, that in the Father's Name the Word is included? Wherefore then not the Spirit also? Or is the Spirit external to the Father? And the Man indeed (if the Word is not Son) is named after the Father, but the Spirit after the Man? And then the Monad, instead of dilating into a Triad, dilates according to them into a Tetrad, Father, Word, Son, and Holy Ghost. Being brought to shame on this ground, they have recourse to another, and say that not the Man by Himself whom the Lord bore, but both together, the Word and the Man, are the Son; for

When this then is urged, they will take refuge in another pretext, saying, neither that the Man is Son, nor both together, but that the Word was Word indeed simply in the beginning, but when He became Man, then He was named Son; for before His appearing He was not Son but Word only; and as the 'Word became flesh,' not being flesh before, so the Word became Son, not being Son before. Such are their idle words; but they admit of an obvious refutation.

23. For if simply, when made Man, He has become Son, the becoming Man is the cause. And if the Man is cause of His being Son, or both together, then the same absurdities result. Next, if He is first Word and then Son, it will appear that He knew the Father afterwards, not before; for not as being Word does He know Him, but as Son. For 'No one knows the Father but the Son.' And this too will result, that He has come afterwards to be 'in the bosom of the Father Matthew 11:27; John 1:18,' and afterwards He and the Father have become One; and afterwards is, 'He that has seen Me, has seen the Father John 14:9.' For all these things are said of the Son. Hence

they will be forced to say, The Word was nothing but a name. For neither is it He who is in us with the Father, nor whoever has seen the Word, has seen the Father, nor was the Father known to any one at all, for through the Son is the Father known (for so it is written, 'And he to whomsoever the Son will reveal Him'), and, the Word not being yet Son, not yet did any know the Father. How then was He seen by Moses, how by the fathers? For He says Himself in the Kingdoms, 'Was I not plainly revealed to the house of your father?' But if God was revealed, there must have been a Son to reveal, as He says Himself, 'And he to whomsoever the Son will reveal Him.' It is irreligious then and foolish to say that the Word is one and the Son another, and whence they gained such an idea it were well to ask them. They answer, Because no mention is made in the Old Testament of the Son, but of the Word; and for this reason they are positive in their opinion that the Son came later than the Word, because not in the Old, but in the New only, is He spoken of. This is what they irreligiously say; for first to separate between the Testaments, so that the one does not hold with the other, is the device of Manichees and Jews, the one of whom oppose the Old, and the other the New. Next, on their showing, if what is contained in the Old is of older date, and what in the New of later, and times depend upon the writing, it follows that 'I and the Father are One,' and 'Only-begotten,' and 'He that has seen Me has seen the Father,' are later, for these testimonies are adduced not from the Old but from the New.

24. But it is not so; for in truth much is said in the Old also about the Son, as in the second Psalm, 'You are My Son, this day have I begotten You;' and in the ninth the title, Unto the 'end concerning the hidden things of the Son, a Psalm of David;' and in the forty-fourth, 'Unto the end, concerning the things that shall be changed to the Sons of Korah for understanding, a song about the Well-beloved;' and in Isaiah, 'I will sing to my Well-beloved a song of my Well-beloved touching my vineyard. My Well-beloved has a vineyard Isaiah 5:1;' Who is this 'Well-beloved' but the Only-begotten Son? As also in the hundred and ninth, 'From the womb I begot You before the morning star,' concerning which I shall speak afterwards; and in the Proverbs, 'Before the hills He begot me;' and in Daniel, 'And the form of the Fourth is like the

Son of God ;' and many others. If then from the Old be ancientness, ancient must be the Son, who is clearly described in the Old Testament in many places. 'Yes,' they say, 'so it is, but it must be taken prophetically.' Therefore also the Word must be said to be spoken of prophetically; for this is not to be taken one way, that another. For if 'You are My Son?' refer to the future, so does 'By the Word of the Lord were the heavens established;' for it is not said 'were brought to be,' nor 'He made.' But that 'established' refers to the future, it states elsewhere: 'The Lord reigned ,' followed by 'He so established the earth that it can never be moved.' And if the words in the forty-fourth Psalm 'for My Well-beloved' refer to the future, so does what follows upon them, 'My heart uttered a good Word.' And if 'From the womb' relates to a man, therefore also 'From the heart.' For if the womb is human, so is the heart corporeal. But if what is from the heart is eternal, then what is 'From the womb' is eternal. And if the 'Only-begotten' is 'in the bosom,' therefore the 'Well-beloved' is 'in the bosom.' For 'Only-begotten' and 'Well-beloved' are the same, as in the words 'This is My Well-beloved Son.' For not as wishing to signify His love towards Him did He say 'Well-beloved,' as if it might appear that He hated others, but He made plain thereby His being Only-begotten, that He might show that He alone was from Him. And hence the Word, with a view of conveying to Abraham the idea of 'Only-begotten,' says, 'Offer your son your well-beloved Genesis 22:2;' but it is plain to any one that Isaac was the only son from Sara. The Word then is Son, not lately come to be, or named Son, but always Son. For if not Son, neither is He Word; and if not Word, neither is He Son. For that which is from the father is a oon; and what is from the Father, but that Word that went forth from the heart, and was born from the womb? For the Father is not Word, nor the Word Father, but the one is Father, and the other Son; and one begets, and the other is begotten.

25. Marcellian illustration from 1 Corinthians 12:4, refuted.

25. Arius then raves in saying that the Son is from nothing, and that once He was not, while Sabellius also raves in saying that the Father is Son, and again, the Son Father , in subsistence One, in name Two; and he raves also in using as an example the grace of the Spirit. For he

says, 'As there are diversities of gifts, but the same Spirit, so also the Father is the same, but is dilated into Son and Spirit.' Now this is full of absurdity; for if as with the Spirit, so it is with God, the Father will be Word and Holy Spirit, to one becoming Father, to another Son, to another Spirit, accommodating himself to the need of each, and in name indeed Son and Spirit, but in reality Father only; having a beginning in that He becomes a Son, and then ceasing to be called Father, and made man in name, but in truth not even coming among us; and untrue in saying 'I and the Father,' but in reality being Himself the Father, and the other absurdities which result in the instance of Sabellius. And the name of the Son and the Spirit will necessarily cease, when the need has been supplied; and what happens will altogether be but make-belief, because it has been displayed, not in truth, but in name. And the Name of Son ceasing, as they hold, then the grace of Baptism will cease too; for it was given in the Son. Nay, what will follow but the annihilation of the creation? For if the Word came forth that we might be created, and when He had come forth, we were, it is plain that when He retires into the Father, as they say, we shall be no longer. For He will be as He was; so also we shall not be, as then we were not; for when He is no more gone forth, there will no more be a creation. This then is absurd.

26-36. That the Son is the Co-existing Word, argued from the New Testament. Texts from the Old Testamentcontinued; especially Psalm 110:3. Besides, the Word in Old Testamentmay be Son in New, as Spirit in Old Testamentis Paraclete in New. Objection from Acts 10:36; answered by parallels, such as 1 Corinthians 1:5. Lev. 9:7. etc. Necessity of the Word's taking flesh, viz. to sanctify, yet without destroying, the flesh.

26. But that the Son has no beginning of being, but before He was made man was ever with the Father, John makes clear in his first Epistle, writing thus: 'That which was from the beginning, which we have heard, which we have seen with our eyes, which we have looked upon, and our hands have handled of the Word of Life; and the Life was manifested, and we have seen it; and we bear witness and declare unto you that Eternal Life, which was with the Father, and was manifested unto us 1 John 1:1-2.' While he says here that 'the Life,' not 'became,' but 'was with the Father,' in the end of his Epistle he says the Son is the

Life, writing, 'And we are in Him that is True, even in His Son, Jesus Christ; this is the True God and Eternal Life.' But if the Son is the Life, and the Life was with the Father, and if the Son was with the Father, and the same Evangelist says, 'And the Word was with God John 1:1,' the Son must be the Word, which is ever with the Father. And as the 'Son' is 'Word,' so 'God' must be 'the Father.' Moreover, the Son, according to John, is not merely 'God' but 'True God;' for according to the same Evangelist, 'And the Word was God;' and the Son said, 'I am the Life.' Therefore the Son is the Word and Life which is with the Father. And again, what is said in the same John, 'The Only-begotten Son which is in the bosom of the Father ,' shows that the Son was ever. For whom John calls Son, Him David mentions in the Psalm as God's Hand , saying, 'Why do You not strech forth Your Right Hand out of Your bosom ?' Therefore if the Hand is in the bosom, and the Son in the bosom, the Son will be the Hand, and the Hand will be the Son, through whom the Father made all things; for it is written, 'Your Hand made all these things,' and 'He led out His people with His Hand ;' therefore through the Son. And if 'this is the changing of the Right Hand of the Most Highest,' and again, 'Unto the end, concerning the things that shall be changed, a song for My Well-beloved ;' the Well-beloved then is the Hand that was changed; concerning whom the Divine Voice also says, 'This is My Beloved Son.' This 'My Hand' then is equivalent to 'This My Son.'

27. But since there are ill-instructed men who, while resisting the doctrine of a Son, think little of the words, 'From the womb before the morning star I begot You ;' as if this referred to His relation to Mary, alleging that He was born of Mary 'before the morning star,' for that to say 'womb' could not refer to His relation towards God, we must say a few words here. If then, because the 'womb' is human, therefore it is foreign to God, plainly 'heart' too has a human meaning , for that which has heart has womb also. Since then both are human, we must deny both, or seek to explain both. Now as a word is from the heart, so is an offspring from the womb; and as when the heart of God is spoken of, we do not conceive of it as human, so if Scripture says 'from the womb,' we must not take it in a corporeal sense. For it is usual with divine Scripture to speak and signify in the way of man what is above man.

Thus speaking of the creation it says, 'Your hands made me and fashioned me,' and, 'Your hand made all these things,' and, 'He commanded and they were created.' Suitable then is its language about everything; attributing to the Son 'propriety' and 'genuineness,' and to the creation 'the beginning of being.' For the one God makes and creates; but Him He begets from Himself, Word or Wisdom. Now 'womb' and 'heart' plainly declare the proper and the genuine; for we too have this from the womb; but our works we make by the hand.

28. What means then, say they, 'Before the morning star?' I would answer, that if 'Before the morning star' shows that His birth from Mary was wonderful, many others besides have been born before the rising of the star. What then is said so wonderful in His instance, that He should record it as some choice prerogative , when it is common to many? Next, to beget differs from bringing forth; for begetting involves the primary foundation, but to bring forth is nothing else than the production of what exists. If then the term belongs to the body, let it be observed that He did not then receive a beginning of coming to be when

he was evangelized to the shepherds by night, but when the Angel spoke to the Virgin. And that was not night, for this is not said; on the contrary, it was night when He issued from the womb. This difference Scripture makes, and says on the one hand that He was begotten before the morning star, and on the other speaks of His proceeding from the womb, as in the twenty-first Psalm, 'You are he that drew Me from the womb.' Besides, He did not say, 'before the rising of the morning star,' but simply 'before the morning star.' If then the phrase must be taken of the body, then either the body must be before Adam, for the stars were before Adam, or we have to investigate the sense of the letter. And this John enables us to do, who says in the Apocalypse, 'I am Alpha and Omega, the first and the last, the beginning and the end. Blessed are they who make broad their robes, that they may have right to the tree of life, and may enter in through the gates into the city. For without are dogs, and sorcerers, and whoremongers, and murderers, and idolaters, and whosoever makes and loves a lie. I Jesus have sent My Angel, to testify these things in the Churches. I am the Root and the Offspring of David, the Bright and Morning Star. And the Spirit and the Bride say, Come; and let him that hears say, Come; and let him that is thirsty, Come; and whosoever will, let him take of the water of life freely.' If then 'the Offspring of David' be the 'Bright and Morning Star,' it is plain that the flesh of the Saviour is called 'the Morning Star,' which the Offspring from God preceded; so that the sense of the Psalm is this, 'I have begotten You from Myself before Your appearance in the flesh;' for 'before the Morning Star' is equivalent to 'before the Incarnation of the Word.'

29. Thus in the Old also, statements are plainly made concerning the Son; at the same time it is superfluous to argue the point; for if what is not stated in the Old is of later date, let them who are thus disputatious, say where in the Old is mention made of the Spirit, the Paraclete? For of the Holy Spirit there is mention, but nowhere of the Paraclete. Is then the Holy Spirit one, and the Paraclete another, and the Paraclete the later, as not mentioned in the Old? But far be it to say that the Spirit is later, or to distinguish the Holy Ghost as one and the Paraclete as another; for the Spirit is one and the same, then and now hallowing and comforting those who are His recipients; as

one and the same Word and Son led even then to adoption of sons those who were worthy. For sons under the Old were made such through no other than the Son. For unless even before Mary there were a Son who was of God, how is He before all, when they are sons before Him? And how also 'First-born,' if He comes second after many? But neither is the Paraclete second, for He was before all, nor the Son later; for 'in the beginning was the Word John 1:1.' And as the Spirit and Paraclete are the same, so the Son and Word are the same; and as the Saviour says concerning the Spirit, 'But the Paraclete which is the Holy Ghost, whom the Father will send in My Name ,' speaking of One and Same, and not distinguishing, so John describes similarly when he says, 'And the Word became flesh, and dwelt among us, and we beheld His glory, glory as of one Only-begotten from the Father.' For here too he does not distinguish but witnesses the identity. And as the Paraclete is not one and the Holy Ghost another, but one and the same, so Word is not one, and Son another, but the Word is Only-Begotten; for He says not the glory of the flesh itself, but of the Word. He then who dares distinguish between Word and Son, let him distinguish between Spirit and Paraclete; but if the

Spirit cannot be distinguished, so neither can the Word, being also Son and Wisdom and Power. Moreover, the word 'Well-beloved' even the Greeks who are skilful in phrases know to be equivalent with 'Only-begotten.' For Homer speaks thus of Telemachus, who was the only-begotten of Ulysses, in the second book of the Odyssey:

O'er the wide earth, dear youth, why seek to run,

An only child, a well-beloved son?

He whom you mourn, divine Ulysses, fell

Far from his country, where the strangers dwell.

Therefore he who is the only son of his father is called well-beloved.

30. Some of the followers of the Samosatene, distinguishing the Word from the Son, pretend that the Son is Christ, and the Word another; and they ground this upon Peter's words in the Acts, which he spoke well, but they explain badly. It is this: 'The Word He sent to the children of Israel, preaching peace by Jesus Christ; this is

Lord of all Acts 10:36.' For they say that since the Word spoke through Christ, as in the instance of the Prophets, 'Thus says the Lord,' the prophet was one and the Lord another. But to this it is parallel to oppose the words in the first to the Corinthians, 'waiting for the revelation of our Lord Jesus Christ, who shall also confirm you unto the end unblameable in the day of our Lord Jesus Christ 1 Corinthians 1:7-8.' For as one Christ does not confirm the day of another Christ, but He Himself confirms in His own day those who wait for Him, so the Father sent the Word made flesh, that being made man He might preach by means of Himself. And therefore he straightway adds, 'This is Lord of all;' but Lord of all is the Word.

31. 'And Moses said to Aaron, Go unto the altar and offer your sin-offering, and your burnt-offering, and make an atonement for yourself and for the people; and offer the offering of the people, and make an atonement for them, as the Lord commanded Moses Leviticus 9:7.' See now here, though Moses be one, Moses himself speaks as if about another Moses, 'as the Lord commanded Moses.' In like manner then, if the blessed Peter speak of the Divine

Word also, as sent to the children of Israel by Jesus Christ, it is not necessary to understand that the Word is one and Christ another, but that they were one and the same by reason of the uniting which took place in His divine and loving condescension and becoming man. And even if He be considered in two ways , still it is without any division of the Word, as when the inspired John says, 'And the Word became flesh, and dwelt among us John 1:14.' What then is said well and rightly by the blessed Peter, the followers of the Samosatene, understanding badly and wrongly, stand not in the truth. For Christ is understood in both ways in Divine Scripture, as when it says Christ 'God's power and God's wisdom 1 Corinthians 1:24.' If then Peter says that the Word was sent through Jesus Christ unto the children of Israel, let him be understood to mean, that the Word incarnate has appeared to the children of Israel, so that it may correspond to 'And the Word became flesh.' But if they understand it otherwise, and, while confessing the Word to be divine, as He is, separate from Him the Man that He has taken, with which also we believe that He is made one, saying that He has been sent through Jesus Christ, they are, without knowing it, contradicting themselves. For those who in this place separate the divine Word from the divine Incarnation, have, it seems, a degraded notion of the doctrine of His having become flesh, and entertain Gentile thoughts, as they do, conceiving that the divine Incarnation is an alteration of the Word. But it is not so; perish the thought.

32. For in the same way that John here preaches that incomprehensible union. 'the mortal being swallowed up of life 2 Corinthians 5:4,' nay, of Him who is Very Life (as the Lord said to Martha, 'I am the Life John 11:25 '), so when the blessed Peter says that through Jesus Christ the Word was sent, he implies the divine union also. For as when a man heard 'The Word became flesh,' he would not think that the Word ceased to be, which is absurd, as has been said before, so also hearing of the Word which has been united to the flesh, let him understand the divine mystery one and simple. More clearly however and indisputably than all reasoning does what was said by the Archangel to the Bearer of God herself, show the oneness of the Divine Word and Man. For he says, 'The Holy Ghost shall come upon you, and the Power of the Highest

shall overshadow you: therefore also that Holy Thing which shall be born of you, shall be called the Son of God Luke 1:35.' Irrationally then do the followers of the Samosatene separate the Word who is clearly declared to be made one with the Man from Mary. He is not therefore sent through that Man; but He rather in Him sent, saying, 'Go, teach all nations Matthew 28:19.'

33. And this is usual with Scripture , to express itself in inartificial and simple phrases. For so also in Numbers we shall find, Moses said to Raguel the Midianite, the father-in-law of Moses; for there was not one Moses who spoke, and another whose father-in-law was Raguel, but Moses was one. And if in like manner the Word of God is called Wisdom and Power and Right-Hand and Arm and the like, and if in His love to man He has become one with us, putting on our first-fruits and blended with it, therefore the other titles also have, as was natural, become the Word's portions. For that John has said, that in the beginning was the Word, and He with God and Himself God, and all things through Him, and without Him nothing made, shows clearly that even man is the

formation of God the Word. If then after taking him, when enfeebled, into Himself, He renews him again through that sure renewal unto endless permanence, and therefore is made one with him in order to raise him to a diviner lot, how can we possibly say that the Word was sent through the Man who was from Mary, and reckon Him, the Lord of Apostles, with the other Apostles, I mean prophets, who were sent by Him? And how can Christ be called a mere man? On the contrary, being made one with the Word, He is with reason called Christ and Son of God, the prophet having long since loudly and clearly ascribed the Father's subsistence to Him, and said, 'And I will send My Son Christ,' and in the Jordan, 'This is My Well-beloved Son.' For when He had fulfilled His promise, He showed, as was suitable, that He was He whom He said He had sent.

34. Let us then consider Christ in both ways, the divine Word made one in Mary with Him which is from Mary. For in her womb the Word fashioned for Himself His house, as at the beginning He formed Adam from the earth; or rather more divinely, concerning whom Solomon

too says openly, knowing that the Word was also called Wisdom, 'Wisdom built herself a house Proverbs 9:1;' which the Apostle interprets when he says, 'Which house are we Hebrews 3:6,' and elsewhere calls us a temple, as far as it is fitting to God to inhabit a temple, of which the image, made of stones, He by Solomon commanded the ancient people to build; whence, on the appearance of the Truth, the image ceased. For when the ruthless men wished to prove the image to be the truth, and to destroy that true habitation which we surely believe His union with us to be, He threatened them not; but knowing that their crime was against themselves, He says to them, 'Destroy this Temple, and in three days I will raise it up John 2:19,' He, our Saviour, surely showing thereby that the things about which men busy themselves, carry their dissolution with them. For unless the Lord had built the house, and kept the city, in vain did the builders toil, and the keepers watch. And so the works of the Jews are undone, for they were a shadow; but the Church is firmly established; it is 'founded on the rock,' and 'the gates of hades shall not prevail against it.' Theirs it was to say, 'Why do You, being a man, make Yourself God ?' and their disciple is the Samosatene; whence to his followers with reason does he teach his heresy. But 'we did not so learn Christ, if so be that we heard' Him, and were taught from Him, 'putting off the old man, which is corrupt according to the deceitful lusts,' and taking up 'the new, which after God is created in righteousness and true holiness.' Let Christ then in both ways be religiously considered.

35. But if Scripture often calls even the body by the name of Christ, as in the blessed Peter's words to Cornelius, when he teaches him of 'Jesus of Nazareth, whom God anointed with the Holy Ghost,' and again to the Jews, 'Jesus of Nazareth, a Man approved of God for you ,' and again the blessed Paul to the Athenians, 'By that Man, whom He ordained, giving assurance to all men, in that He raised Him from the dead Acts 17:31 ' (for we find the appointment and the mission often synonymous with the anointing; from which any one who will may learn, that there is no discordance in the words of the sacred writers, but that they but give various names to the union of God the Word with the Man from Mary, sometimes as anointing, sometimes as mission, sometimes as appointment), it follows that what the blessed Peter says is

right, and he proclaims in purity the Godhead of the Only begotten, without separating the subsistence of God the Word from the Man from Mary (perish the thought! For how should he, who had heard in so many ways, 'I and the Father are one,' and 'He that has seen Me, has seen the Father ?)' In which Man, after the resurrection also, when the doors were shut, we know of His coming to the whole band of the Apostles, and dispersing all that was hard to believe in it by His words, 'Handle Me and see, for a spirit has not flesh and bones, as you see Me have Luke 24:39.' And He did not say, 'This,' or 'this Man which I have taken to Me,' but 'Me.' Wherefore the Samosatene will gain no allowance, being refuted by so many arguments for the union of God the Word, nay by God the Word Himself, who now brings the news to all, and assures them by eating, and permitting to them that handling of Him which then took place. For certainly he who gives food to others, and they who give him, touch hands. For 'they gave Him,' Scripture says, 'a piece of a broiled fish and of an honey-comb, and' when He had 'eaten before them, He took the remains and gave to them.' See now, though not as Thomas was allowed, yet by another way, He afforded to them full assurance, in being touched by them; but if you would now see the scars, learn from Thomas. 'Reach hither your hand and thrust it into My side, and reach hither your finger and behold My hands John 20:27;' so says God the Word, speaking of His own side and hands, and of Himself as whole man and God together, first affording to the Saints even perception of the Word through the body , as we may consider, by entering when the doors were shut; and next standing near them in the body and affording full assurance. So much may be conveniently said for confirmation of the faithful, and correction of the unbelieving.

36. And so let Paul of Samosata also stand corrected on hearing the divine voice of Him who said 'My body,' not 'Christ besides Me who am the Word,' but 'Him with Me, and Me with Him.' For I the Word am the chrism, and that which has the chrism from Me is the Man ; not then without Me could He be called Christ, but being with Me and I in Him. Therefore the mention of the mission of the Word shows the uniting which took place with Jesus, born of Mary, Whose Name means Saviour, not by reason of anything else, but from the Man's being made one with

God the Word. This passage has the same meaning as 'the Father that sent Me,' and 'I came not of Myself, but the Father sent Me.' For he has given the name of mission to the uniting with the Man, with Whom the Invisible nature might be known to men, through the visible. For God changes not place, like us who are hidden in places, when in the fashion of our littleness He displays Himself in His existence in the flesh; for how should He, who fills the heaven and the earth? But on account of the presence in the flesh the just have spoken of His mission. Therefore God the Word Himself is Christ from Mary, God and Man; not some other Christ but One and the Same; He before ages from the Father, He too in the last times from the Virgin; invisible before even to the holy powers of heaven, visible now because of His being one with the Man who is visible; seen, I say, not in His invisible Godhead but in the operation of the Godhead through the human body and whole Man, which He has renewed by its appropriation to Himself. To Him be the adoration and the worship, who was before, and now is, and ever shall be, even to all ages. Amen.

OTHER BOOKS AVAILABLE AT
SCWatchman.space/books

The Deer's Cry By S. C. Watchman (2016) 117 pages

The night was May 1, 433 A.D. Multitudes of people had filled the region of Tara in obedience to the annual summons. On this night no fire in all of Hibernia was to be lit until the great royal fire was ignited by the high king. As the last of the days light faded a small company lead by a man named Patrick made a stand on the nearby Hill of Slane. Outside the fortress of the high king the druids were preparing a great pile of wood for their own bonfire. Suddenly a voice cried out, "Behold, my Lords, The ancient and venerable rights of Tara have been violated with unhallowed fire!" But who was this St. Patrick really? What forces were really fighting against him? Where did his courage come from?

The Gospel of Freedom From Sin and other Articles By S. C. Watchman (2019) 83 pages

This book contains SC Watchman's personal testimony of what Jesus did for him in saving him from Sin along with a compilation of related Facebook Articles. What is wrong with the Gospel of the modern churches? Find out inside.

Milk The Doctrine of Christ By S. C. Watchman (2021) 55 pages

This book is written in order to share the sincere Milk of the word so that Lambs may grow up into young Lions. Jesus commissioned Peter to feed His Lambs (John 21:15). Paul wanted to feed with Meat but most of the time he found himself having to go back to explain and lay the foundations of what is necessary for mankind to understand in order for them to be able to enter into the saving work of God by Jesus Christ. This little book will focus mainly on those most basic doctrines which Jesus & His apostles preached regarding Repentance, Faith and Baptism.

| PUBLIC DOMAIN REPRINTS |

HISTORICAL SERIES:

The Book of Enoch (1917 Translation by R. H. Charles D.D.) 186 pages

The Book of Enoch is not part of the Biblical canon used by either the Christians or Jews. Many Christian groups regard it as non-canonical or non-inspired, but may accept it as having some historical or theological interest. It is commonly known as Pseudepigrapha, meaning that it may not have actually been authored by Enoch. The oldest copies of the Book of Enoch were found among the Dead Sea Scrolls in Aramaic, and have also been preserved in Greek, Latin and Geez Ethiopic. Older sections (The Book of the Watchers, etc) are estimated to date from at least 300–200 BC, and later sections (The Book of Parables, etc) are sometimes estimated to be as recent as 100 BC.

The Apostle Jude however actually quotes from the Book of Enoch attributing the 14th and 15th verses of his letter to "Enoch the seventh from Adam" and says that they were spoken prophetically.

The Apostle Peter also makes reference to the "angels that sinned" being "cast ... down to Tartarus" and bound in "chains of darkness, to be reserved unto judgment" in 2 Peter 2:4.

The Book of Jubilees (1902 Translation by R. H. Charles D.D.) 216 pages

The Book of Jubilees, or The Little Genesis, is an ancient Jewish religious work of 50 chapters. Jubilees is considered one of the Pseudepigrapha by Roman Catholic, Eastern Orthodox, and Protestant Churches.

It was well known to Early Christians, as evidenced by the writings of Epiphanius, Justin Martyr, Origen, Diodorus of Tarsus, Isidore of Alexandria, Isidore of Seville, Eutychius of Alexandria, John Malalas, George Syncellus, and George Kedrenos. The text was also utilized by the community that originally collected the Dead Sea Scrolls. No complete Greek or Latin version is known to have survived, but the Ge'ez version has been shown to be an accurate translation of the versions found in the Dead Sea Scrolls.

The Book of Jubilees claims to present "the history of the division of the days of the Law, of the events of the years, the year-weeks, and the jubilees of the world" as revealed to Moses (in addition to the Torah or "Instruction") by angels while he was on Mount Sinai for forty days and forty nights.

The Books of the Maccabees From The Apocrypha of the Authorized King James Version of the Holy Bible 193 pages

The Books of the Maccabees tells how the Greek ruler Antiochus IV Epiphanes attempted to suppress the practice of basic Jewish law, resulting in the Maccabean Revolt (a Jewish revolt against Seleucid rule). The book covers the whole of the revolt, from 175 to 134 BC, highlighting how the salvation of the Jewish people in this crisis came through Mattathias' family, particularly his sons, Judas Maccabeus, Jonathan Apphus, and Simon Thassi, and Simon's son, John Hyrcanus.

This printing includes illustrations by Paul Gustave Doré for the Apocrypha of the La Grande Bible de Tours

CHRISTIAN PERFECTION SERIES:

CHRISTIAN PERFECTION: Sermon 40 By John Wesley (1741) 42 pages

There is scarce any expression in Holy Writ which has given more offence than this. The word perfect is what many cannot bear. The very sound of it is an abomination to them. And whosoever preaches perfection (as the phrase is,) that is, asserts that it is attainable in this life, runs great hazard of being accounted by them worse than a heathen man or a publican.

CHRISTIAN PERFECTION By Charles G. Finney (1837) 43 pages

The impression of many seems to be, that grace will pardon what it cannot prevent; in other words, that if the grace of the Gospel fails to save people from the commission of sin in this life; it will nevertheless pardon them and save them in sin, if it cannot save them from sin. Now, really, I understand the Gospel as teaching that men are saved from sin first, and as a consequence, from hell; and not that they are saved from hell while they are not saved from sin. Christ sanctifies when he saves. And this is the very first element or idea of salvation, saving from sin. 'Thou shall call his name Jesus," said the angel, 'for he shall save his people from their sins.' 'Having raised up his Son Jesus,' says the apostle, 'he hath sent him to bless you in turning every one of you from his iniquities.' Let no one expect to be saved from hell, unless the grace of the Gospel saves him first from sin.'

SCRIPTURE DOCTRINE OF CHRISTIAN PERFECTION By Rev. Asa Mahan, D.D. (1839) 174 pages

How can a man throw a stone at the sun, aiming or intending to hit the sun? An individual is shooting at a mark, with the full belief that no man, whatever his natural powers may be, ever did or ever will hit that mark. It is an absolute impossibility that he ever should, with that belief, intend to hit it. For the same reason, while a man regards perfection in holiness as impracticable; while he believes that no man ever did, or ever will, in this life, attain to that state, and that it is criminal to suppose the opposite, — to aim at perfection in holiness, or to intend to be perfectly holy, is, then, an absolute impossibility. Now, the church universally affirms, and ministers every where preach the same thing, that no one can be a Christian who does not aim at perfection in holiness, or intend to be perfectly holy. The church and the ministry, then, almost as universally, hold it criminal for any man not to believe a certain fact, to wit, that such perfection is unattainable, the belief of which fact renders the existence of such intention an absolute impossibility. "Thus have ye made void the law of God by your traditions" If a man must aim at perfection in holiness, or he cannot be saved, he must theoretically or practically believe that such perfection is practicable, or he cannot be saved.

CHURCH FATHERS SERIES:

Against Heresies: On the Detection & Overthrow of the So-Called Gnosis By St. Irenaeus of Lyon
(180 A.D.) 249 pages

Against Heresies is a work of Christian theology written in 180 A.D. by Saint Irenaeus, the bishop of Lyon. Irenaeus argued that Christianity was passed down to him from the apostles who knew Jesus personally, while the Gnostics and Marcionites were distorting the faith. While the Gnostics offered salvation through secret knowledge available only to a few, Irenaeus contended that the true doctrines of the Christian faith are the same taught by bishops in different areas. While many of the Gnostics viewed the material world as flawed and from which believers sought to escape to an eternal realm of spirit, Irenaeus saw creation as good and ultimately destined for glorification. "I have spared no pains, not only to make these doctrines known to you, but also to furnish the means of showing their falsity; so shall you, according to the grace given to you by the Lord, prove an earnest and efficient minister to others, that men may no longer be drawn away by the plausible system of these heretics, which I now proceed to describe."
-St. Irenaeus, Bishop of Lyon

The Writings of Athenagoras the Athenian Philosopher & Christian (176 – 177 A.D.) 190 pages

Athenagoras was a Christian apologist who lived in the second half of the second century of whom no more is known than that he was an Athenian philosopher and a convert to Christianity. Of his writings there have been preserved but two genuine pieces; "Apology" or "Embassy for the Christians" which was carefully written to plead justice for the Christians from the Emperors Marcus Aurelius Antoninus and Lucius Aurelius Commodus & "Treatise on the Resurrection" which was written later than the "Apology", and to which it may be considered as an appendix.

ON REPENTANCE & BAPTISM By Tertullian of Carthage (198-203 AD) 97 pages

Tertullian was a prolific early Christian author from Carthage in the Roman province of Africa. He was the first Christian author to produce an extensive corpus of Latin Christian literature. He was an early Christian apologist and a polemicist against heresy, including contemporary Christian Gnosticism. Tertullian has been called "the father of Latin Christianity" and "the founder of Western theology."

"To all sins, then, committed whether by flesh or spirit, whether by deed or will, the same God who has destined penalty by means of judgment, has withal engaged to grant pardon by means of repentance, saying to the people, Repent you, and I will save you; and again, I live, says the Lord, and I will (have) repentance rather than death."

"In the water of Baptism, which (upon a partial quotation of John 3:5) is made necessary, humans are born again; the baptized does not receive the Holy Spirit in the water, but is prepared for the Holy Spirit."
-Tertullian

Against Marcion By Tertullian of Carthage (208 AD) 491 pages

Tertullian was a prolific early Christian author from Carthage in the Roman province of Africa. He was the first Christian author to produce an extensive corpus of Latin Christian literature. He was an early Christian apologist and a polemicist against heresy, including contemporary Christian Gnosticism. Tertullian has been called "the father of Latin Christianity" and "the founder of Western theology."

In Book I Tertullian describes the god of Marcion. In Book II Tertullian shows that Marcion's evil creator which he called "the Demiurge", is the true and good God. In Book III Tertulian shows Christ to be the Son of God, who created the world and who's incarnation in the flesh was predicted by the prophets. In Book IV Tertullian continues with proofs from St. Luke's Gospel; being the only historical portion of the New Testament partially accepted by Marcion. It gives remarkable proof of Tertullian's grasp of Scripture, and proves that the Old Testament is not contrary to the New. It also abounds in striking expositions of Scriptural passages, embracing profound views of Revelation, in connection with the Nature of Man. In Book V Tertullian proves, with respect to St. Paul's epistles, what he had proved in the preceding book.

On The Incarnation of the Word of God By St. Athanasius, Bishop of Alexandria (318 AD) 105 pages

Before the rise of Arianism and the First Council of Nicaea in 325 AD, Athanasius of Alexandria wrote "On the Incarnation of the Word of God" in 318 AD at the age of 20 to answer heathen arguments to the contrary. In it Athanasius explains why God chose to approach His fallen people in the form of man. He states, "The death of all was consummated in the Lord's body; yet, because the Word was in it, death and corruption were in the same act utterly abolished." Athanasius resolves the paradox of the Incarnate by relying heavily on both Scripture and the teachings of the early Church. Athanasius also answers several objections to his account, many of which are still raised against Christians today.

Against the Arians By St. Athanasius, Bishop of Alexandria (356-360 AD) 502 pages

In 325 AD, at the age of 27, Athanasius began his leading role against the Arians as a deacon during the First Council of Nicaea. The Roman emperor Constantine the Great had convened the council in May–August 325 to address the Arian position that the Son of God, Jesus of Nazareth, is of a distinct substance from the Father.

Three years after that council, Athanasius became the bishop of Alexandria. In addition to the conflict with the Arians (including powerful and influential Arian churchmen led by Eusebius of Nicomedia), Athanasius struggled against the Emperors Constantine, Constantius II, Julian the Apostate and Valens.

During the reign of one such emperor it was once said to him that the whole world was against the doctrine of the deity of Jesus Christ to which Athanasius is known to have replied something to the order of, "If the whole world is against the Truth of God's Word, in the strength of the Lord, Athanasius is Against the World!"

During the reign of emperor Constantius, Athanasius was banished from Alexandria for a third time. This was followed, in 356 AD, by an attempt to arrest Athanasius, who fled into Upper Egypt, and completed his work known as the "Four Orations Against the Arians" by 360 AD.

Made in United States
Troutdale, OR
12/22/2024